'For most of my life I was an only child. I didn't mind a bit. And then all of a sudden I get lumbered. I have five and a half stepbrothers _____ .'

When her parents d_____ ____y has to adapt to a new life – _____ which she is now part of two very different families. One week she lives with her mum, who now lives with Bill the Baboon and his three kids. The next week, she lives with her dad, who lives with Carrie and her twins.

It's as easy as A B C . That's what everyone says. But all Andy wants to do is go home – back to the time when there was just her, her mum and her dad, all living happily in Mulberry Cottage . . .

A realistic, moving, yet often very funny tale from the author of the award-winning *The Story of Tracy Beaker*.

www.kidsatrandomhouse.co.uk/jacquelinewilson

The Suitcase Kid

Jacqueline Wilson

Illustrated by Nick Sharratt

CORGI YEARLING BOOKS

Praise for Jacqueline Wilson:

'Jacqueline Wilson is hugely popular with seven- to ten-year-olds: she should be prescribed for all cases of reading reluctance' *The Sunday Independent*

'Reading her stories, which deal both sensitively and humorously with all kinds of issues relating to family break-ups, you can see how easily she retrieves and develops the stuff of her own childhood preoccupations. She writes in the first person, which gives her stories an easy accessibility. Children certainly rate her books . . . And they respond readily to her stories'
Guardian Education

'A brilliant young writer of wit and subtlety whose stories are never patronising and often complex and many-layered' *The Times*

'Jacqueline Wilson's books are perfect for children of the age when they begin to suspect that they've got the wrong parents . . . The author never preaches but the implicit message is clear' *Spectator*

'Jacqueline Wilson has a rare gift for writing lightly and amusingly about emotional issues' *The Bookseller*

'Jacqueline Wilson has the knack of focusing on problems in a child's life with humour and sensitive intuition' *Books for Your Children*

In memory of Hilda Ellen Smeed

THE SUITCASE KID
A CORGI YEARLING BOOK : 0 440 86548 4

First published in Great Britain by Doubleday

PRINTING HISTORY
Doubleday edition published 1992
Corgi Yearling edition published 1993

Set in Linotype Century Schoolbook

Corgi Yearling Books are published by Random House Children's Books,
61–63 Uxbridge Road, Ealing, London W5 5SA,
a division of The Random House Group Ltd,
in Australia by Random House Australia (Pty) Ltd,
20 Alfred Street, Milsons Point, Sydney, NSW 2061, Australia,
in New Zealand by Random House New Zealand Ltd,
18 Poland Road, Glenfield, Auckland 10, New Zealand
and in South Africa by Random House (Pty) Ltd,
Endulini, 5a Jubilee Road, Parktown 2193, South Africa.

Printed and bound in Great Britain by
Cox & Wyman Ltd, Reading, Berkshire.

When my parents split up they didn't know
what to do with me. My mum wanted me to
go and live with her. My dad wanted me to go
and live with him. I didn't want to go and live
at my mum's new place or my dad's new place.
I wanted to stay living in our *old* place, Mulberry Cottage, the three of us together. Four,
counting my pet Sylvanian family spotted rabbit Radish.

There were all these arguments about who would get custody of me. I thought they were talking about custard at first. I hate custard because you can never tell when there's going to be a lump and it sticks in your throat and makes you shudder.

My mum got mad and my dad got mad and I got mad too. I felt *I* was being split up. Half of me wanted to side with Mum. Half of me wanted to side with Dad. It was much easier for Radish. She just sided with me. She lives in my pocket so there's never been any hassle over who gets custody of her.

We had to go for family counselling. It seemed a bit daft because my mum and dad didn't want to be a family any more. This lady chatted to me. She was trying to be ever so casual but I knew she was trying to suss things out. She had some little dolls in her office, a mummy doll and a daddy doll and a whole set of children dolls in different sizes. She wanted me to play with them. I poked the mummy doll and the daddy doll in the stomachs and said I didn't like playing with silly old dolls.

But this lady saw me fiddling about in my pocket and she got a glimpse of Radish. I like to hold her tight when I'm feeling funny.

'Oh, what a dear little toy. Do let me have a look,' she said, in that silly voice grown-ups always use when they're trying to get you to like them.

'She's not a toy, she's a mascot,' I said. I didn't want to show her Radish at all. She's mine and she's private. But I had to let this lady paw her about and undo her frock and turn her upside down in a very rude sort of way.

'What's Bunny's name?' she asked.

You'd have thought I was two years old, not ten. I just shrugged and shook my head.

'That's Radish,' said Mum. 'Andrea's had her for years and years. She's a very important member of our family.'

'Actually, I bought Radish for Andrea. As a silly Saturday present. I like to give her a little treat every now and then,' said Dad.

'You did not give Andrea Radish! *I* bought her one Christmas to go in Andrea's stocking,' said Mum.

'Look, I can vividly remember buying that rabbit in the corner shop—'

'They don't even sell Sylvanian families at the corner shop. I bought it from the toy shop in town and—'

9

I snatched Radish back and put my hand gently over her ears. She can't stand to hear them arguing.

'Never mind,' said the lady, trying to shut them up. She was still smiling at Radish.

'Hello, Radish,' she said, peering right into her little furry face.

I scowled at her. OK, Radish is real for me, but I can't stick it when grown-ups act like she's real too.

'I expect you're feeling a bit sad and worried about where you're going to live, little Radish,' said the lady.

Radish kept her lips buttoned.

'We know what Mummy wants and we know what Daddy wants, but what do you want, Radish?' said the lady.

Radish wouldn't say a word.

'I think she's a bit shy,' said the lady. 'Maybe it's hard to say anything in front of Mummy and Daddy.'

So she asked Mum and Dad to step outside the room for a few minutes. They didn't really want to. They both kept looking at me. You know what it's like at school when you're the team leader and everyone wants to be picked first to go in your team. Pick me, said Mum.

Pick me, said Dad. I stared down at Radish until they'd gone outside.

'Poor Radish. This is a bit tough on her, isn't it,' said the lady.

Radish and I stayed silent. The lady was quiet for a bit too. And Mum and Dad outside. I wondered if they were listening. But then they started up another argument. They whispered at first, but then got really cross and let rip.

'Oh dear,' said the lady. 'Well, Radish. Here's Mummy. And here's Daddy.' She propped these horrible dolls up at either end of her desk. Then she got some toy bricks and built a little house for the mummy doll and a little house for the daddy doll. She reached out and took Radish, putting her in the middle. Then she looked at me. 'Where does Radish want to live, Andrea? Does she want to live in House A?' She pointed to the mummy doll's house. 'Or does she want to live in House B?' She pointed to the daddy doll's house.

'She wants to live in House C. Mulberry Cottage, where we've always lived. With Mum and Dad and me,' I said.

'I know she does. But she can't. Not any more. It wouldn't work out. Just listen to Mum and Dad,' she said. They were shouting now.

'They can't be happy living together. You can see that for yourself, can't you, Andrea? But they both love you very much and they want you to be happy. So which house do you think you and Radish would be happiest in? House A?' She pointed to the mummy doll's house again. 'Or House B?' Daddy doll's turn.

I looked at House A. I looked at House B. I looked at Radish. I made her walk one way. I made her walk the other. I made her trek backwards and forwards across the desk.

'She still wants to live in House C. But if she can't do that – and I still think she could – then she wants to live in House A *and* House B.'

'Ah,' said the lady. 'You mean she wants to live in House A one week and House B the next week?'

So that's how it was decided. Radish lives with me, in my pocket, as she's always done. She's the luckiest one. And I get to live in my mum's house one week and my dad's house the next. It's as easy as A B C. I don't think.

is for Andy

My name is Andrea West but I mostly get called Andy. My sly little stepsister Katie calls me Andy Pandy. Everyone just thinks she's being cute. Katie specializes in cute. We are exactly the same age – in actual fact she's five days older than me – and yet she barely comes up to my waist. I happen to be big. Katie is extremely small. People don't twig she's ten. They think she's only about seven or eight, and she plays up to this for all she's worth. She blinks her blue beady eyes and wrinkles her small pink nose and puts on this squeaky little sugar-mouse voice. People go all drooly and practically nibble her ears. Katie is not a sugar mouse. Katie is a King-Size Rat.

She's very spoilt. She's got her very own television set and video in her bedroom. When it's my week to sleep at my mum's place I have to share with Katie. She always insists that she gets to choose what's on television, and she always gets first pick of the videos. She's got heaps. She's got some pretty impressive creepy gory horror films that her dad knows nothing about. She hides them inside her Care Bears cases. She's also got the usual Walt Disney stuff. And then she's got this WATCH WITH MOTHER video. Have you seen it? It's a bit dopey really, with little kids programmes that my mum and dad used to watch on telly donkey's years ago. Including a little clown puppet called Andy Pandy. We watched it together, and that's when Katie started calling me Andy Pandy.

I couldn't stick it and I told her to shut up and she wouldn't. So I had to make her. My mum saw us thumping each other and she was furious. She didn't say a word to Katie. She just picked on me.

'How dare you hit Katie! I can't believe you could be so mean. You're twice poor Katie's size. I simply won't have this hateful bullying. You make me desperately ashamed of you. Katie's gone out of her way to welcome you into her home and then you behave like this!'

I wanted to hit my mum then as well as Katie.

'It's not fair. You don't know what she's like,' I wailed, only I just sounded like a tell-tale-tit.

I stalked off and shut myself in the bathroom, Radish clutched tight in my hand. We stayed in the bathroom for ages and even when we came out we didn't speak to anyone all the rest of the day. Mum tried to make it up with me when we went to bed, but I still wasn't saying anything, not with Katie grinning away in the dark.

It wasn't until days afterwards that Mum and I were on our own for once. Uncle Bill was working late. Only he's not my uncle. He's my horrible stepfather and I simply can't stick him. I can't understand what my mum sees in him. I take a good look and all I can see is this great hairy baboon. He's got all this thick black hair like a baboon. He's got a squashed-up ugly face like a baboon. I've never caught a glimpse but I bet his bum's bright red like a baboon's too.

Paula was round at her friend's house. Graham was shut up in his bedroom playing computer games. And Katie was out at her ballet class.

'So it's just you and me, pal,' said Mum. 'What shall we do, eh?'

I shrugged and made out I was busy watching the telly. I was still feeling a bit miffed. But Mum came and sat beside me on the sofa and put her arm around me. I made myself go stiff at first but Mum went on cuddling and soon I sort of collapsed against her. I ended up on her lap. My mum's quite little and I'm big and I probably squashed her but she didn't seem to mind.

'Cheer up,' said Mum, fiddling about with my hair, doing it in little tiny plaits.

I'm growing my hair but it's taking forever. It hasn't even got near my shoulders yet. Katie has got long hair right down her back and it's a glossy bright black.

'It's a very unusual combination,' she told me smugly. 'Blue eyes and black hair. I take after my mother.'

16

Her voice always goes all sad and holy when she talks about her mother. It's as if she died only last week and so you've got to be sorry for her. In actual fact Katie's mother died when she was little and so she probably can't remember her properly. Maybe she wouldn't even know her mum had blue eyes and black hair without the colour photo in the silver frame on the window-sill.

My eyes are muddy brown. So is my hair. It's a bit depressing.

'I don't feel like cheering up,' I said grumpily, though I didn't budge off Mum's lap.

'What was all the hoo-ha with Katie the other day?' said Mum.

'She called me names.'

'What?'

'Andy Pandy.'

Mum burst out laughing. 'That's not too dreadful!'

'Yes it is,' I said, and I shifted sideways, back on to the sofa.

'Andy Pandy. That's just a friendly nickname.'

'It's after that television programme.'

'Yes, I know. Well, Andy Pandy's OK. He's the hero. I suppose he's a bit wet. Anyway, *you're* not wet. Why don't you call Katie Looby

Lou and tease her a bit? But don't fight with her, I won't have that.'

'You don't understand.'

'Oh, mums never understand,' said my mum, ruffling my hair. 'Let's watch *Neighbours*, eh?'

She turned the television up. I didn't bother explaining about Andy Pandy. He plays all these daft little games with Teddy and Looby Lou and then the lady with the silly voice says something.

'Time to go home.'

And Andy has to get in his basket while she sings the Time to Go Home song. Katie calls me Andy Pandy and she sings Time to Go Home in this sweet little voice but it's as if she's spitting at me. Because she knows I haven't got a home any more.

is for Bathroom

We're all crammed in together when I'm at Albert Road. That's my un-Uncle Bill's house. I'm never going to call him Uncle. I don't even call him just plain Bill. Though he *is* plain. I don't call him anything at all. I don't even speak to him if I can help it.

I can't stand the way Mum talks to him. She snuggles up to him and hangs on his every word and roars with laughter at his stupid jokes. She doesn't even get cross if he goes out drinking with his mates after work. That's really stupid, because she used to nag my dad like mad if he came home late. Though that was probably when he was seeing that dopey Carrie . . .

My un-Uncle Bill is a painter and decorator though you'd never think it if you saw his house. (That's how he and my mum met. When he came to paint our hall and stairs at Mulberry Cottage, because it was too high for Mum to reach. Bill the Baboon had a special set of planks. I'd like to make him walk his rotten plank. Right to the edge and over.) His own house in Albert Road is dead scruffy, nowhere *near* as nice as Mulberry Cottage, so I can't see why my mum makes out she likes it here. She's starting to do the decorating herself, changing it all around. Making it her place.

There's nowhere that's *my* place though. The others are always barging about the kitchen and the living-room. My mum shares a bedroom with old Billy Baboon, so I'm certainly never going in there.

He's got three children: Paula, Graham and little ratbag Katie. I don't like any of them, but I suppose Paula's the best. She's fourteen and she doesn't think much of my mum and they keep having rows. I encourage this like mad, because then my mum might get fed up and want to leave. And then all I've got to do is get my dad to leave Carrie and we could all be a family again. We might even be able to buy back Mulberry Cottage and start all over again, living happily ever after.

Paula has her own bedroom and she's got pop posters all round the room and she plays her stereo system so loud that the whole house shakes. She's got special earphones but she deliberately doesn't use them. *We're* the ones that need earphones.

It's funny, Paula's so noisy, yet Graham is the most silent boy you could ever imagine. He's twelve, yet I'm much taller than him. If we had a fight I know I'd win, easy-peasy. But he's not the fighting sort. He's pale and twitchy with glasses and he just likes to shut himself up in his box-room and plug into his computer. I think he'll turn into a robot one day. He moves in this jerky sort of way, and the rare times he does speak his voice is flat like a machine.

Katie's got the biggest bedroom so she has to share it with me. It's not *my* fault. I don't want to share with her. I can't stick it. I can't ever dress up or practise pulling silly faces or play a good game with Radish because Katie's always there. I can't even get lost in a good book because Katie turns her television right up or sings some silly song right in my ear to distract me.

So do you know where I go when I need a bit of peace and quiet? I lock myself in the bathroom.

There aren't any really good places to sit. The toilet gets a bit hard after a while. The edge of the bath is too cold. I wouldn't dream of sitting *in* the bath. I always just wash in the basin. The baboon has a bath every day and he leaves dark wisps of hair all over the place, and little crumbs of plaster and flakes of paint.

I collected some of his foul scummy hairs in a matchbox, together with a nail clipping and a shred of one of his dirty tissues. Then I concocted an evil spell and threw the box out of the window. I waited hopefully all the next day for the news that he'd fallen off his ladder. But he didn't. Magic doesn't work. I should know that by now. I wished enough times that Mum and Dad and I could be together again in Mulberry Cottage and it hasn't happened yet.

Even when I'm locked in the bathroom I can't always concentrate on my book. I used to read heaps and heaps and I got through every single story in the Book Box at school, and I went to the library too and I had my own collection of paperbacks, nearly fifty of them, some of them really big hard nearly grown-up books. But now my own books are shoved in a cardboard box somewhere and I can't get at them, and all the books from school and the library suddenly seem boring. I can't get into the stories. I just keep thinking about Mum and Dad and Mulberry Cottage.

So now I choose really babyish books to read, stuff I read years ago, when I was six or seven or eight. I can remember reading the stories the first time round and sometimes I can kid myself I'm little again, and everything's all right.

Sometimes it doesn't work, even in the bathroom by myself. So then I generally play a game with Radish.

She loves the bathroom. It's her favourite best ever place. Don't forget she's only four centimetres tall. The basin and the bath are her very own Leisure Pool. I generally fix up a Superslide by knotting Paula's tights together and hanging them from the door hook to the bath tap. Radish hasn't got a very slippery bottom so I soap her a lot to make her slide satisfactorily. This means Paula's tights get a bit soapy too but that can't be helped.

Radish certainly doesn't fancy a swim in the baboon's hairy lair but she likes a quick dip in the basin, and she's getting very good at dives off the window-sill down into the water. Sometimes she turns somersaults as she goes.

When she starts to get a bit shivery I dry her in the towel, and then she warms up using the sponge as her own Bouncy Castle. When she's tired of this she generally begs me to make her a snowman. I know this will get us into trouble but I don't care. I take the baboon's shaving foam and we make all the snowdrifts and then we start sculpting them into snow people. Last time I got a bit carried away. I made a snow girl and a snow rabbit and then I made a snow cottage. All right, it looked more like a big blob than a cottage, but the snow girl and the snow rabbit liked it a lot. I tried to do a tree too but the shaving foam went *phut* and I realized I'd used it all up. Nearly a whole can.

The baboon beat his chest and bellowed in the morning, but Radish and I didn't care.

is for Cottage

We didn't always live in Mulberry Cottage. We used to live in this pokey flat in the middle of London when I was very little. It was noisy and there was lots of rubbish everywhere and we kept getting burgled. Mum and Dad used to talk about moving to a pretty little cottage in the country but it was always just like a fairy story.

Then one day we went for a run out in the

car and it was very hot and I got bored and started whining and they got cross with me so I howled and wouldn't shut up and Dad stopped at a little corner shop to bribe me into silence. I stopped yelling and started happily slurping my way through an icecream. Mum and Dad had an ice too, and we all went for a little walk in the sunshine. And that was when we saw it. The cottage at the end of the road. A white cottage with a grey slate roof and a black chimney and a bright butter-yellow front door. There were yellow roses and honeysuckle growing up a lattice round the door and the leaded windows, and lots of other flowers growing in the big garden. In the middle of the garden was an old twisted tree with big branches bent almost to the ground. Mum and Dad were so taken by the cottage that they'd stopped keeping an eye on me. I toddled through the gate and made for the tree because it was studded all over with soft dark fruit. I picked a berry and popped it in my mouth. It tasted sweet and sharp and sensational. My very first mulberry.

There was a For Sale notice on the fence. It seemed like we were meant to buy Mulberry Cottage. It wasn't quite in the country. It turned out to have a lot of dry rot and woodworm and for the first year there was dust everywhere and we couldn't use half the rooms. But it didn't matter. We'd found our fairy-tale cottage.

I found it. After all, I was the one who started yelling so they had to stop the car. It was my cottage. I was the one who called it Mulberry Cottage right from the start.

Mum made mulberry pies the first year we were there. And then she made mulberry jam. It didn't set properly but I didn't care. It was fun pouring your jam on your bread. I didn't mind a bit when it ran down my wrist and into my sleeve. I liked licking it off.

When Mum went back to work she stopped doing that sort of cooking. Dad had a go at a pie once, but his pastry was all burnt and crunchy. It didn't really matter though, because the mulberries softened it up. He didn't have another go so I just used to eat my mulberries raw.

Have you ever had a mulberry? They're better than raspberries or strawberries, I'm telling you. You have one mulberry and you want another and another and another. They stain quite a bit no matter how careful you are. You end up looking like Dracula with mulberry juice dripping bloodily down your chin, but who cares? You also often end up stuck in the loo with a tummy upset but honestly, it's worth it.

My mouth is watering. I want a mulberry so much. I can't stand to think that there's someone else living in Mulberry Cottage now, picking my mulberries off my tree. There's someone else in my bedroom with the funny uneven wooden floorboards. I kept trying to prise them up hoping that someone in the past would have hidden treasure underneath. And I was sure there was a secret passage because the walls were so old and thick. I know I'd have found the treasure and the passage if I could only have gone on living there.

is for Dad

Dad came to collect me on Friday evening. I got so excited and fidgety before he came that I couldn't even sit still to watch *Neighbours*. I couldn't wait for him to get here – and yet when he tooted his car horn I suddenly clutched Mum and didn't want to go after all. It's always like that.

Dad doesn't come to the front door any more. Dad and Mum still row a lot if they're together for long. And once Dad and the baboon nearly had a fight. They both had their fists in the air and circled round each other. Mum yelled but they didn't take any notice of her. I kept tugging at Dad but he just brushed my hand away. It was Katie who stopped them fighting.

'Oh please stop, Daddy, you're scaring me,' she squeaked, blinking the famous blue eyes.

I can't stick Katie.

There's one really good thing. My dad can't stand her either.

'I had another fight with Katie,' I told Dad when we were driving over to his place.

'And who won?'

'*I* did.'

Dad chuckled. 'Good for you, Andy. She's a spoilt little brat if ever I saw one.'

'Uncle Bill said I was spoilt the other day,' I said.

I'd made a fuss because I didn't get the cream off the top of the milk for my cornflakes three days running. He said we all had to take turns. I said I never had to take turns in my old house with my mum and my dad. Uncle Bill said it was about time I learnt to share. I said a whole lot of other stuff and I ended up getting severely told off. But I didn't care,

30

because Paula let me have the top of the milk when it was her turn, because she says she's slimming.

'What a cheek that man's got! I don't know what your mother sees in him,' said Dad.

'Yes, he's horrible,' I agreed happily.

'Is he horrible to you, Andy?' Dad asked, reaching out and giving my chin a little tickle.

'Well. Sort of.'

'You tell me straight away if he tells you off again or does anything else horrid, OK? Get on the phone right away. It's madness your having to live with them half the time. You'd be much happier with me, wouldn't you?'

'Mmm,' I said, and I reached for Radish in my pocket.

'I miss you so much when you're at your mum's place,' said Dad.

'I miss you too,' I said.

When I'm with Mum, I miss Dad. When I'm with Dad, I miss Mum. Sometimes I can hardly believe that we all used to live at Mulberry Cottage together.

'Come here, sweetheart,' said Dad, slowing down so he could give me a hug.

I cuddled up against his chest and he kept kissing the top of my head. I felt as if I was a juicy stretch of grass and he was a hungry sheep.

'My little girl,' said Dad.

I love it when he calls me that. Even though I'm not little, I'm big.

He looked at his watch and gave me a squeeze.

'We're quite early you know. Shall we go and have an icecream soda together, just you and me?' He winked. 'No need to tell Carrie.'

Carrie is his new wife. She disapproves of anything that tastes really good, like icecream and fizzy drinks and hamburgers and chips and chocolate. She serves up the most horrible brown muck for our meals. She gives her children Zen and Crystal carrot sticks to eat instead of sweets. (They cheat though. They're always swiping Smarties from the other kids in their Infants class).

Icecream sodas are my all-time favourites. I can never decide whether I like strawberry or chocolate best. My Dad knows I always dither between the two.

'How about two icecream sodas today? One strawberry, one chocolate?' he suggested.

'Wow!' But I hesitated. Seeing he was in such a good mood . . . 'Dad?' I said, trying to sound all sweet and wheedly like Katie. 'Hey Dad, as we've got lots of time could we maybe do something else instead?'

'Instead of icecream sodas? Gosh! OK pet, what do you want to do? Anything for my little girl.'

I took a deep breath.

'Could we take a little drive and go and see Mulberry Cottage?'

Dad's arm went stiff. His face lost its smile.

'Oh Andy. Don't start.'

'Oh Dad, please. I'm not starting anything. I just want to see Mulberry Cottage again, that's all.'

'Why? There's no point. We're not ever going to be living in Mulberry Cottage again. There's another family living there now.'

'I know. I just want to see it, that's all. Because I like it. And the mulberries should be out soon and we could maybe pick some and we could get Mum to make one of her pies and—'

'Don't be silly, Andrea,' said Dad, and he started up the car and we drove off.

I didn't get to go to Mulberry Cottage. I didn't get a strawberry or a chocolate icecream soda. It wasn't fair. It never is.

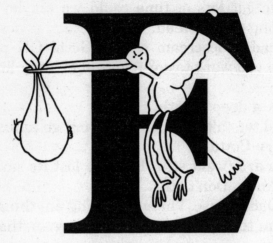

is for Ethel

For most of my life I was an only child. I didn't mind a bit. And then all of a sudden I get lumbered. I have five and a half stepbrothers and sisters.

There's Paula and Graham and horrible little Katie who are my un-Uncle Bill's children. Then there are Zen and Crystal, Carrie's five-year-old twins. Yes, Zen and Crystal. Did you ever hear such dopey names? Mum fell about when she heard.

And then there's the half. Carrie is going to have another baby.

I didn't suss things out for a bit. Carrie is very thin but she often wears long droopy smocky things so I didn't really notice her tummy. But then one Friday night when I was unpacking all my things I started up an argument with Zen. Crystal isn't too bad. She's got long fair hair and a little white face and she sucks her thumb a lot. Zen bites his nails. He's going to chew his fingers right down to the knuckle soon. He's got long fair hair and a little white face too. When I first saw them I thought they were twin girls. But though Zen looks a wet little wimp he's as tough as old boots. He *wears* old boots, sort of miniature Doc Martens, and he doesn't half kick with them too. There's a big poster about the Peace Movement in Carrie's kitchen but no-one gets any peace at all when Zen's around.

He's got his old Teenage Mutant Hero Turtles poster on his side of their bunk-beds. Crystal's got one of a ballet dancer and she's started lessons herself and keeps twirling about in her pink satin ballet slippers. Carrie tried sending her to junior karate instead but Crystal hated it. Carrie tried to get Zen to go to ballet with Crystal but he just mucked about and was silly and the teacher complained. No wonder.

Anyway, I have to sleep in Zen and Crystal's bedroom every other week and it's a right bore. They've got their bunk-beds but otherwise it's not like a bedroom at all. Carrie lets them get all their toys out at once and they never have to put anything away. They have a tent in there too, and a weird Wendy House made out of the clothes-horse, and heaps of cardboard boxes that are supposed to be trains and shops and caves. You have to wade through all this junk to get across the room to the big cupboard. It's falling to bits and half the drawers don't fit properly, but Carrie's painted it with dragons and mermaids and unicorns and all sorts of other fairy-tale stuff so it looks quite pretty if you like that sort of thing.

I think I'd have maybe loved a cupboard like that when I was Crystal's age. I wouldn't mind one now. If I could have it back in my own bedroom at Mulberry Cottage.

Mum says it sounds as if I have to sleep in

a rubbish tip and she gets particularly narked that I don't have a proper bed. Carrie's made this weird cotton sleeping-bag that she says is like a Japanese futon. She embroidered little Japanese ladies and butterflies and birds all over the front and I thought it was specially for me and I couldn't help liking it a lot. But then I found out that Zen and Crystal's creepy little friends come to stay sometimes and they sleep in the Japanese bag too, so I went right off it.

I made a great fuss about my back hurting and my neck hurting and my everything else hurting after a night trussed up in the bag.

'Don't be such a whinge, Andy,' Dad said sharply.

'Whingy-pingy,' said Zen, trampling on my feet in his boots.

'You can share my bunk-bed with me if you like, Andy,' said Crystal.

'No thanks. You wet the bed,' I said.

'Only sometimes,' said Crystal, blushing.

I felt a bit mean then. I wasn't really cross with Crystal. I was cross at Carrie because if my dad hadn't gone off with her then I'm sure we'd all be living happily ever after in Mulberry Cottage.

I say heaps of mean things to Carrie but

she's never mean back. She always acts like she's pleased to see me but I'm sure she's not. She doesn't want me around half the time. She wants my dad to herself. I bet that's why she made the Japanese bed-bag. She can fold it up and stow it away in the cupboard. I bet she'd like to fold me up and stuff me out of sight too.

Anyway *again*, I was busy trying to clear a little bit of space for *my* stuff so I had to chuck some silly junky toys out of the way and Crystal didn't mind when her Barbie went whirling across the room and landed with her legs in the air and she just laughed when her My Little Ponies went flying through the air like Pegasus, but Zen started yelling that I was mucking up all his Transformers and he started kicking me really hard. So I hooked my leg through his and tripped him and he gave a roar of rage and punched me right in the stomach.

'Stop it, Zen!' Crystal shouted. 'You mustn't hit people in the stomach. Carrie said.'

'She said I mustn't hit *her* in the stomach, because she's going to have the new baby,' said Zen. 'I can still hit anyone else.'

'Oh no you can't,' I said, and I pushed him over and sat on him. 'What's all this about a new baby?' I said, breathing hard.

'It's Carrie and Simon's new baby,' said Crystal.

She was sucking her thumb so it came out very indistinctly. I made her repeat it again, while I tried to catch hold of Zen's kicking legs.

'Stop that, Zen, you silly little squirt,' I said, and I pulled his hair which he hates.

He started yelling and Carrie and Dad came running and there was a bit of a fuss because I was the one on top of Zen, and I suppose I am twice his size.

'But he did kick Andy quite a bit,' Crystal said fairly.

Maybe it's not so bad having Crystal for a step-sister. But I know one thing. I can't stick the thought of *another* one. One that will be my dad's little girl too.

'You're having a baby,' I said fiercely to Carrie.

'That's right. Isn't it lovely?' said Carrie, smiling nervously.

'Why do you want more children when you've got Zen and Crystal?' I said.

'I want Simon's child too,' said Carrie.

That made me feel a bit sick. Dad was a bit red in the face too.

'We were going to tell you this weekend, honestly,' he said.

'It's all right. I'm not really interested. I don't like babies,' I said.

'Oh come on. I think you'd like a baby sister,' said Dad.

'No thanks. Anyway, you don't know it's going to be a girl. It could be a boy. A boy like Zen,' I said.

My dad doesn't go a bundle on Zen either. I'm glad. I don't see why Zen and Crystal get to have my dad all the time just because they haven't got one of their own. (Carrie said their dad couldn't face commitment. He probably took one look at Zen and scarpered.)

'*Twin* Zens,' I added triumphantly.

But Carrie shook her head.

'No. I had a scan. In case it was twins again. And it's just one baby. A little girl.'

'Oh.' I couldn't think of anything else to say.

There was this great long silence. Carrie looked at me. Then she looked at Dad. He didn't do anything. So Carrie came and put her arm round me.

'What shall we call your little sister, Andy?' she said.

Dad brightened up. 'Yes, Andy. How about you choosing a name for her?'

Carrie looked a bit worried, but she nodded.

'OK,' I said. 'I'll choose her name.'

They're going to have to let me choose it now. They practically promised. And I'm going to pick the worst name ever.

I used to have this Great-Great-Auntie Ethel who smelt of wee-wee and shouted at everyone. She took one look at me and said 'Who's that great gawky child with enormous feet? Let's hope she's got brains because she's certainly no beauty.'

I've got brains all right. My little step-sister-to-be is going to be called *Ethel*.

is for Friends

Aileen was always my best friend right from the time we were in the first year at Infant school. Her mum and my mum were friends too and Aileen's mum would drive us all home after school. Sometimes we'd go back to Aileen's and her mum would make hot chocolate with marshmallows and Aileen and I would play with her Barbie dolls. Sometimes Aileen and her mum would come back to Mulberry Cottage with us and we'd have fruit juice – once we had *mulberry* juice – and Aileen and I would play Sylvanian families.

Then we got old enough to do things without our mums and so we'd go to the park and play on the swings and we'd go down to the corner shop to buy crisps and Coke and we'd creep through a hole in the fence on this bit of wasteland and play games in the bushes.

We had such a great time. But now it's all different. When we left Mulberry Cottage, I couldn't go on playing with Aileen after school every day. My mum's new house with the baboon is miles and miles away. My dad's flat with Carrie is even further away in the opposite direction. Mum did let me have Aileen round to tea one time, but Katie kept hanging round us and we didn't have anywhere private to play so we just ended up listening to Paula's records. We couldn't be secret and special the way we used to be.

I still see Aileen every day at school but it's not the same. Aileen's mum gives a lift home to Fiona now. Aileen and Fiona play together after school. We go round in this sort of threesome at playtime. Aileen keeps insisting she's still my friend but when we have to join up with a partner in class now she always goes with Fiona.

is for Garden

I come home from school by myself now. There isn't anyone to give me a lift. I have to walk down Seymore Road and round Larkspur Lane and up Victoria Street into the town. I go to the bus station and then, when I'm staying with Mum, I get a 29 as far as *The Cricketers* pub and then I have a ten-minute walk. I have to get two buses when I'm at my dad's, a 62 and a 144 and then I have a fifteen-minute walk even after the two bus rides. I'm exhausted when I get back, I'm telling you.

I'd go crazy if I didn't have Radish to talk to on the way. Once or twice just at first I got lost and forgot the way and got that horrible hot swirly feeling in my stomach. I had to clutch Radish tight to stop myself crying. Then I calmed down and asked a safe-looking lady with children to show me the way to the bus station.

Then another time my purse must have fallen out of my coat pocket because when I was queuing up for the bus I went to get my money out ready and my purse had gone. I thought for a moment I'd lost Radish too but then I found her clinging to the pocket lining. She made me feel a bit better but I still didn't know what to do.

I could simply have told the bus driver I'd lost my purse but I was scared he'd get cross. He was one of those big fat men with a frowny face.

But I didn't have to ask him in the end because an old lady had been watching me frantically searching my pockets.

'What's up, dear? Lost your bus fare? Here, don't you fret, I'll pay your fare today.'

I was very grateful and asked Mum for extra bus fare the next day to pay her back. Mum got ever so fussed when she found out what had happened.

'Poor old Andy. You must have been so worried. Oh dear, I do hate it that you have to come home by yourself now.'

Mum can't come and meet me because she works nine to five in a chemist's shop now to help pay the bills. I wish she'd chosen a more exciting shop, like a cake shop or a toy shop or a pet shop. You can't get very excited when she brings home half-price loo rolls and stale cough sweets.

'*I've* been coming home from school by myself since I was six years old, Auntie Carol,' said Katie smugly.

'That doesn't count. Your stupid old school is just down the road. A baby of six months could crawl it,' I said.

'I wish you'd swop to Katie's school, Andy,' said Mum. 'It would be so much more sensible.'

'But if I went to Katie's school then it would take me hours and hours to get there when I'm staying at Dad's,' I said.

'Well. All this to-ing and fro-ing is getting ridiculous anyway,' said Mum. 'You're getting worn out, Andy. I'm thinking about you, darling. It would be so much better if you settled down in one place for a while and went to the local school.'

'That's what Dad says. He wants me to settle down with him. And go to Zen and Crystal's school,' I said.

I'm not going to go to any other old school. I like *my* school. Even though it isn't really the same any more. Aileen isn't the same. The teachers aren't even the same. They made a bit of a fuss of me at first when Mum and Dad split up but now they often get cross with me. I forget to do things or I lose my books or I don't listen in lessons.

'If you'd only try to *concentrate*, Andrea,' they say.

I am concentrating, but it's not often on lessons nowadays.

There's only one good thing about all these boring journeys to and from school. I've discovered another mulberry tree. It's in a garden in Larkspur Lane so I get to see it whether I'm living at my mum's or living at my dad's. It's not as nice as our mulberry tree at Mulberry Cottage of course. It's very old and knarled and bent over, but it still grows lots of mulberries.

I watched them ripening from red to purple to bright black and brimming with juice. No-one seemed to be picking them. The grass grew lavishly and the flowers were in tangled clumps and the creepers were crawling all over everywhere. Perhaps no-one was living there any more.

I peered over the high fence every day, trying to see the house, though it was hidden by another tree. I never heard a radio or saw a deckchair out in the garden. I started to lean right over the gate, peering in. Sometimes I got Radish out so she could peer too.

The garden would be fairyland for Radish. She could trek through the grass playing Jungle Explorers, swinging on the creepers like a tiny Tarzan. And she could eat mulberries . . .

My mouth watered as I looked at those great big berries. One day I could stand it no longer. I got my leg up over the gate, I jumped down into the garden, I ran through the long grass, I reached the mulberry tree, I snatched a handful of berries and then rushed back. I scratched my hand on the tree and banged my shin badly climbing back over the gate but I had the mulberries safe in my hand. I crammed them into my mouth and the juice spurted over my tongue and I closed my eyes because it was just just just like being back at Mulberry Cottage.

I still stop at the mulberry garden every day. And mostly I slip inside.

is for Haiku

I wish I was
in Mulberry Cottage
with Mum and Dad
and Radish.

That's a Haiku. We did Haikus in English. When the teacher said that we were going to learn about Haikus we all got excited because we thought it was going to be like Kung Fu.

But Haikus are little Japanese poems. She read
us some and there was one about a garden in
the moonlight with a willow and wild berries.
I started listening properly. I decided I liked
Haikus a lot.

> In my dreams
> I am as small as my rabbit
> and I am safe
> at home.

That's another Haiku.

> I live with Mum
> I live with Dad
> I live with Radish
> Can't we join up?

And another.

I

is for Ill

I always seem to be getting ill nowadays. I get these headaches or sometimes they're tummy-aches or other times it's an ache all over and I'm either much too hot or so cold I'm shivering. It's always worse on Fridays. That's change-over day.

A few Fridays ago I had a bit of a sniffle on Friday morning. I burrowed right under the bedclothes till I got boiling hot and sweaty and then I called Mum, sounding all sad and sore and pathetic.

Mum felt my forehead and gave me a worried cuddle. I knew Katie would tease me later about being a baby but I didn't care. Mum always makes far more fuss of me on Fridays. I clung to her and said I felt really lousy.

'I think you've got flu,' said Mum. 'Oh dear. Well, you certainly can't do that awful journey to school, not in this state. You'd better stay in bed.'

'All by myself?' I said, hunching up as small as I could.

Mum hesitated. 'Maybe I'd better stay off work.'

'Oh Mum, would you?' I said.

'They won't like it. But it can't be helped. You're really not at all well, pet. You'd better stay in bed all weekend.'

'What, at Dad's?'

'No, you'll have to stay put here. You're not up to travelling,' said Mum firmly.

I started to feel really sick then. I wanted to stay with Mum and have her making a big fuss of me – but I still wanted to go to Dad's too.

But I made the most of that Friday all the same. Katie flounced off, forbidding me in a

54

whisper to touch any of her videos or records
– 'Or I'll get you later.'

I can beat her in a straight fight but she's
got all sorts of devious hateful ways of hurting
me. She hides my stuff. She scribbles inside my
schoolbooks. Once I found poor Radish floating
miserably down the loo and I just know Katie
threw her there. She had to spend the night in
a bowl of disinfectant and she didn't lose the
smell for days and days, so that whenever I
cuddled her close my eyes stung.

But I didn't need to play Katie's records or
videos or touch any of her boring junk. Mum
came and sat on the edge of my bed and she
read the paper and I read one of my old baby
books and then when I started to act a bit
droopy Mum read some more books aloud to
me. She fixed me a lovely lunch, tomato soup
and a soft white roll and then she made me
a special bowl of green jelly. She even let me
pretend it was lettuce-flavoured so that Radish
could wade through this wonderland and get
her paws all sticky.

We all had a nap after lunch and when I
woke up Mum lent me her white lace hankie
and I played Brides with Radish. I said I was
starting to feel a lot better and suggested I

could get up, but Mum wouldn't hear of it. And then the others came home from school and the baboon came back from his work and then about seven o'clock I heard the car toot outside. It was Dad come to pick me up.

I tried jumping out of bed then but Mum hauled me straight back. She went to speak to Dad. Only they didn't do much speaking. They were shouting in less than a minute. Then Dad stormed right into the house and up the stairs to see me. Un-Uncle Bill said he had no right to come barging in and Dad said he had every right if his daughter was ill. Dad gave me a great big hug but then he held me at arm's length and looked at me.

'You seem fine to me. Maybe you've got a cold, but everyone's got the sniffles just now. Come on, Andy, get dressed and we'll get cracking,' said Dad.

I started to do as I was told, but Mum started shouting that it would be madness taking me out into the cold air when I had flu and that I was to get back into bed this instant.

I stood in my pyjamas shivering in the middle of Katie's bedroom, not knowing what to do. Mum won that battle in the end. Dad stormed out and I was so scared he was blaming me that

56

I started crying. Mum bundled me back to bed, insisting that it was wicked for Dad to get me in such a state.

I had to stay in bed most of that weekend and it stopped being a treat and started to get really boring. I didn't have Mum to myself because all the others were around. And then on Sunday Katie insisted she'd caught my 'flu' and she stayed in bed too. She didn't want my mum nursing her. She just wanted her dad.

So the baboon sat her on his lap and called her his poor little princess and other sickening stuff. He nipped out to the off-licence at lunch-time and bought her a huge box of chocolates. Katie wouldn't eat any of Mum's chicken and roast potatoes and peas but she hogged almost that whole box of chocolates to herself.

I hated seeing her all cuddled up with the baboon. It made me miss my dad even more. I couldn't wait till the next Friday so I could see him again. But then he was all huffy with me for ages, acting like it was my fault I'd stayed on at Mum's.

'You can't kid me, Andy. You were play-acting,' he said crossly, and when I tried to get on his lap he tipped me off and said I was behaving like a big baby.

He was a bit nicer on Saturday and by Sunday he was OK and he played Snap with me and one evening that week he came home early from work and took me out and bought me an icecream soda . . . but it still wasn't such a good visit as usual.

Maybe I'd better not get ill again for a while.

J
is for Jelly

I was ill the very next time I went to Dad's. Not just a little sniffle. I felt a bit shivery and strange on Thursday, but then I generally do at Carrie's house. She has the basement flat and it's always got this sour damp smell even though she burns joss sticks all day long. She's got storage heaters. I don't know what they store but it's certainly not heat. I wear a thick cardi even in the summer and by the

Autumn I wear two of everything, even two pairs of knickers.

Carrie doesn't seem to feel the cold herself and floats around in her filmy smocks without a shiver. Zen and Crystal are the same. They wander around stark naked after a bath or play for hours in their pyjamas while I hop about in the Japanese bag absolutely perished.

I told Dad I felt funny but he didn't take much notice. Carrie tried to put her arm round me to give me a hug.

'It's Friday tomorrow, isn't it. Poor old Andy.'

I wriggled away from her. I don't like her holding me at the best of times. I especially can't stand it now, when she's got this big tummy full of the baby sticking out in front. Zen and Crystal put their hands on her tummy and giggle when they feel the baby moving. It gives me the creeps.

I kept dreaming about the new baby that night. Carrie's tummy swelled and swelled until she got as big as a whale and couldn't even waddle around any more. And then the baby was born and it was huge too, even taller than me, with a great big lolling head and beady blue eyes that glared balefully at me. It bawled whenever I got near it so Dad said I'd better keep out of the way. It went on yelling even when I was in the bathroom so Dad said I had to go right out in the freezing cold garden.

I started yelling too then, and Dad got really cross and said I wasn't setting my little sister Andrea a good example.

'What do you mean, Andrea? *I'm* Andrea. The new baby can't be called Andrea too. I've got to give her a name, you said I could. She's Ethel. I'm calling her Ethel.'

The baby roared and Dad pushed me right out into the road.

'Don't be so silly. You're not Andrea. My baby's my little girl and she's called Andrea,' Dad shouted from the house, struggling with the giant baby.

'*I'm* your little girl! I'm Andy!' I screamed as I dodged in and out of the traffic.

Then a car hit me hard in the chest and I opened my eyes and there was Zen sitting on top of me.

'Wake up, Andy!' he said, jiggling up and down.

'You were shouting, Andy,' Crystal said, bending over me, her long hair tickling my face. 'Were you having a bad dream?'

'Mm. Get off me, Zen,' I said. My voice came

out in a queer croak. It hurt a lot. I wasn't shivery any more. I was boiling hot.

'Get *off* her, Zen,' said Crystal, pushing him. 'I don't think you're very well, Andy.'

'I don't think I am either,' I said, and I started to cry.

'I'll get Mum,' said Crystal.

'No, get my dad,' I croaked.

They both came. Carrie sat cross-legged beside me, her tummy huge under her nightie. She sighed sympathetically.

'Poor little fruitcake, Friday always makes you feel bad, doesn't it,' she said. 'Would you like me to show you the relaxation exercise I do at my childbirth class? It really helps stop you feeling tense.'

'She's not feeling tense, she really is ill,' said Dad, his hand on my forehead. 'She's got a fever, feel, Carrie.'

I squirmed away from Carrie's cool fingers and clutched at Dad.

'My throat hurts. And my head. And my neck and my arms and my legs. Everywhere hurts. Oh Dad, will you stay off work and look after me?' I begged.

'My poor old tuppenny. Yes, you've got a

nasty sore throat. All right, no school. But Carrie will look after you.'

'I want you, Dad.'

'Now you're being silly,' said Dad, but he didn't sound cross. He ruffled my hair and hugged me close. And to my amazement he phoned his office after breakfast and told them he was taking a day's leave.

'I can't help it if it's not convenient,' he said. 'My little girl needs me.'

I was really glad I had a sore throat then, even though it hurt so much. Dad tucked me up in his and Carrie's bed, making a special nest for me, and then we played paper games all morning, noughts and crosses and Hangman and Battleships. We haven't been able to play paper games properly for ages because Zen and Crystal are always around and they're too little to play and just scribble and waste the paper.

Carrie made this bean casserole thing for lunch but the only sort of beans I like are baked beans out of a tin so I wouldn't eat any.

'My throat's too sore,' I said, making it croak a little more.

'Oh dear,' said Carrie, looking sad. 'Isn't

there anything I can get you, Andy? What would you really fancy?'

'Jelly.'

'Jelly. Right. I'll make you a lovely fruit jelly for tea,' said Carrie.

She went out and bought some oranges specially, and spent ages in the kitchen.

'I've never made a jelly before but I *think* it's going to turn out all right,' she said.

'It's easy peasy to make jelly, you just pour on boiling water and stir,' I said.

'Oh, that's jelly out of a packet,' said Carrie, looking shocked. 'I'd never give you junk food, Andy. You need natural fresh food with lots of nourishment.'

Carrie's jelly didn't look very nourishing when she brought me a plate at teatime. It was supposed to be orange jelly but it wasn't orange-coloured. It was a weird sickly brown. It wasn't jelly either. It didn't stick. It sort of slid about the plate. Radish was quivering in my hand, ready for another glorious jelly glut, but when she saw it for herself she jumped back into my pyjama pocket, her ears drooping.

'Come on, Andy, eat up your nice jelly,' said Dad. 'Isn't Carrie kind to make it for you specially?'

'I'm not really hungry now.'

'Don't be silly, Andy. You've got to eat something.'

'I feel sick.'

'Now don't start.'

But I did feel sick, and it wasn't just to do with the jelly. Mum was due to come and collect me and I knew there was going to be trouble.

I lay waiting. I heard my un-Uncle Bill's van draw up outside. I heard Mum's footsteps and the tap on the steps down to the basement flat. I heard the door-knocker. And then I heard the quarrel.

'What do you *mean*, Andrea's in bed? My God, I simply can't believe this! I didn't think even you could stoop so low! Just because Andrea was genuinely ill the other weekend ... Oh, of course she's not ill this time! You're just being deliberately obstructive, trying to get your own back in as nasty and spiteful a way as possible ... It's just typical! Come on, hand Andrea over this minute.'

'The child is very ill. She has a sore throat, and a fever—'

'Well, I'm not surprised, stuck in this damp old flat. It's disgraceful, no place for young children—'

65

'Well, if you hadn't bled me dry over the divorce we could afford a better place—'

'Oh don't give me that rubbish. And you don't even make sure Andy has a proper bed. She's told me about having to sleep on the floor. I can't believe it, you're too mean to buy a proper bed for your own little girl – and yet *her* kids have got bunk-beds, I know. Well, if Andy really *is* ill then I insist she comes home with me where I can nurse her properly. Andrea? Andrea, where are you, darling? It's Mummy. I've come to take you home with me.'

I heard her blundering about the flat for quite a while before she got the right room.

'You poor little lamb!' she said, rushing to me. 'Why have they stuck you in here? Ugh, in their bed. Come on, let's put your coat on over your pyjamas. You're coming home with me this instant.'

I jumped out of bed obediently and stepped straight into the plate of jelly. I stood shivering, up to my ankles in brown slime.

'Oh my God! *What's that?*' Mum screeched.

'It's jelly. Carrie made it for me.'

'Jelly!' snorted Mum. 'That stupid hippy's been feeding you that muck and calling it *jelly*?'

66

'Will you quit calling Carrie names?' Dad roared.

'I'll call her anything I like, the dirty slut! She's not looking after my daughter again, do you hear me? I'll send the social services round. You're daft enough to take on her hippy twins and she looks as if she's about to have your baby any minute, but I'm telling you one thing – she's not looking after *my* daughter, not any more.'

is for Katie

Mum took me home with her and said I wasn't ever going to go back to Dad's. Dad phoned up and came round and sent furious letters. I stayed in bed with my sore throat and tried to forget about them both. I played lots of Under-the-Bedcovers games with Radish. She had a sore throat too and we knew the only possible cure would be a sip of magical mulberry juice so we searched high and low across the dark and barren land (you try crawling around under your bedcovers) but our throats remained sorely parched.

'What are you doing under there, you daft berk?'

It was Katie, back from school.

'How's the poor lickle invalid then?' she said nastily. 'When are you going to shove off back to your boring old dad, eh? I'm getting sick of you cluttering up my bedroom. Your mum's not *serious*, is she? You're not going to be here always?'

I emerged red-faced from under the covers.

'I don't know,' I mumbled.

Katie slotted a video into place and pressed the button. A horribly familiar little puppet wobbled into view.

'Oh ha ha, very funny,' I said.

Katie played the fast forward so Andy Pandy and Teddy jerked about like crazies and then stopped the tape the moment she spotted the basket.

'Time to get into your basket, Andy,' Katie said, in the lady's silly high-pitched tone. 'Did you get that, Andy Pandy? Fold up your great huge horrible arms and legs and stuff your fat head into your basket, right? I'll post you off to

69

your dad. Only once the new baby's born they won't have room for you there either so you'll just have to stay stuffed up in your basket for ever, OK, because nobody wants you.'

I clutched Radish tightly. I knew Katie was just winding me up deliberately. But it was working. I *felt* wound up. Tied up so tight I could hardly breathe.

'They do so want me,' I croaked. 'My mum wants me. My dad wants me. That's what all the fuss is about now. They both want me so much.'

'Oh no they don't,' said Katie. 'They only go on about you because they want to get at each other. If they really truly wanted you then they'd have stayed in that boring old cottage you keep going on about. But your dad left and your mum left. Your dad wants his new lady. Your mum wants my dad. They want them, not you.'

'Shut *up*!' I said, and I reached out of bed and tried to hit her.

It was just a flabby punch, it couldn't have hurt her at all, but she immediately started squealing and Mum came running.

'Whatever's the matter now?' Mum shouted above the racket, taking hold of Katie.

70

'Andy's poked my eye out and it *hurts*!' Katie roared.

'Andrea! I thought I'd put a stop to this nonsense! I won't have you bullying poor little Katie. Come here, Katie, let's see. Of course your eye's all right. Although, oh dear, yes, it is a bit red. Andrea, how *could* you?'

'I didn't touch her silly old eye,' I protested truthfully. But then I looked at my fist. Radish's ears were sticking out of it. It looked as if Radish had done the poking for me.

I tried to explain but Mum wouldn't listen. She was very very cross. Then the baboon came home and I eavesdropped anxiously and she told him. And Katie started crying all over again just so that he would make a fuss of her. Then he came into the bedroom to see me and I got really scared.

I decided to poke his eye too if he shouted or smacked me. He had no right to tell me off. He wasn't my dad. I suddenly badly wanted my own dad and burst into tears.

'Yes, well, I'm glad to see you're feeling sorry, Andrea,' he said. 'Dear oh dear, you little girls! And I thought it would be smashing for you both, being the same age and that. But listen to me, Andrea. I know you've had a hard time

71

and you're not very well just now but that still isn't really any excuse. You must stop hitting Katie or you'll really hurt her. She's only small and she's not used to such rough and tumble. Her poor old eye is very sore. It could have been really nasty, you know. I don't want my baby to end up getting badly hurt. She's been a good little girl sharing her bedroom and all her precious bits and bobs with you. So I'd like you to try to be a bit grateful, Andrea. I know you're a nice little girl underneath even though you've got a bit of a quick temper. You've inherited that from your dad, obviously. But you've got to learn to control yourself, dear.'

I had the greatest difficulty controlling myself right that minute. I wanted to scream and kick and hit and rage because it wasn't fair. Katie always hurts me far more than I can hurt her. And I don't want to share her horrid bedroom. I want my *own* bedroom, back in Mulberry Cottage. My own place with my own things where I can be with my own rabbit.

is for Lake

The garden in Larkspur Lane has got a lake! Well, not a *proper* lake. It's really a round brick goldfish pond – but it's a magnificent lake for Radish.

We go there nearly every day after school, even though the mulberries are finished now. We've started to explore the garden properly. Once we thought we saw a face at the window and we had to run like mad. We didn't go back for several days, walking quickly past the gate without even looking in, but we missed the garden badly.

Radish jumped over the gate by herself so I had to go after her. I wanted to stay close to the mulberry tree, but Radish found a crazy-paving path and followed it round a corner behind a hedge and there were three mossy steps down into another garden. The lawn was long and lush there too, right up past Radish's ears, and if I crouched down at her level I couldn't see the lake until we were right on top of it.

I don't think I've ever seen Radish so excited. She loves her dips and diving sessions in the bathroom at Mum's place (there's no proper lock on the door at Dad's and there's a gap under the bath where the spiders live so Radish doesn't like playing there) but the lake was pure paradise by comparison.

She wanted to wade right in straight away, but I kept her paddling cautiously at the edge in case it got too deep. We both got a shock when an orange whale suddenly rose up out of the water and nibbled Radish's paws. I snatched Radish out of the way. We've done the story of Jonah and the Whale at school and

I didn't fancy the idea of gutting a goldfish to retrieve my Radish. But she didn't seem too bothered by the fish. I looked very carefully at their mouths. They just opened and shut as if they were blowing harmless kisses. They didn't seem to have *teeth*. Still, maybe they could suck at Radish and then swallow her down whole.

I decided Radish had better go boating. I found various big leaves but as soon as I stood her on board the leaves started sinking. I tried collecting twigs but I needed something to stick them all together. I snaffled some Sellotape from the kitchen drawer at Mum's place and stuck the twigs together the next day and made quite a good little raft but Radish didn't seem too happy on it. It tipped about too much. I was scared she'd sail right into the middle of the lake and then slide in under the water, out of her depth.

She needed a proper boat, not a raft.

I sidled up to Graham after tea the next day.

'Hey Graham,' I said, smiling at him.

He blinked a bit behind his glasses. We've barely spoken to each other ever since my mum's lived at his place. He generally makes himself scarce in his room with his computer.

He's clever and gets a lot of extra home-work. The baboon calls him the Boy Wonder. I don't like the way he says it. He doesn't seem to think that much of Graham. He's dotty about Katie and he cares a lot about Paula too though he's always nagging at her for wearing too much make-up and staying out late. But he often makes these snide remarks about Graham. Graham doesn't say anything back. Graham hardly ever says anything very much.

'Graham, you haven't got a toy boat, have you? I mean, I know you're too old for toys now, but did you use to have one?'

Graham shook his head. 'I made myself one with a second-hand Meccano set once.'

'Did you? Did it float OK?'

'No, it's metal, so it wouldn't float.'

'Well then it was a pretty stupid boat, wasn't it?' I said, disappointed. 'What does float, Graham? I've tried wood, but it's not right.'

'Cork.'

'Cork. What's that? Oh, I know, like in the top of a bottle. But it wouldn't be big enough. What else floats?'

'Rubber.'

I shook my head, thinking about the eraser in my pencil case.

'Still too small. Come on, Graham, what else?'

'Plastic.'

I thought hard. I went back to the living-room. I borrowed one of the baboon's tapes, making sure no-one was looking. I tried floating the plastic case in the bath. It did OK, but as soon as I tried to launch Radish on it they both sunk. It needed to be bigger. A video case. Aha.

The next day after school Radish sailed the good ship *Video* from one side of the lake to the other. She had the sail up and stood on the sun deck, her black eyes bright with bliss.

is for My Mate Graham

Mum still said I couldn't go back to Dad's. Dad got on to his solicitor. We had to have another family counselling session. It was the same lady, the one with the mummy doll and the daddy doll and the bricks to make House A and House B.

'Hello Andrea. How's Radish?' she said.

I just shrugged, but I was impressed that she'd actually remembered Radish's name.

Mum and Dad ranted on and on. I didn't say much at all. Neither did Radish. The lady kept looking in my direction and asking me what we thought. We shrugged so often our shoulders ached.

It was quite good fun hearing Mum slagging off Carrie and Zen and Crystal and it was quite good fun hearing Dad slagging off the baboon and Paula and Graham and Katie but it was no fun at all hearing them slagging off each other. I started to get my sore throat back, and I felt sick and I had a pain in my tummy. I went off to the toilet down the corridor to see if that might help the pain. I crept back and listened for a bit outside the door.

'How do you think Andrea's coping with all this?' said the lady.

'It's awful for the poor little lamb,' said Mum.

'Yes, it's really unsettling her,' said Dad. 'Though when she's been with me a few days she calms down – and by the end of the week she's almost her old happy self.'

'That's because she knows she can come back to me soon.'

'That's absolute rubbish! The poor kid's been missing me dreadfully, she says so herself.'

'Have there been any behaviour problems at all?' asked the lady.

I tensed a little.

'She's always fine with me.'

'We get on like a house on fire, always have done.'

'It's just that the school says she's rather withdrawn and isn't doing very well at her lessons.'

'What do you mean, withdrawn? She's always been very outgoing and she's got heaps of friends.'

'And she's extremely bright, nearly always top of the class.'

'Yes, of course, but she has had quite a lot to cope with recently.'

I nodded bitterly behind the door.

'Children in these circumstances often develop worrying little habits which show they're under stress. They get whiny and demanding. They bite their nails. They often wet the bed.'

'Cheek!' I whispered. 'I do *not* wet my rotten old beds.'

'Sometimes they start stealing, but it's not as serious as it sounds. It's simply a way of looking for affection, taking a few treats because they feel very hard done by.'

'Oh dear,' said Mum, her voice catching. 'You see the thing is, Andrea has started taking a few things recently.'

· '*What????*' I whispered. 'I haven't! I'm not a thief! What are you *on* about, Mum?'

'Well, Andrea's never stolen anything when she's with me. So it just shows she wants her dad.'

'It's not really stealing. And she takes such silly things. Things she can't possibly want. It's not as if she helps herself to money or chocolates or anything like that,' said Mum, sounding nearly in tears. 'I haven't said anything to her, but I've been getting really worried. It started off with her taking my Sellotape. And then she took one of Bill's cassettes. I knew she doesn't like his music so I thought she was just trying to be annoying. But then she took Katie's video case. That's what's really puzzled us. She doesn't like that video, the *Watch with Mother* one, the Andy Pandy puppet gets on her nerves. But she didn't take the video, just the *case*. What in the world would she want the case for? It doesn't make sense.'

I stuck my tongue out at the door. It made perfect sense.

'Perhaps she just wanted to annoy Katie?' said the lady.

'Perhaps,' said Mum. 'She certainly doesn't get on with her. They're always fighting.'

'She fights a lot with Zen and Crystal too,' said Dad, 'but if only Andrea could be with us for longer then I'm sure she'd put down roots and we'd be like one big happy family, especially when the new baby's here.'

'She needs to be with me,' said Mum. 'She can't cope with the idea of a new stepsister, she's talked about it to me.'

'Yet she's already having to cope with five ready-made siblings,' said the lady. 'You can't expect Andrea to get on with them. She doesn't want to be with them, she doesn't want to be with your new partners – she simply wants to be with you two.'

I nod, clutching Radish.

'And of course that's not possible.'

It *is*.

'I wonder where Andrea's got to? I'd better go and look for her.'

I take my cue and go back into the room. They all three give me big false smiles. I don't smile back. I still don't say anything. They think they've sussed me out but they know nothing.

82

And they're wrong about my new brothers and sisters, as a matter of fact. I don't think much of Zen but Crystal's OK, she can be quite sweet sometimes. I detest and despise little sugar-mouse Katie but Paula's funny, though she gets narked with me when I use her drying tights as a slide for Radish. But the best one of all is Graham. We are now mates.

He kept out of the way as usual for a few days and then he suddenly waylaid me on the stairs.

'I've got something in my room for you,' he muttered.

It was a boat. He'd made me a real little Radish-sized boat out of pieces of wood carefully nailed together and then painted. There's a real sail made from an old hankie and a little red ribbon flag on top.

'This one floats,' said Graham. 'I've tried it out in the bath. And it'll take one passenger easily.'

'Oh Graham!' I gave him a big hug. He went very pink and his glasses misted over. 'It's a lovely boat. It must have taken you ages. Why did you do it for me?'

'Because I like the way you keep bashing Katie,' said Graham, grinning. 'I can't stick her either. She always used to get on to me and tease me and muck up my stuff. Now she leaves me alone because she's got you to plague.'

'Yeah, it's not fair. And I can't ever get away from her.' I considered, my head on one side. 'It's awful sharing a room with her. Tell you what, Graham, I could come in here with you sometimes, couldn't I?'

'Oh, this is too small for two people what with my computer and everything,' Graham stammered, blinking anxiously.

'It's OK. I've got my own secret place where I go actually.'

'The bathroom?'

'No, much much better than the bathroom. I go there after school. That's where I'll sail my boat. Thanks ever so much, Graham. Here, we're mates now, aren't we, you and me?'

'Yes OK, if you like,' said Graham.

I do like. And so does Radish. She liked the video vessel very much but she *adores* her real sailing boat. She'd sail the lake all day long if I let her.

is for Night

Katie keeps me awake half the night. She won't have the light out for a start. Well, she'll switch the main light off but she's got this little china lamp in the shape of a toadstool with all these dinky rabbits and squirrels perched on little china chairs inside (Radish squeezed through the little door and tried to make friends but they didn't want to know). The lamp glows all night long, and then Katie has her own torch and she nearly always has her television on too. She turns the sound down low but the picture goes on flickering.

The only way I can find a bit of proper dark is right under the bedclothes and then I nearly suffocate.

'Switch that stupid set *off*!'

'It's my telly. It's my bedroom. I can do what I want.'

'I'll tell my mum.'

'I'll tell my dad.'

'I want to go to sleep.'

'Well *I* want to stay awake.'

'Look, I'm turning it off, so tough titty,' I said, jumping out of bed and switching off the set.

'And *I'm* turning it on, so tough titties with knobs on,' said Katie, bouncing out of bed and switching it straight back on.

She likes it when we have these long arguments late at night. She likes to stay wide awake. Sometimes I have a bad dream and I wake up at two or three in the morning and if I look over at Katie's bed her eyes are nearly always open, big and blue and unblinking.

It's not that she can't go to sleep. She fights terribly hard not to. She almost never lies down comfortably. She sits up with all her pillows propped behind her. She eats biscuits and drinks a lot of water so she has to keep nipping along to the bathroom. She even wears an old angora jumper under her pyjamas. It's so tight and tickly it does a splendid job keeping her awake.

'You aren't half a baby, Katie. Ten years old and scared of the dark.'

'Oh, I'm scared am I?' said Katie, and she touched the volume control on the television. She was watching one of those awful *Nightmare* films and just the sound of the creepy music made me put my head back under the covers.

It was my mate Graham who helped me suss things out. He gets a bit fussed and fidgety if I barge into his bedroom but we sometimes have these little chats on the stairs now. He used to share a bedroom with Katie when they were both little so he knows what it's like.

'She didn't have a television then so she used to make me play all these games with her and then we'd have to take turns telling ghost stories and whenever I fell asleep she'd pinch me and once she hit me so hard with her torch I had a black eye in the morning *and* I got into trouble with Dad for it because he said I was a right little wimp if my kid sister could get the better of me in a scrap,' Graham said, sighing.

'Doesn't she get tired like other people?'

'Yes, of course she does. Haven't you seen the dark circles under her eyes? And she sometimes falls asleep at school.'

'So why won't she go to sleep at night like anyone else?'

'Because she's scared.'

'But she *makes* herself scared, watching all those horrid videos.'

'No, that's to keep her awake. She's scared of going to sleep.'

'Mm?' I stared at him. 'What's there to be scared of in going to sleep?'

Graham fidgeted quite a bit. He screwed up his face several times and took his glasses off and polished them.

'She's just scared, that's all.'

'But what *of*?'

Graham's eyes looked very strange and bare and pink without his glasses. They blinked a lot.

'When our mum died they told us she'd gone to sleep,' he said, swallowing. 'Paula and I knew she'd been ill and then we knew she was dead. But Katie was just this little squirt and she didn't know what dead meant. So they said it was just like going to sleep. They meant to be kind but she got very scared of going to sleep after that.'

'I *see*.'

'Andy?'

'What?'

'Don't tease her about it, eh? I mean, I know she's a right pain, she's my own sister and yet I can't stick her, but all the same, don't go on about it.'

'I won't.'

And I didn't. That night I didn't even moan when she kept bumbling about the bedroom hour after hour. I settled down and went to sleep myself. I woke up about midnight. I looked over. Katie was still awake, sitting bolt upright staring at the television screen.

'Katie.' I reached out and touched her. She was icy cold. 'Hey. Why don't you switch that off and come in my bed for a cuddle, eh?'

She paused. There was a little silence. Then she gave a sniff.

'What on earth makes you think I want to come in your bed, Andy Pandy? You're so big and fat I'd get squashed flat in five minutes.'

I *still* didn't tease her. But I didn't half want to.

is for Old People

I don't like Old People. They really get on my nerves.

Miss Maynard is old. She's my headmistress. I had to go and see her the other day. She started off being quite matey and she even offered me one of her special toffees but then she started in on me.

'It's just not good enough, Andrea. Your schoolwork's gone to pieces this year. You don't hand your homework in on time, or you don't even bother to do it. You don't have your P.E. kit for your lessons. You don't bring a proper sick note when you've been off school. What's going on, mmm?'

My teeth got jammed in this huge wodge of toffee so I could only manage to urgle-urgle in response. Anyway, how could I explain properly? I'm so busy flitting from my mum's place to Dad's and back again that I leave half my stuff behind. I hand Mum my P.E. stuff to go in the wash and then I forget to take it with me to Dad's. It's no use expecting Carrie to do it. She washes but she doesn't ever iron anything and I get teased when I'm at Dad's because my school blouses are all crumpled and once they went shocking pink because Carrie shoved my stuff in with Zen's scarlet sweater. Carrie didn't even say she was sorry. She said she thought the pink shirt looked lovely with my bottle-green uniform, much better than boring old white.

I don't always bring a sick note because I forget to ask Mum or Dad . . . and maybe just occasionally I'm not exactly sick, I'm just staying off school because I've got fed up with it.

No-one knows. I pretend to Mum or Dad that I'm going to school and I get on all the right buses but I don't always get off in the right place. I slope about the town instead. Sometimes I go to the garden in Larkspur Lane and Radish and I spend hours and hours there. She sails backwards and forwards across the lake and then she treks through the jungle or climbs the north face of Mount Mulberry . . .

'Andrea!' Miss Maynard put her thin wrinkly face close to mine. 'You've gone off into a daydream! For goodness sake, girl, you must stop this silly habit. I know things have been difficult for you at home.'

'I haven't *got* a home any more. Mum and Dad—'

'Yes, I know. And I do sympathize. But I can't help thinking you're making a rather unnecessary fuss. You know as well as I do that lots and lots of parents divorce and move house. It's very upsetting, but it's not the end of the world. We've been making allowances for you long enough, Andrea. Now it's time you started pulling yourself together.'

She gave my shoulders a little shake as if she was really pulling me together. I felt that if she went on pulling I'd go twang like elastic.

Mr Roberts is old too. Really old, with white hair and whiskers, but he still serves in his sweet shop though he can't bend any more because he says his knees have gone. You can't see whether they really have gone or not because of his corduroy trousers. Bill the baboon doles out pocket money on Saturdays. I get it too when I'm around, and then we all go down the road to the local shops. Paula's always fussing about her figure so she doesn't go to Mr Roberts' sweet shop, she buys tapes and magazines from the newsagent's on the corner. Graham and Katie and I go to the sweet shop.

'Hello, my darlings,' Mr Roberts says as soon as he sees us. He's always twinkling and stroking his beard. You expect him to go Ho-ho-ho like Father Christmas.

Graham is very shy with most people but he gets quite chatty with Mr Roberts. But it's Katie who is the favourite. Naturally. She twirls about the shop like a sugar-plum fairy and Mr Roberts chuckles and claps and calls her his Little Precious and his Cute Little Sweetheart. He always lets her have a free go in his Lucky Bag, five pence a dip.

He offers me a free go too but I just stick my nose in the air and say no thanks. I have to buy my sweets and chocolate from him because there's nowhere else to get it, but I'm not going to make friends.

Mr Roberts and I are deadly enemies. The very first time I went into his shop with Graham and Katie he looked me up and down and then he whispered to Katie, 'Who's the Jolly Green Giant then?'

It was a loud whisper and I heard. Katie sniggered and snorted and even Graham smiled. He said later that Mr Roberts just called me that because I was wearing my green school raincoat. Rubbish. It was a studied insult because of my size.

The grannies and grandads are all old too. I can't stick any of them. I have my own Nan and Grandad but they live in Canada with my auntie so they're no use. They're Dad's mum and dad. Mum's mum and dad are dead so they're no use either. It's not fair, because Paula and Graham and Katie have got two full sets of grandparents and they're always coming to see them, and Zen and Crystal have a granny and grandpa too. *They* aren't too bad, because they took me to the zoo with them, and we all got icecream and an animal colouring book. Paula and Graham and Katie's lot are awful. The baboon's parents are squat and hairy like him, even the granny. I'd hate to kiss her because she has a moustache. But the worst ones of all are the other gran and grandad. They used to help look after Paula and Graham and Katie after their mum died. They still come and visit a lot. They don't think much of my mum. They keep going on about the past, and how devoted Bill was to his first wife, and Mum gets very pink in the face. They practically ignore her. And me. You will never believe this but when they come on a visit they always bring presents for Paula and Graham and Katie. Sometimes they're really big presents, new clothes or books or records. Sometimes it's just boxes of chocolates. But whatever it is, I don't get anything at all. Not a sausage.

Mum got pinker than ever, pinker than my spoiled school shirts, and eventually I heard her ask the gran and grandad if they could include me in the present-giving so that I wouldn't feel left out.

'But Paula and Graham and Katie are our grandchildren,' they said. 'Andrea's nothing to do with us.'

Well, good. Catch *me* wanting anything to do with *them*.

P

is for Photographs

Dad's got a camera. We're back to the old
routine now. One week at Mum's. One week
at Dad's. You know. As easy as A B C. Carrie
was a bit huffy at first because she'd had a
social worker round to check up on things.

'And she said everywhere is spotless,' said
Carrie. 'You tell your mother that. We might be
a bit untidy, but the flat is perfectly clean and
she said that Zen and Crystal are delightful

intelligent children who have obviously had a lot of loving care and stimulation.'

The delightful and intelligent twins were having a fierce pillowfight as she spoke, lovingly and carefully stimulating the pillows until they both burst simultaneously and scattered a snow of feathers.

Carrie just laughed. Even Dad didn't get cross. He got his camera and took lots of photos.

'You'll wear that camera out before the baby's even born,' said Carrie, still laughing. She turned to me. 'I bought your dad this second-hand camera so he can take lots of photos when the baby's being born. Won't that be lovely?'

I stared at her. I know how babies are born of course. I didn't think they were going to be the sort of photos you could put in a silver frame and prop on top of the television set.

Dad saw me looking doubtful.

'I want to take lots of photos of my number one daughter too,' he said. 'Come on, Andy, give us a smile.'

I gave him a smile. And then another. And then I put my hand on my hip and gave him a little wave. Then I pointed a toe. Then I pirouetted round the room, Dad going *snap snap snap*.

'That's the girl, Andy. Hey, that's great. You've really got the idea, haven't you?'

It was wonderful. I felt like a film star. Crystal came and joined in and she smiled and waved and pointed too, but she didn't do it as naturally as me. And Zen was hopeless, galumphing about and pulling hideous faces at the camera.

'No, Andy's the star model,' said Carrie. 'Here, let's dress her up like a real model, eh? Come and help me choose some clothes, Crystal. And we'll make her up and give her a posh hair-do. Would you like that, Andy?'

I liked it enormously. Carrie dressed me up in one of her long droopy fancy frocks and Crystal draped a shawl round my shoulders and stuck a ring on every finger. Carrie stroked dark shadow on my eyelids and purple lipstick round my mouth and then brushed my hair up into a crazy kind of bun. Crystal squirted me all over with scent even though it wouldn't show in a photograph.

Then we had a long, long, posing session, Dad snapping away until he eventually ran out of film. He developed the photographs himself, blundering round the bathroom in the pitch dark. I couldn't wait to see the finished photographs. I felt as if I'd been transformed into this new grown-up magical pretty person. I looked for her in the photographs – but I just saw myself, looking a bit funny in a long frock with stuff smeared all over my face.

'I don't like them. Tear them up, Dad. Ugh, I look awful,' I said hastily.

'No, they're very good. The lighting's a bit haywire and you're out of focus here and there, but on the whole they're great,' said Dad.

'*You* look great, Andy,' said Carrie. 'You know what? You'll have to be a fashion model when you grow up. You're nice and tall already. Fashion models have to be very tall.'

I didn't know that. I thought about the idea. Maybe the photographs weren't too bad after all.

Dad gave me some copies to show to Mum when it was her turn to have me.

'Oh for Heaven's sake!' said Mum. 'Look at the way they've got you up! You look awful, Andy. All that dreadful make-up. And you're wearing that Carrie's clothes. Why on earth couldn't your father take some proper photos of you in your own clothes, instead of all dolled up like a dog's dinner.'

'I was being a fashion model, Mum. Carrie

said I could be a model when I grow up, she did, Mum, honestly.'

'She would,' said Mum, shuddering.

'Fashion models aren't *fat*,' said Katie, poking me in the tummy.

'I can go on a diet when I grow up,' I said, but I was starting to wish I hadn't taken the photos with me.

But then Paula came and had a look.

'Don't you look grown-up, Andy? No-one would ever think you were only ten. You look almost as old as me.'

That pleased me quite a lot.

And then Graham had a quick shuffle through the photos too.

'Don't, Graham. I look such a twit,' I said, going hot.

'Yeah, you said it, Andy Pandy,' said Katie.

'I think you look pretty,' said Graham.

That pleased me even more.

is for Questions

'What's Miss Maynard on about in this letter, Andy? She's moaning about all your dental appointments, saying it would be better if you could go after school. But you haven't *had* any dental appointments, have you? You went for a check-up in the summer and you didn't even need any fillings. So what's going on, Andy? *Andy??*'

*

'How did you do in your English test, Andy? And how's the old arithmetic getting on? Why won't you let me see your schoolbooks nowadays? You are still top of the class, aren't you? Andy, what's the matter?'

'Come along, Andrea, answer the question. It's no use looking at Aileen, she's not going to tell you. You weren't paying attention, were you? It's simply not good enough. Do you want to end up a complete dunce, is that it?'

'Who's been mucking around with my tights? They're all wet and soapy. You've been messing about with your little rabbit again, haven't you?'

'How are things working out for you and Radish, Andrea? Do you mind going from House A to House B and back again?'

'Do you know what time it is, Andy Pandy? Time to go home. Only you haven't got a home any more, have you?'

is for Radish

I didn't dare stay off school for a bit because Mum went to see Miss Maynard and they had a Long Talk. I'm not ever going to be able to make out I've got to go to the dentist now even if I get a gum boil and half my fillings fall out. I can't even get a cold or a cough or a tummy upset. Miss Maynard showed Mum my forged sick notes. And then Mum told Dad so I won't even be able to swing things when

I'm at his place. I have to stay at boring old school even though the teachers just shout at me now and Aileen and Fiona whisper secrets and won't play with me properly and I keep coming bottom in all the tests.

I can't even go to the garden for long after school because Mum knows what time I should get back to her place and even though she's not there Katie always tells on me. It's even worse when I'm at Dad's. Carrie comes to meet me off the bus and she looks awful now with her great huge bump and I'm scared people will think she's a proper relative instead of just a stupid stepmother. I just have time to charge down Larkspur Lane, climb over the gate, give Radish one quick sail across the lake and back, maybe let her take a two minute trek in the grassy jungle, and then it's home again home again *jiggetty jig* only I haven't got a home any more and Radish seems to be getting a bit fed up with my pocket.

I wish I could make a real home for her. I tried making her a Japanese bag out of one of Dad's hankies and then I thought about making her a proper little Japanese house but Crystal kept trailing round after me asking what I was doing, and then when I got the big box of kitchen matches to construct a wooden house Carrie suddenly swooped and snatched them away.

'I'm sorry, Andy, but I can't let you play with matches.'

'I'm not going to *play* with them. I'm going to make something with them.'

'Yes, it's going to be a little house and she's made a tiny screen out of a cigarette packet and a baby tree out of a bit of twig and she's going to make Radish a special frock called a kimona,' Crystal burbled.

'Shut *up*, Crystal,' I hissed, because it would all get spoilt if everyone knew.

It was spoilt anyway. Carrie still wouldn't let me have the matches. I did try to think of making the house with something else but then Zen trod on the screen after I'd spent ages colouring in little tiny Japanese things all over it. Carrie helped me a bit. In fact she did the drawing part and she had the ideas and Zen kept pestering and eventually he just went *stamp*. Carrie said we could do another screen but I said no thanks. I didn't really want her poking her nose in anyway. I wanted it to be a secret for Radish and me with no-one else involved, not even Crystal.

I tried again when I was at Mum's. I snaffled an old shoe-box and I spent ages getting all the thread off some cotton reels but Katie was poisonous.

'Oh how sweet. Little Andy Pandy's playing house with her dinky toy rabbit. But I think it's rather a dodgy site. I have a feeling this is an earthquake area. What's that? Did you feel a tremor? Whoops!'

She reached out and Radish and her home went flying. So then I reached out and Katie went flying.

Mum was furious and wouldn't even listen why.

'I've told you and told you, Andy. You are *not* to hit Katie, no matter what. You *must* stop this disgraceful bullying, especially when Katie's so much smaller than you.'

And as if that wasn't enough, Katie deliberately pulled two buttons off her school blouse. Mum saw and tutted and went to her sewing-box – and then I got into another row because she said I'd mucked up all her thread.

I was in so much trouble that I decided I might just as well stay for ages in the Larkspur Lane garden and miss my bus. Miss two buses, even three. Katie could blab all she liked to Mum as I'd stopped caring.

'Do you hear that, Radish?' I said, as we climbed over the gate. 'We can stay here as long as you like.'

Radish wriggled excitedly in my hand. She could hardly wait till I got her boat unpacked from my satchel. She hopped on board and was soon sailing across the lake, expertly skimming her way through the shoals of orange whales. I let her sail under her own steam, squatting down on the muddy shore and watching her, but after a while it got a bit cold and damp so I found a long twiggy stick and started propelling her round the lake in uncharted territory. Together we discovered Step Creek and Lily Land and for a while we were caught up in the foetid swamps of Waterweed Bog but we escaped at last after Radish heroically hacked her way through with her bare paws and my scrabbling fingernails.

She was a bit tired of sailing after that and we'd both got very wet so we ran round and round the lake to get warm. We were hungry too and looked longingly at the mulberry tree but the berries were long since over. I searched the lining of my satchel and salvaged a few biscuit crumbs but they weren't much of a feast for Radish and they didn't help my hunger at all.

I don't have a watch but I knew it was teatime. I was really really late now. It was starting to get dark. Mum would be back from work and she'd be so cross. She'd tell the baboon and he'd have another go at me. And Katie would give a smug little smile and then whisper about it half the night. I wouldn't even be able to cry because she'd see.

I leant against the mulberry tree clutching Radish in my fist and had a bit of a cry there. But then as I moved about to stop my face getting scratched my hand holding Radish suddenly slipped under a branch and went into a little hole.

'Radish? Come back!'

But Radish was running about inside the dark little hole, getting excited. It was just like a secret cave. I tried to peer in but it was getting too dark to see properly. Radish insisted that she could see. She loved the little hole. Only it wasn't a hole to her. She wanted me to help her make it into a proper home. Not a proper permanent home, but a holiday home for her visits to the lake.

'OK, Radish. We'll make it really cosy for you. We could get some moss for a soft green carpet. And I could stick some shiny leaves together to make matching curtains. And we'll have to see about some sort of light because I can't see in the dark even if you can.'

And at that moment a light went on. Not inside the hole. Outside. In the big house behind me. It made me jump and my hand jerked and then suddenly Radish wasn't there.

'Radish? Radish, where are you? Come back! Come here!' I said, feeling frantically. And then I felt the drop at the back of the hole. I pushed my arm in as far as it would go. I scrabbled and stretched but it was no use. Radish had fallen out of my reach.

'Radish!' I screamed.

And then the door opened and there was a dark figure in the garden and I had to tear my arm out of the tree and run for it.

is for Starlight

'Where on earth have you *been*?' Mum shouted.

I was too choked up to answer properly.

'I was just . . . playing,' I mumbled.

'Playing!' said Mum, and she smacked me hard across the face.

We both gasped. She's never hit me before. Then I burst into tears. And Mum did too.

'Oh Andy,' she said, and she was suddenly hugging me tight. 'I'm sorry. I was just so

111

worried and I've been phoning everyone. I phoned Miss Maynard, and I had to phone your father and he blames me for going out to work and yet if he'd pay his share of the bills then I wouldn't have to and— Oh darling, never mind all that. All that matters is you're safe.'

'But Radish isn't,' I said, and I started really howling. I'd held it in while waiting for the first bus and then on the journey and then on the second bus and then on the walk back to Mum's place but now the full awfulness washed over me like a giant wave.

'I've lost Radish,' I sobbed, and I buried my head in Mum's shoulder so I could shut out all the other faces round me. Graham looked sympathetic and Paula patted my shoulder but Katie had her eyebrows raised in mock amazement and the baboon looked impatient.

'For goodness sake, is that why she's so late? Because she's lost her little toy?' he said, sighing.

'She's *not* a toy, she's a mascot,' I shouted.

'Hey hey! No need to take that tone. Look, your poor mum's been worried sick. You're two hours late home, young lady. It's just not good enough.'

'Yes, I know, Bill, but Radish is very special to Andy,' said Mum, still holding me close.

'All the same, it seems a bit daft to have the whole family going demented because she's lost a little rabbit that isn't even real.'

'She *is* real to me!'

'Come on now, Andy, calm down. You really are being a bit of a baby, you know,' said Mum. She said it quietly but the others could still hear. I pulled away from her. 'Andy? Now don't be like that. Look, maybe Radish isn't lost for ever. When did you last see her? Did she drop out of your pocket on the way home?'

'She fell down inside a tree,' I whispered, thinking of poor little Radish tumbling backwards down that dark hole.

'Which tree?' said Mum, but I couldn't tell her because I'd get into more trouble for going into someone else's garden. Oh how could I have run off like that and left my Radish down in the depths of the mulberry tree? And she wasn't the only thing I'd abandoned in my hurry to save my own skin.

'I've lost your lovely little boat too, Graham,' I said crying harder.

'Never mind. Look, I can easily make you another,' Graham said gruffly.

113

'But there can't ever be another Radish,' I said, sobbing.

'Of course there can,' said the baboon. 'I'll get you a new one in the morning. They sell them in the toy shop down the road. Katie had some of those Sylvanian family things when she was little.'

The 'little' stung, but I was so overwhelmed with misery and guilt I hardly cared.

'I don't want a new Sylvanian family. I want *Radish.*'

Radish hadn't died. She hadn't stopped being. She was still there, alone in the dark tree, probably hurt, certainly very lonely and scared. She'd be wondering where on earth I was, why I wasn't coming to rescue her . . .

'I've got to go back,' I said desperately. 'I can't reach her, but I could call down to her, try to comfort her—'

'Don't be so silly, darling,' said Mum. 'You're certainly not going out again. You're going to have some tea and a nice hot bath and then you're going straight to bed.'

There was no arguing with her. There *was* a lot of arguing going on, but that was between Mum and Dad, because Dad came round to see if I was safe and then started up all the old rows. My hand kept reaching out for Radish and then clenching in despair.

It was even worse when I went to bed. I couldn't remember ever going to sleep without Radish. She always tucked into my hand and I put my finger in between her dear little ears and rubbed her soft furry forehead until I went to sleep. So now of course I couldn't possibly sleep. I lay awake for hour after hour. Mum crept in to see me and gave me a special kiss and tucked me up while Katie made vomit noises from the next bed, but it didn't help. I heard Graham go to bed. Then Paula. Then Mum and the baboon. Soon the whole household was asleep except me. And Katie. She started.

'Down a tree, is she, Andy Pandy? In with all the bugs and spiders, eh? You get lots of creepy crawlies inside trees. And maybe some bird's fallen down the hole too and died and your little Radish is lying on its *corpse*. Yeah, all the maggots are going *wiggle wiggle wiggle* all over her and she won't even be able to cry for help because rabbits don't talk. She's just opening her little mouth and screaming silently, wondering why you don't come.'

'I *am* coming,' I said. I got out of bed and started pulling on my clothes.

'What are you doing, you dope?' Katie whispered.

'What do you *think* I'm doing? I'm going to comfort Radish,' I said, pulling on a jumper.

'But it's after midnight. You can't go *out*.'

'Just watch.'

'But your mum—'

'I don't care. She won't know. And if you tell her I'll . . . I'll tell you're such a scared baby you won't even lie down properly to go to sleep. And I know why and I'll tell everyone – if you tell on me. Understand?'

She understood all right. She still looked worried.

'Andy, you are just kidding, aren't you? You can't really go out in the middle of the night. Look, those things I said about Radish, I was just making them up to annoy you, they're not true.'

'They could be,' I said, and I put on my coat and wound a scarf round my neck.

'But it's so dark outside,' said Katie.

She was wrong about that. When I'd crept down the stairs and out the front door I looked up and saw there was a big round moon and hundreds of stars shining in the sky. I saw the Pole star shining brighter than all the others. I threw back my head, staring at it until my eyes watered, and I whispered the wishing song.

Starlight, star bright
First little star I see tonight
Wish that I may, wish that I might
Have the first wish that I wish tonight.

'I wish that I can find Radish and work out a way of reaching her so that I can have her back, please, please, *please*.'

is for Time To Go Home

There aren't any buses in the middle of the night. Larkspur Lane is a long bus ride away. I wasn't sure how long it would take me to walk. I'd never been out that late at night before. Certainly not by myself. The stars and the street lights stopped it being too dark, but it was still pretty scary. It was cold and strange and all the streets seemed so empty, and yet whenever a car went by or a man walked past I shrank away from them.

I tried to think of poor little Radish stuck down the tree – but I couldn't stop thinking about poor little *me* too. I remembered all the things Mum and Dad had said about strangers and when a man slowed down when he saw me and said 'What's up, dear? Why are you out all on your own at this time?' I shot past and went flying off down the street. He called after me and then started running too.

I ran faster, heart thudding, feet pounding, dodging down an alley and round someone's garden and down another passage and out into another road and then another, running and running and running – and when at last I stopped, spread-eagled against a wall with a great tearing stitch in my side the man was nowhere to be seen.

He might have been a kind man trying to look after me. He might have been a monster ready to make off with me. There was no way of telling.

I didn't even know where I was any more. I stared round at the dark unfamiliar buildings in panic. I could try going back along the alley but the man might be waiting . . .

I started shaking and shivering. My cheeks

got a bit wet. My hand seemed horribly empty – but then I tucked my thumb inside my fist and tried to kid myself it was Radish and it helped just a little bit. I ran on down the road and when I turned the corner I was at the shops. I knew how to get back to Mum's place in less than five minutes. But I couldn't go back. Katie would be still lying awake, and how she'd sneer if I came creeping back so soon. And Radish was still down the tree, so lost and lonely and frightened. I thought of her tiny heart beating violently under her soft fur and my face screwed up in pain.

'I'm coming, Radish,' I whispered. I stared up at the stars. 'You've *got* to make my wish come true.'

So I set off walking. I walked and walked and walked. I walked until I was so tired I started to wonder if I was dreaming. Everything seemed so strange and silvery in the starlight and every so often my head would nod and I'd stumble and start. I kept expecting to blink my eyes and find myself tucked up in bed at Mum's, but it didn't happen. So I just walked some more, my head down, shoulders hunched, feet going *left right left right left right*.

I missed my way several times but then I'd

suddenly recognize a shop or a house and I'd know I was back on course again. But then I found myself in streets I was certain I'd never seen before. I walked on and yet it was all new and different and I realized I was lost again. I tried going back but I kept getting to corners and not knowing whether to take the left turn or the right. So in the end I kept on walking anyway, and after a while I stopped thinking about finding the way. I just looked up at the stars and whispered Radish's name and walked on and on and on.

Then I suddenly recognized a house at the end of a road, with gables and a curly iron gate and a caravan parked in the front drive. It was Aileen's house and she went on her holidays in that caravan and we'd swung on that gate together and she was probably asleep in her bedroom under the gables right this minute.

'Aileen's house?' I whispered. Then I'd somehow missed Larkspur Lane altogether. I'd bypassed the school. I was back in my own old territory, the other side of the school. The part of the town where I never went any more. If this was Aileen's house then I knew what was down the road and round the corner.

I stood still, shivering. No. I had to go to

Larkspur Lane and find Radish. I couldn't waste time going anywhere else. But I had to. My feet started walking and I couldn't stop them.

I went past Aileen's house. Past all the other houses in the road with their neat privet hedges and their pointed roofs making a zig-zag pattern against the starry sky. I got to the corner. I stood still again, holding my thumb. Then I started walking, very very slowly.

I could see it in the starlight. A cottage at the end of the road. I could only see in black and white but it was easy to paint in the colours. A white cottage with a grey slate roof and a black chimney and a bright butter-yellow front door. There were yellow roses and honeysuckle growing up a lattice round the door and the leaded windows, and lots of other flowers growing in the big garden. And in the middle of the garden was the old twisted tree with the big branches bent almost to the ground, and at the tip of each twig grew big bunches of black mulberries . . .

No, no mulberries. The berries had long ago withered on the tree. No roses, just tangled thorny branches. No sweet-smelling honeysuckle, just leathery stems trailing untidily. But it was still Mulberry Cottage. I was back. I was home.

is for Unconscious

'Andy? Andy darling, is that you?' Mum's at the door, smiling at me. 'Come in, sugar-lump, I've got tea all ready on the table.'

'Yes, come on, Andy, Mum's made a lovely mulberry pie and my mouth's watering,' Dad calls.

'Dad?' I step inside, shaking my head. 'Dad, what are you doing here?'

'He got off work early, didn't you, darling,' says Mum.

'But what are *we* doing here?' I say, dazed.

'We live here, silly,' says Mum, and she ruffles my hair. 'What's up, Andy? Don't you feel very well?'

'No, I feel . . . wonderful. I can't believe it. Was it all a dream then – all that about leaving Mulberry Cottage and you having Bill and Dad having Carrie and . . . ?'

'I think you're still half asleep, pet. Come on, let's have tea, we're all hungry.'

Mum takes my hand and leads me into the living-room. Dad's sitting at the table, smiling at me. There's a big bunch of our own pink roses in a pretty white vase, and there are little fairy cakes with pink icing and white rosettes and the newly-baked mulberry pie, dark wine-red juice bubbling up through a crack in the golden pastry and filling the whole room with the rich fruity smell.

Mum cuts me a huge slice and tops it with vanilla icecream. I bite into hot and cold, crunchy and smooth, sweet and sharp, and close my eyes with the bliss of it.

'Mmmmm,' I say, and Mum and Dad laugh.

'Doesn't Radish want some too?' says Mum.

'Radish?' I say, and there she is, safe and sound, tucked up in my pocket, half asleep too.

Mum lets me fetch a doll's-house saucer and a china thimble and Radish eats and drinks with us.

'But wait. This is the thimble I swopped with Aileen ages ago,' I say, puzzled.

'Well, you must have swopped it back again,' says Mum.

'And maybe you'll get swopping yet again because I've got a little surprise in my pocket for you and your Radish,' says Dad.

'A present!' I jump up and run to Dad.

'Oh darling, you do spoil her,' says Mum.

'I like spoiling both my best girls,' says Dad, and he gives me a present out of one pocket and Mum a present from the other.

Mine is a small square cardboard box and inside is a tiny Radish-size gilt table and chair, and sellotaped safely to the table top is a tiny pink china cup and saucer and plate, delicately edged with a wisp of gold paint. Mum's present is in another cardboard box and it's a proper size pink china teacup and saucer with cherubs flying all round the rim, and a little message in looping writing at the bottom of the cup. The message says 'I love you'. Dad says it too. Mum goes as pink as her cup and they give each other a long kiss. Radish and I grin at each other. We are all very pleased with our presents.

We eat up the pie and icecream and every one of the fairy cakes and then we all do the washing-up together, making it a game. Dad keeps flapping the tea towel and I put my fingers on my head to make horns and rush around pretending to be a little bull and Mum makes out we're getting on her nerves but she keeps laughing, and we're still all in a giggly mood when we go back into the living-room, as if it's a special day like Christmas.

We switch on the television and my very favourite film *The Wizard of Oz* is just starting and so Mum and Dad and Radish and I all cuddle up to watch it. I've got my red slippers on and Mum and Dad keep calling me Dorothy and I turn Radish into Toto and make her give little barks. We sing along to all the songs and at the end of the film when Dorothy clicks the heels of her ruby slippers and whispers 'There's no place like home' I suddenly start crying.

'What's up, darling?' says Mum.

'Don't be sad, little sausage,' says Dad.

'I'm not sad. I'm crying because I'm so happy,' I say, sniffling.

'You funny old thing,' says Mum, and she pulls me on to her lap for a cuddle.

When the film finishes I climb on to Dad's lap instead and he reads me a story, lots of stories, from all the story books I had when I was little.

'But they got lost somewhere, I'm sure they did,' I say.

'Well, we found them again, specially for you,' says Dad, giving me a kiss.

'You don't mind reading me such babyish stuff, Dad?'

'You're our baby, aren't you?' says Dad, giving me a tickle. 'Come on, little babykins, say *cootchy-coo* for your Dad-Dad.'

'Oh Dad, don't be so daft,' I say, shrieking with laughter.

'I don't know – tears one minute, a great big fit of the giggles the next. I think it must be bed-time,' says Mum.

'Oh no,' I say, but I don't argue too much because I don't want to spoil anything and it's easy to be good when I'm so happy. I get in the bath and Radish gets in with me and floats about as merry as a little duck. Then we both get dry and powdered and into our nighties and then Dad comes and carries me into bed as if I really am a baby. He tucks me up and he tucks Radish up too, and he kisses both our noses which makes me giggle again. Then Mum comes and she tickles us both under the chin and we giggle some more. Then Mum and Dad stand arm in arm at the foot of my bed, chatting softly to each other while Radish and I snuggle up. The bed's so soft and I feel so safe with all my own things round me, my own rabbit pictures on the wall, my own wardrobe, my own toy cupboard, my own bookshelf, my own Radish in my hand, my own Mum and Dad right by my bed, together. I'm so happy I want this moment to last forever but I'm so sleepy too and I can't stop my eyes closing and I know I'm going to sleep and I'm suddenly worried because I know it can't last and that it's going to be very different when I wake up and I try to open my eyes wide but they're so heavy and I have to rest them just for a second and then they won't open again and I'm going to sleep in spite of myself, I'm going to sleep . . .

V

is for Vagrant

I woke up and it was dark and I was so cold and I felt for Radish but I couldn't find her and then I remembered and I couldn't bear it and I huddled under an old sack at the bottom of the garden and tried to get back into the dream . . .

And then I woke up again and it was light and I heard someone out in the garden, over by the bird-table.

'Come on, little sparrows, nice toast crumbs for breakfast. Come and have a little peck. And I've got some nuts for you too and— Oh my goodness! Harry, come quick! There's some little old vagrant sleeping under the mulberry tree!'

A vagrant. For a moment I thought she meant a real vagrant sleeping somewhere beside me. And then I realized. She meant me.

Vagrants sleep rough. They don't have their own bed. They don't have a proper home. Nobody wants them. They keep shifting around and getting moved on and everyone acts like they're a general nuisance.

I'm a vagrant.

I scrambled out of the old sack and struggled to my feet, and then I started running, staggering once or twice because I was so stiff. The woman gasped and then called after me but I wouldn't stop. I couldn't get the gate open so I jumped right over it. They'd painted it green instead of black. And when I chanced one last look round I saw they'd painted the front door green too. It didn't look like my Mulberry Cottage without a butter-yellow front door. But it isn't my Mulberry Cottage any more.

I ran away, blundering down the road, round

corners, along lanes, no longer watching where I was going, not even knowing any more, just wanting to run and run. I ran right across the road and a car hooted at me and made me jump so I didn't cross any more roads for a bit and then another car hooted and I blinked at it, bewildered because I was still safely on the pavement, and it hooted again and someone shouted and I saw it was Dad. Only maybe I was still dreaming because Mum was with him too, Mum and Dad together in our car, and they stopped the car with a squeal of brakes and then they were both running towards me – and suddenly I was swept up in their arms and we were having a big hug together, Mum and Dad and me, hugging the way we used to, the three of us together. No, we used to be four. Radish!

'Oh Andy, darling, don't cry! It's all right, you're safe and we've got you back and—'

'And half the police in the country are out looking for you but we found you ourselves and just so long as you're OK—'

'Oh Andy, why did you run away? We've been so *worried*—'

'We've been going out of our minds. Everyone's been searching—'

I cried harder. 'I haven't been searching. I just gave up. And she'll be so scared without me,' I sob. 'Oh I've *got* to go and rescue Radish!'

'But you dropped her down some tree, darling, you said—'

'I know which tree. It's in a garden where I go a lot.'

'You don't mean . . . our old garden? At Mulberry Cottage?'

'No, this is a different garden. In Larkspur Lane, near my school. I was looking for it last night but I got lost and then I was back at Mulberry Cottage and you were there, both of you were, and we all had tea together and then you both put me to bed—'

'That must have been a dream, Andy.'

'Yes, I know. It wasn't ever like that, even before you split up,' I say sadly. 'But Radish isn't a dream. She really is in the tree and I must go and try to get her back.'

'That blooming rabbit,' said Dad, only he didn't say blooming. But he drove us in the car to Larkspur Lane and I pointed out the right cottage.

'It's still very early. We can't just barge into a private garden and start searching their trees,' said Mum. 'Maybe we ought to wait a while,

Andy. You're still frozen stiff. We ought to take you straight back home and—'

'And we've got to phone the police, tell them you're safe.'

'And I must let Bill and the children know. They're all so worried. Katie's been in floods of tears.'

'Katie?'

'Carrie and the twins are very upset too – and it's bad for Carrie to get in a state when the baby's nearly due.'

'But I've *got* to get Radish,' I said, starting to climb over the gate.

I was up and over the other side before they could stop me.

'Andy, come back!'

'We must knock at the front door first to ask permission.'

'No, we can't. I'll get into trouble,' I hissed, running across the wet grass towards the mulberry tree. 'It's OK, I know exactly where Radish is, and if you could try to get your arm down the hole, Dad, you can reach much further than me—'

But before I could get to the tree I heard the door of the house opening, and someone coming out. Two people. They'd caught us.

is for Welcome

They were two small plump elderly people, both in their dressing-gowns. The woman was wearing a pink quilted satin affair, the man a woollen red-and-blue tartan job. They both had those old-fashioned slippers with pompoms. They certainly didn't look very frightening but I was in such a silly state I was frightened all the same.

'Please. I just want to look for Radish. I'll only be a moment,' I stammered.

'We're so sorry to disturb you like this,' said Mum.

'I know she's very naughty playing in your garden, but my daughter's lost her toy rabbit down your tree and that's why we're here at this God-forsaken hour, you see, to try to find it,' said Dad.

'Oh, it's perfectly all right. We were expecting you,' said the old man.

'Expecting the little girl. She's our little visitor,' said the old woman. 'She comes nearly every day and we're always so pleased to see her.'

I blink at them in astonishment.

'It's been grand to see her enjoying our garden. All our grandchildren are in Australia so we've no children of our own to come and play,' said the old man.

'Of course we didn't like to intrude. We've been careful to keep our distance, but we couldn't help having little peeps at you now and then,' said the old woman, smiling at me. 'You and your little rabbit seemed to be having such fun. And yesterday you stayed such a long time and it was such a pleasure to us. But it started to get dark and we wondered if you might have lost track of the time. We hoped you might come indoors and take a bite of tea with us but when I came out to ask I must have startled you, because you ran away.'

'I'm sorry,' I said, blushing. 'That was silly. And I left Radish. I dropped her down inside the mulberry tree. Do you mind if my dad tries to get her back?'

'Not at all, my dear, not at all. Although you can easily reach her yourself, you know,' said the old man, and he gave his wife a little nudge.

'Why don't you go and look,' she said, her eyes twinkling.

So I ran to the mulberry tree. I found the little hole under the branch. But it wasn't just a hole any more. Someone had stuck some little net curtains up at the entrance, turning it into a tiny window. I peered inside – but I couldn't see Radish.

'That's upstairs,' said the old woman. 'I think she's downstairs now.'

I put my hand in the hole and felt, but the old woman was shaking her head.

'No dear, there's a much easier way to see downstairs. Run round to the other side of the tree and crouch down just a little,' she said.

I ran. I crouched. I saw another hole in the tree. There was a small doll-size doormat at the edge, with WELCOME in very tiny cross-stitch. I peeped past the mat and there was my own darling Radish stretched out happily on her own little wooden sofa, her head propped on a blue velvet cushion.

I gazed at her until my eyes blurred.

'How did . . . ?' I whispered.

'Just our little bit of fun, my dear,' said the old woman, putting her soft hand on my shoulder. 'My daughter used to play games with her little dolls inside the old mulberry, turning it into a real tree-house. Arthur and I were sure you'd be back so he did a bit of whittling and made the sofa and I did a bit of stitching to make the hole look a bit homey.'

'It looks very very homey,' I said. 'And do you know what it's called? It's Radish's own Mulberry Cottage.'

We all went inside the couple's own cottage because they were starting to shiver in their dressing-gowns, and we all had tea and hot buttered toast and Mum and Dad explained about our own Mulberry Cottage and it was all so cosy and everyone was chatting away so happily that I started to wonder if my dream might really come true . . .

But then when we were back in Dad's car he started blaming Mum for not looking after me properly when I was in bed and she got furious and started on about my not even having a proper bed at Dad's place and I clutched Radish and realized that some dreams can't ever come true.

Radish still lives with me in my pocket most of the time because I need her so much. But she has her own Mulberry Cottage too and now, nearly every day after school, I take her there. She goes boating on her lake and then she has an acorn cup of mulberry juice in her own little cottage while I have cocoa and seed cake with Mr and Mrs Peters. That's the name of the old couple. They asked if I'd like to call them Uncle Arthur and Auntie Gladys but I've got too many uncles and aunties already. Sometimes, just in my head, I call them Granny and Grandad. I never thought I'd like any old people. Mr and Mrs Peters are very old, but I like them ever such a lot.

is for Xmas

You should have seen Mulberry Cottage at Christmas. I dipped a pine cone in green paint and then I splodged on little red berries and gold stars so that Radish had her very own Christmas tree. I even made her a teeny weeny paper chain though Mrs Peters had to help me because I just kept tearing it. Mrs Peters' hands are like little claws because she has arthritis and yet she can still make them move like magic.

She gave me my own sewing-box for Christmas. It's got all these little compartments stuffed with threads and needles and a silver thimble and a tape measure that snaps back into place when you touch the button. The compartment tray lifts out and at the bottom are all sorts of materials from her own scrap bag, soft silks and velvets and different cottons with tiny sprigs of flowers and minute checks and pin-head dots, all perfect for making into dresses for Radish. She's got so many little outfits now she wants me to change her all day long so that she can show them all off.

I've made her a dance-frock that covers her paws, a velvet cloak lined with cotton wool fur, even a little sailor-suit with a big white collar and a white cap with special ear-holes. Mrs Peters had to help quite a lot with that little outfit, but I did all the designing. Maybe I won't be a fashion model after all. Maybe I'll be a fashion designer. Then I don't have to bother about getting thin. Mrs Peters is such a good cook that I'm getting bigger than ever. She doesn't mind. She says I'm a growing girl and I should eat my fill. I told Katie and she said yes I was growing all right, growing gi-normous, and she puffed out her cheeks and strutted round pretending to be me. People laughed and I wanted to cry but I didn't. I didn't hit Katie either. I just made out I didn't care and said I'd sooner be gi-normous than a silly little squirt like her, and got on with my sewing.

Mr Peters gave me a whole suite of wooden furniture to go in Mulberry Cottage. There's a big wardrobe that really opens, and a wonderful wooden trunk so Radish has got plenty of space to store her magnificent new ensembles. Mr Peters also gave me my own big penknife with a pearl handle, so that I can do a bit of whittling myself. Mum panicked and asked Mr Peters to look after the knife for me, so that I can only whittle when I'm with him. I think Mum worried that I might run amok and stick my penknife straight into Katie. I must admit it's a tempting thought. No, I'm joking, don't worry. Katie's still foul most of the time but just occasionally she's not too bad.

She gave me a little plaster ornament of Andy Pandy for my Christmas present and I was not particularly amused, especially as I'd sewn her a special velvet Alice band to tie back her lovely long hair. But then she cleared half the window-sill of all her stuff and said that it was mine now, and I could keep my

Andy Pandy ornament there. So now I own half the window-sill and Mum found the box with some of my old stuff from our Mulberry Cottage and I've got my china rabbits and a Father Christmas in a glass snowstorm to keep Andy Pandy company, and all my books and some old photos of Mum and Dad and me back at Mulberry Cottage. Dad took a special flashlight photo of Radish in her Mulberry Cottage and I've got that too, and Radish has got her own copy hanging on her wall like a big poster.

I gave Mr and Mrs Peters one of the fashion-modelly photos of me for a Christmas present. I wasn't sure they'd like it but they put it in a special silver frame and I'm in the middle of their mantelpiece with their grandchildren either side of me.

I can never get to be one on my own nowadays.

is for Yacht

My second best Christmas present was from Graham. I bet you can guess what it is. It begins with Y. Not a yak. A yacht. A wonderful, magnificent, correct in every detail Bunny *Britannia* for Radish.

Mr Peters helped Graham to make it. Mr Peters saw Radish sailing in the modest Mark One yacht and wondered if I'd made it myself.

'You've done quite a professional little job

there, Andy. You've quite a way with wood,' he said, turning the boat backwards and forwards admiringly (but making Radish feel terribly seasick in the process).

'Not me. Graham made it for me. He's my sort-of brother,' I said proudly.

'I thought you always moaned about all these sisters and brothers of yours,' said Mr Peters.

'Not Graham. We're mates, Graham and me.'

'That's good. Well any time you want to bring him along with you he'd be very welcome. Some Saturday, say?'

'Oh. Well. He's got lots of homework to do. And he shuts himself up with his computer for hours. I'm not sure he could spare the time,' I said.

Mr Peters just nodded. He didn't seem to mind either way. But I did.

I wanted to keep Mr and Mrs Peters all to myself. They'd become my sort-of grandparents and I didn't see why I should have to share them. It was enough bother having to share my mum and my dad.

And yet I liked Graham a lot. He wasn't busy *all* the time on Saturdays. He'd like to see Radish sailing his boat on the pond. He'd like Mrs Peters and her seed cake. He'd especially like Mr Peters and the little lean-to at the back of the house where he did his woodwork.

But what if it all got spoiled? What if Mr and Mrs Peters fussed round after Graham and I got left out again?

But what if it was fun? I could show Graham all my secret places in the garden and all the special things Mr and Mrs Peters had made for me and Radish, and maybe they'd fuss over me a bit while he was there so he could see they liked me a lot. And maybe Graham could do some whittling with Mr Peters while I did some sewing with Mrs Peters and then we could all join up for tea and cakes and that way no-one would be left out.

I stayed awake even longer than Katie trying to sort it all out in my head. (There was no problem about asking Katie. No way. Never.)

But the next morning I waylaid Graham on the stairs and asked him over to the Peters' place on Saturday.

'Oh, I'm not sure I could make it. I've got lots to do. No, thanks Andy, but I'd much rather not,' he gabbled.

I was mad. I thought he'd be thrilled to bits. Well, *grateful* at the very least. But it turned out I had to go down on my knees and beg before he'd agree to go with me. And even then he moaned and groaned all the way.

'This is mad, Andy. They're your friends, not mine. This old man won't really want to meet me. And I wish you hadn't shown him that boat. It was just these bits of old wood nailed together. I made it too quickly, it wasn't any good at all.'

'Well, Mr Peters thought it was *ever* so good. He's dying to meet you, Graham. He wants to show you all his woodwork stuff and you can have a go at making something together.'

'I can't do things with anyone watching. I go all fingers and thumbs. Dad says I'm useless. Oh Andy, why can't you mind your own business,' said Graham, giving me a shove.

But I didn't shove back. I understood. No wonder Graham was a bit of a wimp. Anyone would be, with the baboon for their dad. I suppose he loved Graham but he certainly didn't seem to like him. He was always nagging at him to act like a *real boy*. If the baboon was an example of a *real man* then they're a pretty duff species. My mum is *mad* wanting a bloke like the baboon. Mad mad mad. Still, I don't suppose there's any way I can like it so I'll just have to lump it. Even though un-Uncle Bill is a blooming big lump.

'It's OK, Graham,' I said. 'You don't have to feel shy. Mr Peters is ever so nice and he never ever shouts or gets shirty.'

'I don't feel a bit shy,' said Graham fiercely, going red.

He went even redder when he met the Peters. He hung his head and didn't say anything and when Mr Peters asked if he'd like to see all his woodwork things Graham just shrugged and didn't look interested. But it was all right after all. Mr Peters nodded and didn't make a big deal about it and talked to me instead and Mrs Peters talked to me too and Graham just sat and fidgeted in the armchair, but gradually his face went back to its usual pale creamy colour and his hand crept out to touch the smooth wooden fruit bowl by his side.

'Take an apple, dearie,' said Mrs Peters, but he wasn't bothered about the apples, he was looking to see how the bowl was made. And then he tiptoed over to the sideboard to have a proper look at the fancy fretwork and Mr Peters went to stand beside him and they started chatting. Graham didn't say much more than 'yes' or 'no' at first but eventually he started asking all sorts of questions and they ambled off to the lean-to together – and that was that. We practically had to drag them away when it was tea-time, even though Mrs Peters had made a treacle tart and iced fairy cakes as well as her famous seed cake.

Graham came with me to the Peters every second Saturday after that. He sometimes came over the Saturdays I was staying round at my dad's too. He and Mr Peters worked together on his Christmas present to me. My magnificent yacht. Radish can sail across her lake in seconds now. She's hankering to take to the open sea and attempt to cross the great pond in the park. She thinks her yacht is the best Christmas present ever.

Guess what *my* best Christmas present is.

is for Zoë

Carrie gave birth to my half-sister a week after Christmas. She should have hurried things up a bit so that she arrived on the proper present day but that's typical of Carrie, she's always late for everything.

It was my week to stay at Mum's but Dad came round and asked if he could take me to the hospital to see the new baby all the same. I thought Mum might make a fuss but she was in a good mood because un-Uncle Bill had got a new decorating job and they were celebrating on the sofa with drinks and chocolates and a smoochy video so Mum said yes quite happily – and she even gave Dad a little kiss on the cheek and said congratulations.

Dad looked pleased and I dared hope that they might get back together after all if they were actually kissing each other nowadays – but when I saw the way Dad kissed Carrie at the hospital I realized there are all sorts of different kisses and some mean you love someone a great deal and others mean you maybe still love someone a little tiny bit but that's all.

'Yuck yuck yuck!' said Zen, who had to come to the hospital with us. 'Do you have to do all that stupid slurpy kissy stuff?'

'I want to see my sister,' said Crystal, jumping up and down excitedly, her hair all over her face (Dad was looking after the twins single-handedly and they both looked even more ruffled and rumpled than usual).

'Here she is,' said Carrie, holding up this little bundle in a blanket.

I was right down at the end of the bed and couldn't see much. Just a tiny nose and a little red mouth. It opened and the new sister started making a lot of noise.

'She's saying hello,' said Carrie, grinning.

'Can I hold her, oh please can I hold her?' Crystal begged.

'Maybe you're a bit little,' said Dad anxiously.

'No I'm not, am I, Mum?' said Crystal, pouting.

'I think you're big enough to hold the baby – but sit on the bed and lean against me so that she can snuggle up comfortably,' said Carrie, getting Crystal and the baby carefully arranged.

'Look at me, I'm holding my sister,' said Crystal, her face bright pink with pleasure.

The baby's face was pink too because she was crying.

'I'm not big, I'm little, I'm a lickle wickle baby,' said Zen, and he started making loud *waaa-waaa* noises, imitating the baby.

'Come here, little baby,' said Carrie, and she scooped Zen up into her arms and held him as if he really was her baby again. He wriggled and protested but you could tell he liked it.

I stood watching them. Dad had his arm round Carrie, Carrie was cuddling Zen, Crystal was holding the new baby. I fidgeted in my pocket and found Radish.

Dad saw and smiled at me.

'Do you want to hold your sister too, Andy?'

'No thanks. I'm not really that bothered about babies,' I said, stroking Radish's ears.

'Why don't you take a turn? You might be able to stop her crying,' said Carrie.

'But there's no room on the bed.'

'You're big enough to hold her properly,' said Crystal enviously, and Dad handed the baby over to me.

I popped Radish back in my pocket and took hold of the baby. She was heavier than I'd thought she would be. I didn't know how to balance her at first but then her head lolled against my chest and my arms made a sort of cradle for her. She seemed to find it comfortable. She gave one last cry, several squeaks and splutters, and then quietened completely. I looked down at her. She looked up at me. She had big blue eyes but her hair wasn't fair like Carrie and Crystal and Zen. She had toffee-coloured curls. She was going to be dark like Dad. Muddy-brown like me.

I gently touched her starfish hand and her tiny fingers closed round my thumb.

'She's holding my hand!' I whispered.

'She likes you. She's stopped crying,' said Dad.

'She's so little,' I said, looking at her tiny fingernails, all so perfect in every detail.

'She's actually quite big for a baby,' said Carrie. 'Much longer and stronger than Zen and Crystal were at that stage. I think she's going to be tall.'

'She's like me,' I said.

'Well, she's your sister, so it's not really surprising,' said Dad.

'Is she still going to be called Ethel?' said Carrie.

'Yuck, Ethel's a *stupid* name,' said Zen.

I swallowed. I looked down at my sister.

'Yes, it is a stupid name,' I said. 'She's pretty. She ought to have a pretty name.'

'Well, what shall it be?' said Dad. 'We've already got A for Andy and C for Crystal. What about B for . . . Bella?'

'Belly-button,' said Zen, sniggering.

I wasn't too keen on a B name. Dad and Carrie might carry on then and have D for Dora and E for Emma and on and on all the way through the alphabet. One little half-sister was fine, but I didn't want a whole crowd of them.

'What about a Z name?' I said.

'Yeah, Z's the best. Z for Zen. That's my name,' said Zen, pleased.

'Z for . . . Zoë,' I said.

Zoë's my special favourite sister now. She really does like me. I can nearly always stop her crying. And I can give her a bottle and wash her in the bath and change her nappy, though I'm not sure that's such a treat. Mrs Peters is helping me make Zoë a little smock with a Z for Zoë embroidered on the front.

I'll maybe have to try to make something for Crystal too. She's my second favourite sister and she gets fed up quite a bit of the time because she's not big enough to do lots of things for the baby. I found her all curled up and crying in the Japanese bag the other day. I let her play with Radish for a special treat and it cheered her up a lot.

Zen gets fed up too but catch me letting Radish anywhere near him!

I like helping look after Zoë so much that I never really want to pack my things on Fridays when I'm at Dad's. But then when I get to Mum's I can pal around with Graham and Paula's given me some of her old make-up though Mum says I'm nowhere near old enough to use it yet. I look super with it on though, really grown-up. Katie smeared a whole lot of make-up on too, but she just looked silly, like a little kid with face paints. Poor old Katie.

I went to see the Family Counselling lady the other day because she wanted to know how Radish and I were getting on.

'We're OK,' I said.

'You still go to your mum's house one week and your dad's house the next?' she said.

'I've got a House A and a House B *and* a House C now,' I said. 'I go to Mum's House A one week and Dad's House B the next week and I go to Mr and Mrs Peters' House C nearly every day and Radish gets to play in her own Mulberry Cottage when she's there, though she still lives in my pocket most of the time.'

'It must take a lot of organizing,' said the lady, smiling.

'Oh it does. But I've got it under control now,' I said, smiling back at her. 'It's as easy as A B C. Really.'

THE END

ABOUT THE AUTHOR

Jacqueline Wilson was born in Somerset. She began her working life at a publishing company, then spent two years working as a magazine journalist before turning her hand very successfully to a career as a full-time author. She has written a number of books for children, as well as a series of crime novels and several plays which have been broadcast on Radio 4; she has also run classes for children in creative writing. An avid reader herself, Jacqueline has a personal collection of more than 10,000 books!

She lives in Surrey and has one grown-up daughter.

THE BED AND BREAKFAST STAR
Jacqueline Wilson

Where do baby apes sleep?
In apricots!

I'm Elsa, and that's one of my jokes (I tell
lots of jokes and I'm going to be a big star
one day). I do my best to cheer my family
up – but no-one seems to laugh much any
more. Not since we lost our lovely house
and had to move into a bed and
breakfast hotel . . .

'The book's chirpy narrative tone, amusing
illustrations and happy ending enlighten its
load without diminishing its concern'
The School Librarian

0 440 863244

CLIFFHANGER
Jacqueline Wilson

*I slipped backwards and suddenly . . .
there I was! Suspended. In mid-air. 'Help!'*

From climbing and abseiling to canoeing
and a Crazy Bucket Race, the adventure
holiday promises to be full of action.
There's just one problem as far as Tim is
concerned: he is *hopeless* at sports of any
kind . . .

Can Tim survive the horrors of a week
absolutely *packed* with activity? Can his
team – the Tigers – be the overall
champions? There are some surprises in
store for everyone!

**From the award-winning author of *The
Story of Tracy Beaker*, *The Suitcase Kid*
and *Double Act*.**

0 440 863384

DOUBLE ACT
Jacqueline Wilson

*No-one can be like a mother to us. NO-ONE.
NO-ONE AT ALL. ESPECIALLY NOT
STUPID FRIZZY DIZZY ROSE . . .*

Ruby and Garnet are ten-year-old twins.
Identical. They do *everything* together,
especially since their mother died three years
earlier. But can being a double act work for
ever? When so much around them is
changing . . .

'Wonderfully perceptive'
BOOKS FOR YOUR CHILDREN

'Hilarious' THE TIMES

WINNER OF THE 1995 CHILDREN'S BOOK
AWARD

WINNER OF THE SMARTIES PRIZE

0 440 863341

THE TM TECHNIQUE

Peter Russell was an honorary scholar at Gonville and Caius College, Cambridge, where he studied mathematics, theoretical physics, experimental psychology and, later, computer science. He has undertaken research on the psychology of meditation and has appeared frequently on radio and television. His other books include *The Brain Book*, *The Awakening Earth* and *The Creative Manager*. He is now a consultant on creativity, mind set and stress management to several major corporations, and lectures frequently on human consciousness in both Europe and the USA.

THE
TM
TECHNIQUE

*An Introduction to Transcendental
Meditation and the Teachings of
Maharishi Mahesh Yogi*

Peter Russell

ARKANA
PENGUIN BOOKS

ARKANA

Published by the Penguin Group
Penguin Books Ltd, 27 Wrights Lane, London W8 5TZ, England
Penguin Books USA Inc., 375 Hudson Street, New York, New York 10014, USA
Penguin Books Australia Ltd, Ringwood, Victoria, Australia
Penguin Books Canada Ltd, 10 Alcorn Avenue, Toronto, Ontario, Canada M4V 3B2
Penguin Books (NZ) Ltd, 182–190 Wairau Road, Auckland 10, New Zealand

Penguin Books Ltd, Registered Offices: Harmondsworth, Middlesex, England

First published by Routledge & Kegan Paul Ltd 1976
Published in the USA by Routledge & Kegan Paul Inc.
in association with Methuen Inc. 1976
Reprinted and first published as a paperback 1977
2nd (US) edition 1977
3rd edition 1978
Published in Arkana 1990
5 7 9 10 8 6 4

Printed in England by Clays Ltd, St Ives plc

Contents

v

Contents

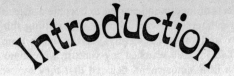

Introduction

Towards the end of 1967 I was browsing through the shelves of my local library when I came across a book entitled *The Science of Being and Art of Living* by Maharishi Mahesh Yogi. Having a growing interest in various forms of meditation, I added the book to the half dozen others I had picked out and carried on browsing down the shelves.

It was some days before I got round to opening Maharishi's book, but when I did I was taken by surprise. Throughout the book he was saying the exact opposite of everything I had read about meditation, and even appeared to be contradicting the 'authorities' in the field. Meditation, he said, could be easy; it did not require effort or control; anyone could meditate whatever their disposition or life-style. He was turning most of the traditional teachings upside down: yet he seemed to make a lot more sense than many of the other teachers I had come across. Having studied the book at length I decided that if the practice of Transcendental Meditation (TM) was even half as remarkable as his book then I must try it.

My initial experience was not, I must admit, all that I had hoped for, but this I soon realized was not the fault of the technique: the error lay in my being too analytical about the process. At this stage my academic training was more of a hindrance than a help. Over the next few months, however, the long-term effects of meditation started to become noticeable. I was feeling much calmer, more self-assured, and getting things done more quickly and more effectively. At the same time several friends who had initially watched my venture with some caution, and perhaps a little amusement, decided that they too would like to try it, and I found my own experiences being confirmed by the changes I observed in others.

My appreciation of the technique grew steadily, and when in 1969 I had the chance of taking a year to myself I decided to travel to India to study TM further. It was obvious that if I was to go deeper into the subject I needed to spend some time at the source of the teaching. My trip was well rewarded: both my experience and understanding of the field increased beyond all measure and before leaving India I decided to train as a teacher of TM. In the five years since then I have been researching further into the theory and practice of TM. This, together with the experience of teaching the technique to several hundred others, has convinced me that here is a most valuable, although largely misunderstood, practice.

The popular image of TM has generally been one of something a little mystical and not really suited to us living in the West in the twentieth century. This is to some extent understandable. Meditation has generally been associated with a withdrawn monastic life-style and thought to be of interest only to the spiritually inclined But this is not because meditation is itself an inherently reclusive practice. Teachings such as Maharishi's have always been formulated in the language of the times. If today meditation is thought to be something of an anachronism and of little relevance to a scientific-technological society it is only because it has not yet been formulated in the language of the present day. Maharishi is putting the theory and practice of meditation into a twentieth-century context and showing that far from being a vague metaphysical ideal it is a practical teaching which can be investigated and understood in terms of physiology, psychology, sociology, etc. He is proving that it is just as valuable – if not more valuable – today as it ever was. And for just this reason it is even more important that the subject be given a contemporary formulation.

In view of my personal interest in TM one might wonder whether I was not biased towards the subject. Certainly I have come to regard TM as a most valuable technique – indeed, if I did not believe it was of such value I would hardly be so willing to sit down for a year and write a book about it – but I challenge any implication that my personal involvement prevents me from writing as fair an account of the subject as someone who is looking at it from the outside. On the contrary, the person who has not spent some time acquainting himself with both the technique and the teachings behind it is hardly in a good position to present a comprehensive account of the subject.

TM validated itself to me not through critical analysis but through personal experience supported by the experiences of others I have taught, by Maharishi's writings and lectures on the subject, by a comparison with similar teachings which have arisen in most cultures at one time or another, by a consideration of TM in the light of contemporary physiology, psychology and physics, and by the recent experimental studies of the subject. In this book I have tried to bring these various approaches together in the belief that by throwing light upon the subject from as many different angles as possible the general reader may more readily gain a comprehensive vision of what TM is.

The specialist may feel some dissatisfaction when his or her own subject has not been dealt with as adequately as they would wish. This is inevitable with a book which takes a general, multidisciplinary approach. I must however emphasize that none of the various approaches are meant to prove that TM works: they are merely different windows into the subject. To take one specific example, the scientific research into TM is still very much in its infancy. Much more detailed analysis will be necessary before any degree of proof is possible. What to me is important is that none of the scientific work to date has disproved the claims of meditators. This alone makes TM a subject worthy of further investigation and it is for this reason that a brief account of the scientific experimentation has been included.

Although I have in many instances drawn upon similar teachings from other cultures and other ages in order to illustrate particular points I have not attempted to make a comparative study of TM with respect to other techniques. Such a comparative study may well be due; but if so it must be based upon a clear understanding of what TM is and what it is not. I hope that by laying down a fairly comprehensive picture of TM future analyses of TM may at least be based on a reasonably faithful understanding of TM – though ideally they should also be based on a clear personal experience of the subject.

Finally a word on the use of analogies. Throughout history teachers of meditation have made liberal use of analogies and parables, and Maharishi is no exception. The ideas being put forward are often very foreign to our own way of thinking and by likening the situation to a more familiar experience an abstract point can be made more concrete and the pupil given a better idea of what the teacher is trying to say. The various analogies used in this book are not therefore meant to prove any points; only to relate the points to everyday experience. One must also remember that an analogy is only a similarity: as much as it is like the situation under consideration it is also unlike it, and any analogy will, if taken too far, break down.

Introduction to the Third Edition

Since the original writing of this book Maharishi has brought forth a new set of practices, known as the TM Sidhi techniques, which build upon the basic technique of Transcendental Meditation. The basic TM technique allows the individual to transcend the active mind and experience a deep unitive silence beyond all thought. The TM Sidhi techniques allow one to begin to operate from this level of silence, and, it is claimed, when one does so many seemingly impossible things become possible.

In the third edition of the book I have added a new chapter called 'The Art of the Impossible' which briefly discusses these new developments in the TM movement. In the long term these additional techniques will probably have as profound an effect upon personal development as the TM technique itself, and it is impossible to give them their full due in just one chapter. All I have done in this edition is to give the reader a brief outline of their history, how they work, their effects and their values, with the hope that a little of the mystery surrounding them may be removed.

PR
May 1978

Acknowledgments

My indebtedness to Maharishi Mahesh Yogi for the knowledge and inspiration he has given me goes without saying. I also owe much to Dr John Allison whose personal guidance in the practice and theory of meditation laid a firm foundation to my interest in TM.

With regard to the production of this book I would like to thank Charmian Campbell for going through much of the earlier work with me and making many valuable contributions to both the structure and style of the book; Dr Ivor Pleydell-Pearce who also managed to struggle through and comment upon my rather untidy first draft; Chris Robertson for being a continual source of feedback, discussing at length with me many of the finer arguments and pointing out several interesting cross-connections which I would otherwise have missed; and Dr Diana Surman for helping to tidy up my rather cumbersome use of the English language. I would also like to thank Marion Fisken, Phil and Harriet Jump, Gill Robertson, and Penny and Philip Townsend, each of whom helped in more material and domestic matters at various stages of the book's preparation.

Part One

This book falls naturally into three parts. The first part deals mainly with the technique of Transcendental Meditation. Chapter 1 starts with a brief introduction to the subject, explaining what TM is, its role in life, and how it is taught. This is followed in Chapter 2 by a look at the origins and history of the practice, and how it is spreading through the world today. Chapter 3 is more theoretical and looks at Maharishi's description of the human thinking process and the principles which underlie TM, and Chapter 4 describes how the technique itself works. The last three chapters of this section deal with the effects of TM upon the individual. In Chapter 5 some of the scientific research into TM is reviewed, looking particularly at the state of rest which results in both the body and the brain. Chapter 6 shows how this deep rest dissolves accumulated stresses and Chapter 7 considers the all-round improvement in the quality of life which such relief from stress brings.

Part Two goes on to look at the changes in awareness of both oneself and the world around which come with the regular practice of TM, and Part Three considers the implications of such changes for society as a whole.

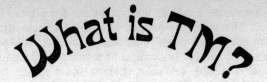

What is TM?

1

Every minute of the day someone new learns to practise Transcendental Meditation. He or she may be a doctor, a teacher, an artist, a labourer, a business executive, a housewife, a policeman, a student, a politician, a university professor, or someone from any other walk of life. What is it they are all learning to do and why?

Transcendental Meditation (or TM, as it is commonly abbreviated) is a technique which allows the mind to settle down to a less excited state. The person experiences quieter and quieter levels of thinking till he or she arrives at a state of complete mental stillness. In this state the attention is said to have gone beyond, or transcended, the everyday levels of thought – hence the name Transcendental Meditation.

As the mind settles down the body follows suit, becoming more relaxed than during sleep. One does not however go to sleep: one remains fully conscious and is usually aware of all that is happening in the world around. It is not a state of unconsciousness or hypnotic trance: it is simply a state of mental and physical quiet along with full inner wakefulness.

To practise TM takes about twenty minutes twice a day, once in the morning and again in the early evening. One simply sits down comfortably, closes the eyes and begins the mental technique. As a result the mind is allowed to settle down into a state of complete rest.

Now notice that I said 'as a *result* the mind is *allowed* to settle down...'. This is very important. In TM there is no attempt to make the mind settle down; once started the process happens of its own accord without any control or coercion on the part of the individual – indeed, any such attempt would almost certainly disturb the process. This complete lack of effort and control distinguishes TM from most other techniques of relaxation and meditation.

The word 'meditation' covers a wide range of techniques with many different associations. For some the word may imply holding the mind to some mental image or possibly to the idea of nothing; to others it may mean speculating on some chosen theme, or meticulously examining the contents of one's mind. Since all these meanings and many more have, at one time or another, passed under the umbrella of 'meditation' it is often presumed that 'Transcendental Meditation' must involve one or other of these practices. But this is not the case. As we shall see in Chapter 4 TM is unlike any of these concepts of 'meditation'. In fact the word 'meditation' is probably something of a misnomer as far as TM is concerned. But there is no other word in the English language which seems adequately to describe the practice without being equally ambivalent and misleading, so we shall have to accept it as the most approximate description of the technique.

Unlike some other forms of meditation TM does not advocate any renunciation of worldly affairs. The actual practice of meditation, it is true, does involve a temporary withdrawal from activity, but it is a withdrawal in order that one may return to activity that much more effectively. It is a re-charging of one's mental and physical resources and on returning to their daily tasks meditators find they have far greater energy and efficiency. Rather than being a withdrawal from the world TM is a balancing of the intense activity to which most of us are fully committed by a corresponding degree of profound rest. Rather than reducing activity, TM enhances it.

The practice of Transcendental Meditation is the same for everyone. The process is not concerned with the meaning of thoughts but with the way thoughts develop in the mind. And whether a person be an artist or scientist, young or old, English or Indian the way thoughts develop is essentially the same, and the practice of TM is essentially the same.

TM does not involve sitting in any strange physical postures, any change of life-style, or the adoption of any philosophy. There is, as will become apparent later, a large body of theory which accompanies TM and which may well be regarded as a philosophy, but it is not necessary to accept this in order for meditation to have its effects. Being independent of what you are thinking *about* TM is not affected by your own personal beliefs. Indeed you do not even have to believe that it will work; providing you follow the correct practice the effects follow automatically.

Until a few years ago science had regarded meditation as a very subjective affair and had had very little to say about it. But now that states of consciousness are becoming of increasing importance in many fields of science, and recent developments in physiology and psychology have made it possible to study in some detail the effects of meditation, the subject is rapidly gaining respectability. Since 1970 there has been considerable research into the effects of TM and many of the claims of meditators have been confirmed. Physiologists have shown that the technique does indeed produce a state of profound rest and relief from stress, and psychologists have found that people are more peaceful, relaxed and efficient after meditation. This scientific support together with the personal experience of the many people who have tried the technique has led to a marked reduction of the scepticism which initially surrounded TM.

Dissolving Stress

Another factor which has contributed to the rapid expansion of TM over the last few years is its effectiveness in reducing stress. Technological advances and large-scale industrialization may have relieved us of many of our physical burdens and helped increase our material standards of living but in their wake has come a significant increase in our mental burdens. It is this mental load which we commonly refer to as stress.

The actual sources of stress are numerous. Walking down a city street, driving in traffic, working amidst the din of factory machinery, living near a busy airport, struggling through the rush hour and having to deal with other tense people are all common causes of stress. Increased competition and insecurity result in so much tension and anxiety that 'mental breakdowns' and heart diseases have become more or less an occupational hazard in many professions. The more demanding the job the greater the stress. Air traffic controllers, for instance, who may each be responsible for the safety of a hundred lives once a minute show one of the highest incidences of peptic ulcers. At the other end of the spectrum the boredom and monotony of a production line can have similar effects.

The rapidly accelerating pace of modern life means that we are meeting new situations, making new decisions, and even changing life-styles faster and faster. The body has to adapt and readapt to each new change, and when the environment starts changing faster than the body can adapt we begin to accumulate stress. The faster the changes come the more stress is accumulated. The pressure is now becoming so intense that normal sleep no longer gives the body sufficient chance to recover from the overload and many people end up permanently stressed and tense.

Today it is no longer infectious diseases which are the major killers but 'stress diseases'. Many doctors now believe that over 75 per cent of our illnesses have their roots in stress and over 50 per cent of all deaths are from stress-related disorders. British doctors write over 60,000,000 prescriptions a year for tranquillizers and anti-depressants. On top of this there are the many other drugs such as aspirin which are bought over the counter, and a thousand million pounds spent each year on cigarettes. But suppressing the symptoms, which is essentially what this approach is doing, does not remove the stress and sooner or later it will reappear in some other form. Moreover, as well as depressing the physiological excitement most drugs also depress the person's sensitivity and alertness as well.

What then is the solution? The pressures in the world are there and they're not going to disappear in the foreseeable future. It is not, however, the pressures themselves which are the trouble so much as our inability to cope with them. The increasing pace of life is demanding that we take extra rest to balance the extra pressures, yet at the same time it is itself prohibiting us from taking this rest. What we need is a more intense form of daily rest.

Indeed, if the body is not given this rest it eventually falls ill forcing us to take extra rest – or at least it makes abundantly clear that it needs more rest. If we continue to ignore its natural needs then we may find ourselves heading for a rest of a more permanent nature.

The question is how to relax. It is not always as easy as it sounds. It is very easy to raise your blood pressure. Just to think of a frightening experience will do it for you immediately. But you cannot lower it as quickly by simply thinking of a soothing experience. Paradoxically the more tense a person is the harder it is to relax. The anxious person is prone to *try* to relax and becomes even more anxious on finding that he or she cannot. It is here that TM is so beneficial. Firstly, there is no deliberate attempt to relax, the whole process happens quite automatically. And secondly, the practice can be comfortably integrated into a normal daily routine and so neutralize stresses and tension as they arise.

Physiological research indicates that the process of TM is the exact opposite of that by which the body accumulates stress. Whereas stress results in higher heart rate, increased breathing, raised blood pressure and general physiological excitement: TM produces a slower heart rate, decreased breathing, lower blood pressure and general relaxation. By giving the body and mind two periods of additional deep rest, twice a day. TM neutralizes tensions as they are incurred and simultaneously dissolves the many accumulated stresses that were untouched by normal sleep. Moreover, it does this without decreasing mental alertness or sensitivity. The effect is very much as if one had fitted the rest and refreshment of a weekend into just twenty minutes.

Having this much rest twice a day instead of just once a week leads not only to an all-round improvement in health, but to a greater clarity of thought, a much better use of personal resources, more efficient action, and a greater resilience to further stress. In short the whole of life becomes more enjoyable, rewarding and fulfilling.

Learning TM

The basic instruction in TM is very simple. It is usually taught in four lessons over four consecutive days, each lesson lasting between one and one and a half hours. The instruction is carried out by qualified teachers of TM, of whom there are now some eight thousand throughout the world, and weekly courses are available at most of the thousand or so teaching centres which have been established (see Appendix).

The teaching has been standardized so that the procedure is the same no matter who the teacher or what the country, and takes place in seven steps.

The first step is an introductory lecture which gives 'a vision of possibilities' offered by TM. It is concerned primarily with the benefits which the person who starts TM is likely to experience, and with a very general understanding of the basic principles on which TM is based. This is followed by a 'Preparatory Talk' which deals more with the theory of meditation, and covers all that it is necessary for a person to know before starting the practice.

After the Preparatory Talk those wishing to start TM have a short private interview with their teacher. This is in order that both may get to know each other a little and deal with any personal queries.

The fourth step is one of personal instruction in the technique and takes about one hour. The fifth, sixth and seventh steps are for 'verification and validation of experiences'. During these days one meditates at home twice a day and receives additional instruction and explanation during the teaching periods. These next three sessions are usually given in groups, so that one may also gain from the experience of others, although there is always the opportunity of private consultations with the teacher.

After these four days of instruction most people are well established in the technique of meditation and continue the practice without any trouble. But although very simple the technique of TM is also very delicate, and the new meditator may unintentionally introduce some slight modification into the practice, with the result that meditation is no longer so effective, and probably not so enjoyable. In order to catch any such intrusions at an early stage it is important that the new meditator returns to see a teacher periodically for what is called 'checking'. In the beginning this may mean meeting with the teacher once a fortnight, or once a month. Later it is reduced to about once every few months. As well as keeping the technique of meditation in trim, these meetings also give the meditator a chance to understand more about his experiences and personal development.

The History of TM

2

Transcendental Meditation is not a new technique: it has a long and distinguished history stretching back several thousand years. It may not have always had the same name but the same basic technique has been taught many times in the past. But although the technique of TM may have been known and taught before, its history has not been a continuous one. The knowledge has been lost many times.

This loss is the inevitable consequence of the teaching becoming slightly distorted each time it is passed on from one person to another. When this happens time after time the teachings become so diluted and shrouded in misunderstanding that very little of the original remains. One is reminded of the legend of the First World War army officer who sent the message 'Send reinforcements we're going to advance' only to have it arrive at his headquarters as 'Send three-and-fourpence we're going to a dance'. It is rather like taking a copy of a copy of a copy of a .... each copy becomes a little more distorted and unintelligible until finally the original has disappeared.

As the practices become distorted they rapidly lose their effectiveness and no longer work so well. They are then, quite naturally, cast aside and all that remains are the empty verbal descriptions of meditation and its effects. Any further suggestion that meditation could in fact be easy is inevitably treated with scorn.

Although the practices may become lost to the world at large the seeds from which the teachings originally sprang live on and from time to time some teacher comes and tries to spread the original techniques once again. Today we are witnessing such a revival of this ancient teaching, and one which is spreading right across the world. The teacher who at this time has brought the technique out to the world is Maharishi Mahesh Yogi, commonly known as just Maharishi.

Brahmananda Saraswati

Before Maharishi came out of the Himalayas in 1955, he had been a devoted disciple of the renowned Indian sage Brahmananda Saraswati. His full title was Swami Brahmananda Saraswati, Maharaj, Jagat-Guru Bhagwan Shankaracharya of Jyotir-Math, but he is referred to by Maharishi as simply 'Guru Dev'. This is a common title in India and is used to refer to the master who leads a tradition. It can be simply translated as 'Divine Teacher'.

Guru Dev was born in 1868 and started his spiritual quest at the early age of nine. As a small boy he felt that there was no lasting satisfaction to be gained from worldly 'pleasures' and that true fulfilment came from within. So he set off in search of a spiritual master. He travelled up to the Himalayas where he searched for four years before coming across a teacher who satisfied his high criteria: not only had he to be learned in philosophy but also an enlightened man and a lifelong celibate.

Although Maharishi rarely talks of his master's life, maintaining that incidents from his outer life can never do justice to such a man's true significance (his inner state of consciousness), he does nevertheless tell one story which illustrates the strict care which the young boy took in his search for a master.

During his travels the boy came across a certain sannyasin who was purported to be an 'enlightened man'. A sannyasin is a recluse and one who has renounced all material possessions and worldly pleasures. By tradition such people are not allowed to cook their own food for it is part of their austerity that they do not use fire. When the boy met the sannyasin the first thing he did was to ask if he might have some fire. The man immediately became angered and reprimanded the child for having asked such a thing: didn't he know that sannyasis never had any fire and that it was a great insult to request such a thing? The boy simply replied that if he had no fire from where had it flared up? The man calmed down and recognizing that this was more than a simple child standing before him entreated the boy to stay and become his disciple. But the boy had seen enough to know that this 'saint' failed to meet his requirements.

After four years of searching through the Himalayas he eventually came across a man who satisfied his requirements. This was Swami Shri Krishanand Saraswati, a great sage of the time, who lived deep in the mountains at a place called Uttar Kashi, often called 'The Valley of the Saints'. The boy soon became his closest disciple and remained with him for twenty years.

At the age of thirty-four he left his master's side and retired to a cave in central India to live in solitude for forty years. He was almost completely cut off from any other people, these mountains being some of the thickest and wildest in India, yet even from the little contact that he did have with others he became widely renowned as an enlightened man.

After twenty years of solitude he was requested to leave the mountains and take up the chair of Shankaracharya of Jyotir-Math in northern India. This was one of the four seats of learning that Shankara had set up many centuries before in an attempt to preserve his teaching from distortion, but for the last hundred and fifty years no one had been found worthy enough of this position. It was clear to the custodians of Shankara's tradition that Brahmananda Saraswati was a fully realized man and one who could lead the people of India back to the original teachings, and they asked him to take up the chair. But he refused. Repeatedly messages were sent to him urging him to come out of the forest and fill this important position but just as consistently he refused. It was to be another twenty years before he finally took the position and this time he was given no chance of refusal.

Every twelve years in India there is a large gathering of 'saints' and holy men at Allahabad where two of the holy rivers, the Ganges and the Yamuna, meet. This festival is called the Kumbla Mela and it is customary for many of the recluses to come down from the mountains for this occasion. Along with thousands of others Guru Dev had left his cave to attend. Making the best of the opportunity his proponents performed the inauguration ceremony and having been officially invested as Shankaracharya for

North India Guru Dev had little choice but to accept the honour. He did not return to the mountains but spent the rest of his life travelling and teaching throughout northern India trying to re-establish a correct understanding of the ancient teachings.

Maharishi

At this time Maharishi was studying physics and chemistry at Allahabad University. Besides his studies he also maintained a lively interest in spiritual teachers, and on hearing that Brahmananda Saraswati was in Allahabad for a while he went along one evening to the house where he was staying.

Maharishi relates how he had been quietly ushered on to the flat roof of the house and was sitting there in darkness and silence unable to see or hear anything of this renowned saint. After some time a car swung round in the distance and the beam from the headlights momentarily caught the sage's face. Immediately, without having spoken to him, Maharishi saw that here was a profoundly serene and wise individual. After several more visits he decided to become a disciple of this man. Guru Dev accepted him on the condition that he first went back to finish his studies. This Maharishi did then returned and spent the next twelve years studying, learning and working with Guru Dev.

During this time Maharishi had become Guru Dev's closest disciple and at his master's death inherited all the knowledge of his tradition. With this knowledge he retired to live in solitude in an isolated mountain cave deep in the Himalayas. He had no particular plans at this time; he just wanted to be alone and still. But after two years of silence he gradually felt drawn back into the world. The recluses of that area tried to dissuade him, they felt that the outside world was like mud and there could be no reason why an enlightened man should want to dirty himself. Maharishi's feeling, however, grew stronger and stronger, and eventually he left the peace and solitude of his mountain cave and made his way down to the plains of northen India. From there he travelled on to the south of India and it was here that he found himself being asked to teach meditation.

These two years of silence have since been followed by nearly twenty years of the most intense activity. Maharishi works continually, morning, afternoon, evening, and far into the night, day after day and month after month. He has no time to engage in idle gossip or read newspapers; every minute is devoted to the task of teaching TM as effectively and quickly as possible.

But in spite of the time and effort he pours into his work Maharishi never takes any personal credit for his successes. If ever any credit is due it always goes to his master, Guru Dev. For this reason he will always be heard to end any lecture or discussion with the phrase 'Jai Guru Dev', meaning simply 'By the grace of Guru Dev'. With this expression he is acknowledging that it is only through Guru Dev that the teaching has been made available again today.

The Growth of TM

The first place that Maharishi went to when he left the Himalayas was the state of Kerala in the south of India. He had made no specific preparations to talk there, he had simply been drawn to visit the place, but a couple of days after his arrival he was approached by a man who, recognizing him as a monk from the north, asked him to give a week of lectures. Maharishi accepted and the popularity of his first lectures was such that by the seventh talk the hall that had been hired was overfilled. He was immediately asked to speak in other towns around the area and ended up spending the next six months lecturing and teaching TM throughout the state.

At the end of this period the first book on TM was published, *The Beacon Light of the Himalayas.* Only a small number were printed and sadly it is now out of print. In essence it tried to show how through TM, or rather Transcendental Deep Meditation as it was then called, Maharishi was once more bringing out the original teachings of the Indian scriptures.

After leaving Kerala he spent two years travelling and teaching around India, rapidly gaining acceptance both for himself as a teacher and for TM as a technique. In 1958 he established the Spiritual Regeneration Movement (SRM) in Madras laying a more permanent foundation to his movement and set off to take his message further afield.

He argued that one reason why many Western nations were more prosperous than India was because they were more open to accepting change; they were able freely to try out and take up new ideas. So if he was to succeed in getting the world interested in meditation he must go to the more 'progressive' nations first. In 1958 he left India and travelling east through Singapore and Hawaii arrived in California early in 1959. He stayed there for several months teaching TM and establishing a permanent national centre for the SRM, then went on eastwards to New York and Europe.

By the end of one year so many people were wanting to learn TM that Maharishi realized he could no longer personally cope with the demand. So he decided to embark upon the training of teachers of meditation. This decision represented a radical change in the Indian tradition. Previously the teaching of meditation had always been undertaken by the master of the tradition, or by his closer disciples, but Maharishi was taking ordinary Westerners and training them to teach meditation. This does not mean that he was creating Western gurus or spiritual masters: he was simply instructing people in the art of teaching meditation and this can be done by most people who have had some experience of TM and who have undergone the appropriate training.

Initially this training took place in India near Rishikesh, a little town situated at the point where the Ganges emerges from the Himalayas, and the start of a major pilgrimage for many Hindus. Just outside the town, a little way up the wooded and sharply rising slopes, Maharishi had built a meditation centre, or 'ashram' as such places are known in India. Here would-be teachers spent three months learning the art of teaching meditation.

The first course consisted of about thirty participants but by 1970 they had expanded to two hundred. Faced with an ever-increasing demand for teachers he moved the courses to Europe and set up facilities for training a thousand or more teachers at a time. More recently he has extended the teacher training programme so that the first stage of the training can be completed at home. By 1975 he had trained a total of nearly ten thousand people as teachers of TM.

When Maharishi first came to the West he found that many people were a little wary of anything 'spiritual' and were often put off TM by the name of his organization, i.e. The Spiritual Regeneration Movement. So in 1960 he established the more neutral sounding 'International Meditation Society' (IMS), and in 1965 the 'Student's International Meditation Society' (SIMS) to cope with the rapidly increasing demand for TM amongst the student population and others of that age-group.

The initial rapid growth of interest among students is probably accounted for by the increasing disillusionment with the 'consumer society' and conventional education, and the realization that the drug experience did not appear to be providing the anticipated 'alternative consciousness'. At the same time scientists in the West began to take a greater interest in the physiological and psychological effects of meditation, and as a result TM has gained in respectability. This has led to the establishment of two more organizations: the Maharishi International University (MIU), which is integrating the study of TM with conventional academic disciplines (see Chapter 14), and the Foundation for the Science of Creative Intelligence which is primarily concerned with introducing the benefits of TM to business and industry. Over the last ten years TM in America has enjoyed an annual growth rate of between 100 and 150 per cent – a figure which makes it the fastest growing organization in the world. By mid-1975 there were 550,000 people who had learnt TM in America and more than a million across the world, and the figure was growing at the rate of 35,000 per month.

The rapid growth of interest in TM has not been confined to America and Europe. With the present exception of Russia and China, meditation is being taught in almost every country of the world. Some of the greatest interest has been shown by India itself to which TM has now returned wearing the clothes of the West.

But whatever its packaging the teaching always remains the same. The different styles of presentation which Maharishi has created are just different ways of putting the same message across to different audiences. And, just as apples will continue to fall whether you think that the reason lies in the apple's tendency to fall, the force of gravity, or the curvature of space-time, so TM will have the same effects on the mind and body whether you understand the process in terms of the release of stress, the development of Creative Intelligence, or the expansion of consciousness.

Maintaining the Purity of the Teaching

With many other meditation practices and systems of self-development one finds the benefits and rewards which the teacher is describing bear little or no relation to the concerns of the man-in-the-street. The listener is often left puzzled and confused, if not highly incredulous. Maharishi, however, is always at great

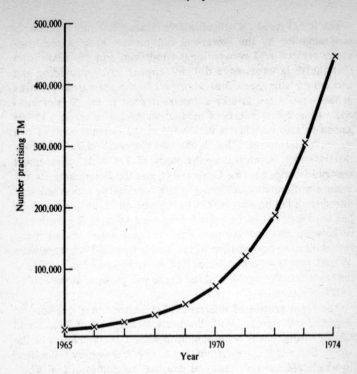

Figure 1   *The growth of TM in the United States (Data supplied by SIMS National HQ, Los Angeles). The growth in other countries has followed a similar exponential pattern although involving smaller numbers. (An extrapolation of this curve shows the whole of the US meditating by 1979. This state of affairs is unlikely to come about quite so rapidly because exponential growth rates only occur when the growing group is small compared with the total population. As the proportion of people meditating becomes a sizeable proportion of the total population the curve will tend to flatten out. Nevertheless the present trends do indicate that a large proportion of the US population will have learnt TM by 1979!)*

pains to ensure that his pupils are receiving the teaching on a level they can relate to and comprehend.

Inseparable from his desire to bring TM to the world is his aim to keep the teaching as pure as possible. He wants to ensure that this present revival of the tradition is not distorted and lost as rapidly as it has been in the past. Eventually, of course, it will suffer the same fate but Maharishi is trying to take steps to ensure that with TM this loss occurs as slowly as possible.

Every lecture he gives is being recorded, all on audio- and most on video-tape, in order to provide a more permanent and faithful record of what he has taught. This is the first time in history that it has been possible to preserve such a teaching so faithfully and hopefully this will help it retain its purity for much longer.

But one must also ensure that the individuals who are practising TM do not themselves distort the practice. Although TM is simple and easy it is also very delicate and the novice may inadvertently distort the technique a little before he or she has grasped it completely. This invariably leads to some control or restraint being introduced and the practice which has been modified in this way is seldom so effective. In order to prevent this Maharishi always advises frequent 'checking' in the first few months of the practice and also insists that one does not deliberately mix TM with any other technique. This is not necessarily because the other practices are in themselves of no value, only that the technique of TM is complete in itself. Any attempt to add to TM invariably turns out to be a subtraction.

From my own experience of teaching TM I have found that when occasionally people complain that meditation is no longer working for them it is often because they have unconsciously modified the practice a little. In effect they are no longer doing TM but something slightly different. It is not that TM is no longer working but that the modified practice is not so effective as TM.

As well as not mixing up the practice of TM with other practices, Maharishi insists that the theory behind TM is kept separate from other philosophies or metaphysical systems. Again this is not because other points of view are necessarily wrong, within their own frame of reference they may well be perfectly valid, but because they will usually muddle one's understanding of the TM process. The slightest turn away from the correct teaching may not seem very significant today but in a generation or so that innocuous seed could have grown up to become the source of considerable misunderstanding and distortion of the practice.

Maharishi is also effecting a fundamental change in the mode of propagation of the teaching. In the past it was virtually impossible to prevent distortion creeping in. In the absence of 'mass media', telecommunications or air travel, the only way in which a teaching could be spread was by personally handing it on. Maharishi has tried to eliminate this treacherous process of dissemination by effectively bringing everyone who learns TM back to the source so that they have the practice first hand. It is obviously impossible for everyone to learn TM personally from Maharishi, nevertheless it has been possible for him personally to train enough teachers. Only when Maharishi is satisfied that the student has fully grasped the fundamentals of this teaching will he permit him or her to go out and teach other people. In this way he is ensuring that everyone who teaches TM has the knowledge in its purity and that everyone who learns TM is effectively coming back to the source to receive the practice in its purity.

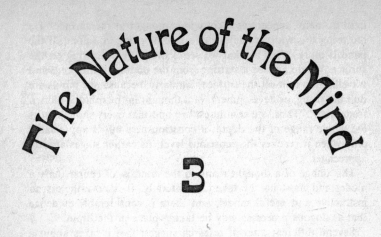

The Nature of the Mind

3

Maharishi's teachings are notably different from many of the others which have emerged from India and the East in that he never belittles the material side of life or the importance of physical well-being. Other teachers can be found claiming that spiritual or inner development should be one's prime or even sole ambition. Some go so far as to deny the reality of the physical world, relegating it to the realm of illusion to be ignored or even rejected. Maharishi, however, will have none of this. He continually emphasizes the reality of the world around us, the importance of physical well-being, and the intimate interdependence of the physical and the mental.

It is a basic premise of modern psychology that for every mental change, for every thought, experience, desire and feeling, there is a corresponding activity or change in the brain. It is now being recognized that the converse is also true: that for every physiological change and activity in the brain there is a corresponding change in mental activity; that *everything* that happens inside our brains affects our mental state in some way or other. Most of these mental changes pass unnoticed, only the strongest changes being consciously appreciated.

'A thought,' writes Maharishi, 'starts from the deepest level of consciousness and rises through the whole depth ... of the mind until it finally appears as a conscious thought at the surface.' He illustrates this with an analogy of a bubble rising in a pond. If the pond is murky then all that we see is the bubble bursting on the surface. We do not see it starting from the bottom of the pond and travelling up to meet the surface. Similarly, because our minds are dull the rising, or development, of a thought in the mind is hidden from 'view'. 'Thus,' he continues, 'we find that every thought stirs the whole range of the depth of consciousness but is appreciated only when it reaches the conscious level; its earlier stages are not appreciated.'[1]

This image of a thought rising in the mind is, of course, only a model and must not be taken too literally. It is nevertheless an instructive and useful model, and there is considerable evidence that analogous processes may be taking place in the brain.

Several different lines of research suggest that it takes about a tenth of a second for the brain to generate a conscious experience. Now a tenth of a second might seem a very brief time but by neurological standards it is pretty long. When we consider that one neuron is able to excite another in about one thousandth of a second and that each neuron may interact with a thousand or more others it rapidly becomes apparent that an immensely complex activity can be established in one tenth of a second: complex not only in the sense of there being many neurons involved but also in the sense of being highly organized and structured.

If we are to become aware of one specific neural activity, a visual event say, then that activity must somehow be distinguished from the vast amount of other activity that is going on in the brain. It is probable that the distinguishing factor is organization. Those neural processes which give rise to conscious experiences are those which possess a greater degree of order and structure. Indeed, there is a good case to be made for the view that conscious experience is the mental counterpart of organization on the physical level; that consciousness is the complement of a highly structured nervous system, and that specific mental experiences are the complementary aspects of coherent activity within the nervous system.[2] Sir John Eccles, the celebrated neurophysiologist, has remarked that the activity of the human brain is the most complex process in the entire solar system. It should, therefore, also be the most conscious process in the solar system.

A mathematical analysis of the situation suggests that it is only necessary for a very small percentage (0.001 per cent) of the neurons throughout the brain to be coherent in order that a neural activity be distinguishable from the less coherent background activity. It is likely that it is this ordering of a small percentage of the neurons which occurs in the tenth of a second taken to generate a thought.

In cybernetic terms the process of organization increases the signal-to-noise ratio. The signal is the experience being attended to and the noise is all the other unwanted activity. By increasing the coherence of the 'desired' information it is differentiated more clearly from all the background noise and therefore gives rise to a stronger conscious experience.

The actual degree of coherence necessary for a thought to break through into consciousness will depend upon the level of the background activity. There is in effect a threshold for conscious experience. Activities with a relatively poor degree of coherence remain subliminal (literally, below the threshold), masked out by other more coherent activities; activities with sufficient coherence just to pass the threshold will give rise to dim, hazy thoughts; while more strongly ordered activities will be appreciated as clear conscious experiences.

The parallels with Maharishi's model of the mind are fairly obvious. The rising of the 'thought bubble' corresponds to the progressive complexification and organization of the neural signals in the brain. The thought gets stronger and stronger as the coherence increases until it breaks through above the surrounding mental 'noise' to be appreciated as a thought on 'the conscious level of the mind'.

Figure 2 illustrates Maharishi's description of the process. The same diagram could equally well be used to illustrate the concurrent processes in the brain and so I have added to Maharishi's labelling a parallel physical one.

The Source of Thought

Every thought starts from the deepest levels of the mind as the faintest impulse and as it rises towards the surface it begins to gain structure. The structure of a thought determines its meaning and the meaning distinguishes one thought from another. At the moment of their inception all thoughts are qualityless and indistinguishable one from another, but as they rise towards cons-

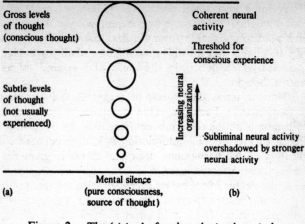

Figure 2   *The 'rising' of a thought in the mind.*
(a) Maharishi's description of process.
(b) Possible physical counterpart.

ciousness they each become more specific and more differentiated from other possible thoughts until, on arriving at the gross conscious levels of everyday thinking, each thought is a unique, clearly defined, experience.

If we were to reverse time and trace a particular mental experience back through progressively earlier stages in its development we would encounter softer and softer levels of mental activity. Eventually, when we arrived at the point in time when the thought was only on the point of being generated, we would reach a state of zero mental activity, a state of non-vibrating consciousness.

This state of mental stillness can be thought of in terms of pure consciousness or the true Self (see Chapter 8). In terms of the bubble analogy it is the bed of the pond from which the thought bubbles begin their journey upwards. Maharishi talks of it as the source of thought and a field of pure creative intelligence.

Every mental activity is, by virtue of its being an activity, a change of some kind. Maharishi sees change as a manifestation of the creative principle in nature. For him 'creativity' signifies not just inspired or original change but any change.

All thoughts also have a meaning of some kind; they are concerned with some thing. This directedness of thinking

Maharishi sees as the expression of 'intelligence' – 'that which gives order and direction to change'.

He sees creativity and intelligence (in his sense of the words) in every thought and at every level of thought. Therefore, he argues, the source of thought from which all thoughts arise must be a field of pure creativity and pure intelligence – pure creative intelligence.

Many people might find this a bewildering concept. For the present we could interpret Maharishi as saying that the source of thought is a field of potential change and potential order. Most people learn to meditate quite happily without fully grasping this point and for the present it will not affect our understanding of the process of TM. We shall, however, return to it later (pp. 101 and 158).

It is important that we should make ourselves clear of the distinction between the 'source of a thought' and the 'cause of a thought'. By the *source* of thought Maharishi denotes the field from which all thinking springs, every thought we ever have starts from deep within the mind as the faintest mental impulse and grows until it reaches consciousness. This is true of all thoughts whatever their meaning. It is the fundamental mechanism of all mental activity and is happening continuously from birth to death. What *causes* a thought to have a particular meaning is, however, a different process. We all know how one thought can spark off another and how some outside event will set us thinking about something else. When we ask what causes a certain thought we usually mean what previous ideas or incidents have given rise to this particular idea? We could say that the source relates to the medium in which mental activity is structured, whereas the cause determines the specific form this structure takes on.

This distinction can be made clearer by considering the analogous process which happens with a television picture. The picture is generated by a beam of electrons streaming from the cathode at the back of the tube. These are shaped and ordered by electrical and magnetic fields so that by the time the beam reaches the screen it produces a meaningful pattern of dots. The *source* of the picture is the cathode sitting at the back of the tube. What *causes* the initially unstructured stream of electrons to take on the form of one particular image is a chain of events which can be traced back through the electronics of the set, the aerial and the transmitter to the studio, and back further to producers, script writers, audience demands, political pressures, financial limitations, etc. In a similar way infinitely complex chains of events taking place in the world and in our brains *cause* the stream of thought impulses to take on a specific structure and meaning. But the *source* from which they spring is always the same.

The Process of TM

The process of TM is one of allowing the stronger levels of mental activity to reduce permitting the subtler underlying levels to enter consciousness. Maharishi defines the technique as 'turning the attention inwards towards the subtler levels of a thought until the mind transcends the subtlest state of the thought and arrives at the source of thought'.[3]

As the whole of mental activity settles down the threshold for conscious experience (the dotted line in Figure 2) is lowered and thoughts begin to enter the conscious mind at earlier stages in their development.

It is rather like being in a group of people at a cocktail party. In order to make yourself heard against all the background activity you have to raise your voice. This corresponds to the normal levels of thinking where thoughts have to become 'loud' enough to be experienced. If everybody in the room began to talk very softly you would no longer need to shout in order to be heard. Similarly during TM all other mental 'chatter' has died away and the mind only needs to whisper an idea for it to be consciously appreciated. Finally, when the whole mind becomes perfectly still, thinking as we normally know it ceases and one is left in a state of 'pure consciousness' – the still source of thought.

When all mental activity has ceased one arrives at a state which is not only peaceful but also profoundly satisfying. Now it might seem paradoxical that the source of thought which by definition is without qualities could be a source of joy (a question which I shall take up later, in Chapter 8). But, paradoxical as it may sound, we find that many mystics who have experienced states remarkably similar to those found in TM have made the same assertion. They repeatedly emphasize that as well as being a state of complete mental silence the experience is also a state of peaceful and serene contentment. St Theresa, for instance, the sixteenth-century Spanish mystic, says that, 'the soul is completely happy in this ... quiet.' Two thousand years previously the Upanishads described the state as one of 'Sat-Chit-Ananda', Eternal-*Bliss*-Consciousness, and in the present century R. M. Bucke described his mystical experience as one of 'a sense of exaltation, or immense joyousness . . .'

It is because the goal of meditation is itself a most enjoyable state that it is not necessary to control the mind during meditation. Once one has begun to experience the satisfaction of the goal then the attention will spontaneously settle down of its own accord without any individual coercion or control.

Why, one might ask, does this not happen anyway, without a technique of meditation?

From early childhood onwards we have been encouraged to seek satisfaction in the world of sensory experience. Western society encourages this outer-directedness further by providing endless sources of entertainment, continually re-affirming that satisfaction can be gained through sensory experience of one form or another. So we keep looking for a source of stable satisfaction in the outer world – a world where all satisfactions are transitory – because this is the only way we know how to look.

Idries Shah, the Sufi teacher, makes this point in one of his Nasrudin stories.[4] A man saw Nasrudin searching for something on the ground. 'What have you lost, Mulla?' he asked.

'My key,' said the Mulla.

So the man went down on his knees too, and they both looked for it.

After a time, the other man asked: 'Where exactly did you drop it?'

'In my own house.'

'Then why are you looking here?'

'There is more light here than inside my own house.'

Similarly we have lost the inner 'key' to true fulfilment. It is lost within ourselves but we search for it outwardly because that is the only way we know how to look.

But why does this inner source of satisfaction remain hidden? The answer is that it is over-shadowed by the grosser levels of mental activity. Indeed, the more we bombard the senses in our search for satisfaction the more mental noise increases, the stronger thoughts have to become in order to be consciously appreciated, and the more the inner fields are hidden from the awareness.

But although the source of thought itself remains hidden from the awareness the qualities associated with this field do nevertheless radiate out to some extent. In much the same way a light will shine out through a fog although the lamp itself may remain invisible, and the closer that one approaches the source the brighter the light becomes. Similarly, the subtler levels of thought are found to be of a more charming nature and once turned in the right direction the attention is drawn in spontaneously. As layer after layer is progressively peeled away the brilliance of the source increases and the attention is led on by the increasing charm to be found at every step, till finally it passes beyond even the finest level of thinking and arrives at a state of inner silence. The whole process is self-reinforcing; no control or effort is needed, it simply happens of its own accord.

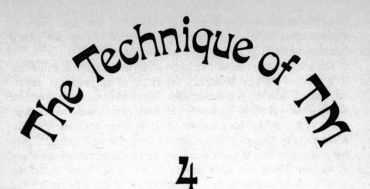

The Technique of TM

4

'I think I'll go and meet her,' said Alice, for, though the flowers were very interesting, she felt that it would be far grander to have a talk with a real Queen.

'You can't possibly do that,' said the Rose: 'I should advise you to walk the other way.'

This sounded nonsense to Alice so she said nothing, but set off at once towards the Red Queen. To her surprise, she lost sight of her in a moment, and found herself walking in at the front-door again.

A little provoked, she drew back and, after looking everywhere for the Queen (whom she spied out at last, a long way off), she thought she would try the plan, this time, of walking in the opposite direction.

It succeeded beautifully. She had not been walking a minute before she found herself face to face with the Red Queen, and full in sight of the hill she had been so long aiming at.

Alice Through the Looking Glass

One of the commonest mistakes made in meditation is to *try* to reach the state of pure consciousness. But it turns out that trying only takes one further from the goal and like Alice one keeps returning to the starting point. It is only when one stops *trying* to meditate that the whole process starts happening of its own accord bringing one full in sight of the goal so long aimed at.

The idea that the mind has to be controlled before it will come to a state of stillness is usually the result of an incorrect understanding of how the mind functions. Many have noticed how their minds always seem to be wandering from one thought to another; never being still for long on one idea, let alone completely silent; a continually changing panorama of thoughts and images. They have assumed that it must therefore be in the nature of the mind to wander. From this false premise it is then deduced that if the mind is to be stilled it must be controlled: it must be prohibited from following its natural inclination.

Indian writings have summed this up by likening the mind to a monkey continually jumping from branch to branch. Monkeys, it is said, are naturally mischievous creatures and the only way in which you will keep a monkey still is to tie it down. The same, it is said, is true of the mind. The only way in which the continually wandering mind can be 'tamed' is to tie it down. And, since the mind loves to wander, this will be very difficult and require great effort.

As a result a vast range of practices have developed with the expressed intention of 'controlling the mind'. Some of these aim at holding the attention to one thought while others try to keep the mind empty of all thoughts. Whatever the technique it is invariably taught that effort and discipline will be essential if any success is to be gained.

But unless the thought or image to which the mind is being held is a particularly charming one the mind will soon become bored and start wandering off in search of more enjoyable experience. It becomes 'obvious' that severe mental discipline will be essential if the mind is to be kept on the chosen theme. So one tries hard, and, lo and behold, it is indeed found to be difficult. Experience supports the argument and the fundamental flaw is never suspected. It is the initial premise that is wrong – the premise that it is the essential nature of the mind to wander.

A wise monkey-catcher realizes that the monkey is leaping from branch to branch for a reason; it is looking for something – more bananas perhaps. He realizes that to chase the monkey round and round the tree is a waste of time. It is much simpler and much quicker to place a pile of bananas at the foot of the tree and the

monkey will soon come down of its own accord. By recognizing
the inner needs of the monkey he brings it to a state of stillness
without any effort, control or chaining down.

Similarly with the wandering mind. The essential nature of the
mind is not to wander but to move towards sources of greater
satisfaction. When the world changes or when we become bored
the attention shifts elsewhere looking for more satisfaction. It is
only because nothing in the external world offers a lasting satisfaction that the mind is continually wandering. Thus it is much
simpler and quicker to open the awareness to the source of
satisfaction lying within and then allow the mind to settle down of
its own accord without any effort or control.

The Path of Effortlessness

Looking back over history we find that time and again the original
teachings affirmed that meditation should be easy and gentle. But
the passage of time has caused the original practices to become
distorted and lose their effectiveness. Any claims that meditation
was simple were quickly scoffed at and people began to interpret
the original teachings in terms of control and effort.

Reading through the ancient texts one may often come across
statements such as 'the mind must become still', or words to that
effect. Now such a statement is very neutral. It merely states what
must come to pass if any progress is to be made. It does not
explicitly advocate effort or control in the process. But those who
lacked the means to fulfil this recommendation saw this in the
only way they could, in terms of control. They tended to translate
it more in the sense that 'the mind must be made still'.

A controlled mind, however, is one of the fruits of meditation
not a path to it. The very act of trying causes mental activity to
increase and hinders meditation. Like *trying* to go to sleep at
night: if you worry about going to sleep you only become more
active and restless, but if you can completely forget about sleep –
by counting sheep perhaps – then you will usually drop off
without realizing it.

The purpose of meditation is to let the whole mind become
completely still. But so long as there is any control or effort some
mental activity must be continuing and it will be impossible for
the *whole* mind to become still. Like trying to pull oneself up by
one's own bootstraps – the more one tries the more one has to

overcome. If one succeeds at all through effort then it is more than likely that one only succeeds in *thinking* that the mind has become still. (This does not necessarily mean that such practices can never work. They may eventually bear fruit, but only after a long and arduous ordeal – indeed, their proponents have never claimed otherwise. One possible explanation of how these techniques may eventually succeed is that after the mind has been stretched to its furthest limits for long periods of time it eventually gives up. When it does give up it lets go of *everything* and the person spontaneously 'transcends'.)

Likewise, concentration plays no part in TM. Strictly speaking 'to concentrate' means to focus, to bring together, to become one-pointed; it does not necessarily signify control or effort. In most practical situations, however, some effort is usually necessary. Firstly the mind has to be held to the chosen thought against its natural tendency to roam off in search of more charming ideas. And secondly more energy has to be put into the thinking process itself in order to increase the signal-to-noise ratio and make the chosen thought clearer in consciousness. Thus the word 'concentration' has generally become synonymous with 'effort'.

In TM the mind becomes concentrated of its own accord without any effort. The state of complete mental stillness is itself charming to the attention. One is now flowing *with* the natural tendency of the mind rather than struggling *against* it and control is no longer necessary. Moreover, since the background mental noise is decreasing, there is no need to think 'harder' in order to increase the clarity of thought – it becomes clearer automatically.

Another common error has been to mistake the source of thought for the cause of a thought. Various techniques have developed in which the person attempts to follow a thought back through its causal chain and through memory to its origin at some distant point in the past. But this is not the same as tracing a thought back to its source, i.e. experiencing the *same* thought at quieter and quieter levels of activity. Such practices are still concerned with the meaning of thoughts and hold the attention to the grosser levels of mental activity. They may be of some psychoanalytic value, but they are unlikely to lead the mind to a state of stillness.

With TM there is no concern with the meaning of thoughts. It does not matter what one is thinking about, only that one can think. A point which Maharishi sums up by: 'Anyone who can think can meditate.' One's ideas may be useful, boring, clear, dull, brilliant or nonsensical but as far as TM is concerned they are all thoughts of one form or another, and all thoughts, no matter what they are about or who is thinking them, start from the faintest impulse and develop until they are strong enough to be consciously appreciated. It is this structure of the thinking process which is the concern of TM.

Some people have had the good fortune to arrive spontaneously at states of deep meditation, often without any prior knowledge of their existence let alone any deliberate attempt to reach them. In such cases one usually finds that the experience came when the person was relaxed and doing nothing in particular, letting the mind just wander according to its own nature. Here is part of R. M. Bucke's description of the state which preceded his experience of 'Cosmic Consciousness'. Note the relaxed, non-disciplined attitude of mind:[1]

> My mind ... was calm and peaceful. I was sitting in a state
> of quiet, even passive enjoyment, not actually thinking, but
> letting ideas, images, and emotions flow of themselves....

It is this passive attitude of letting things flow by themselves which is so important: not control or effort. The principal reason why these experiences do not happen more frequently is that we are always making an effort to succeed. In most spheres of life it may be true that the harder we try at something the more likely we are to achieve the goal, but it is simply not true of meditation. Here the less effort the better. Thus our attitude of continually trying and focusing the mind effectively removes the possibility of this natural occurrence from our lives.

TM, by letting the mind slip into a state of silence of its own accord, is a means of allowing this natural state to occur more frequently and regularly and makes the experience available to everyone rather than just the fortunate or 'chosen' few.

Turning the Attention Within

The process of TM might be summarily described as turning the attention through 180°: away from the outer world of sensory experience towards the subtler inner levels of the mind.

But this does not entail thinking about inner experiences, or about pure consciousness, for thinking *about something* inevitably keeps the attention on the level of meaning, i.e. on the surface levels of the mind. It does not have the effect of turning the attention within in the sense in which I use it here – the direct *experience* of the quieter underlying levels of thinking. As far as TM is concerned thinking about meditation is as much an outward directed activity as driving a car is. The inward turn that is necessary is a turning of the attention away from the meaning of thoughts and from all sensory experience.

When people first hear of TM they quite naturally try to conceive of the process in terms of experiences with which they are already familiar. That is they form a mental image of the state. If then, without any further guidance they were to attempt to meditate they would almost certainly expect something similar to their image of meditation to be happening. But this would keep the attention on the senses and would still be a mental activity of some kind: it could not therefore be a true state of inner silence. This was emphasized six hundred years ago by the anonymous author of *The Cloud of Unknowing*, one of the first English works on contemplative mysticism:[2]

> They read and hear it said that they should stop the 'exterior' working with their mind, and work interiorly. And because they do not know what this 'interior' work means, they do it wrong. For they turn their actual physical minds inwards towards their bodies, which is an unnatural thing, and they strain as if to see spiritually with their physical eyes, and to hear within with their outward ears, and to smell and taste and feel and so on inwardly in the same way. So they pervert the natural order, and with this false ingenuity they put their minds to such unnecessary strains that ultimately their brains are turned. And at once the devil is able to deceive them with false lights and sounds, sweet odours and wonderful tastes, glowing and burning in their hearts or stomachs, backs or loins or limbs.

Any preconceptions or expectations of what will happen cannot help the process one iota. They can only hinder it. Moreover, any intellectual analysis or scrutiny of what is taking place will pull the mind back towards meaning and the surface levels of thought. Thus Maharishi, in common with many teachers in the past, refrains from giving detailed descriptions of the meditative experience lest the pupil, in his eagerness to reach the goal, turn himself away from the correct path.

Maharishi also emphasizes that one should not make any attempt to forget about the surface levels of thought:[3]

> Trying to forget amounts to remembering what one aims to forget. This should not be done because the process of meditation does not advance on the basis of forgetting the gross material objective world of possessions, but on the basis of entertaining finer fields of experience. The attempt to forget is based on hatred and condemnation, whereas the spontaneous experience of finer fields of thought during the meditation is based on that willing acceptance which is the natural tendency of the mind on the way to greater happiness. . . .

But equally one should not *try* not to anticipate, not to analyse, or not to forget. Trying of any kind increases mental activity and just as fatally holds the attention to the surface levels of thought.

Nor, therefore, should you *try* not to try!

It is impossible to coerce the mind inwards, it must be allowed to retire effortlessly and gradually of its own accord. Nothing can be done to hasten the process: 'Once begun, it should be allowed to proceed by itself . . . quietly and patiently, without any anxiety or hurry . . . naturally and innocently.'

The Technique of No-Technique

The technique of TM is simply that of taking the correct starting point, the *effect* of which is that the attention begins to experience a thought at slightly earlier stages in its development. The whole system settles down a little and the attention, attracted by the charm of a slightly quieter level of thinking steps down again. And so it continues. The process entails nothing more than setting the correct initial conditions – the effortless inward turn of the attention – and letting go. The rest follows as surely and naturally as an apple falls to the ground.

Maharishi brings out a parallel here with the principle of least action in physics. The quantity 'action' is a measure of the energy exchange in any physical interaction and is the product of energy and time (or momentum and distance moved). The principle of least action states that for any given change in the physical world the total action involved will be the minimum possible within the limits imposed by the physical constraints of the given situation. This principle determines the path and velocity of a ball rolling down a slope. It determines the shape of the field around a magnet and the path of light rays as they are bent by different mediums. In fact given the initial conditions of any physical system and the constraints applying to it one may predict all future states of the system on the one assumption that any changes will satisfy the principle of least action. The principle is fundamental to the whole of classical mechanics.

Maharishi, however, sees it as being even more fundamental. It is not, he claims, restricted to the physical world, but can be applied to mental processes as well. We cannot test this statement in any quantitative way since at present we have no way of measuring 'mental energy'. Here I shall be concerned only with the qualitative implications of this hypothesis. Applying it to the specific process of TM he states that having set the correct initial conditions the mind will not only settle down to quieter levels of thinking automatically but will do so in the most efficient manner possible. Once set on the correct path there is nothing that we can do to hasten the process. It is as predetermined and as effortless as the arc of a diver.

Moreover you do not have to believe in TM for it to work. Providing that you do make the correct start and do let go you will be carried down by the mind's search for satisfaction – by mental gravity one could say – whether you believe in it or not, just as the diver is carried down by physical gravity whether he believes it or not.

It may seem paradoxical, but the less you believe in it, the better. Those who come to learn TM with the expectation that here is something fantastic which will produce amazing experiences and immediate changes in their lives are apt to anticipate and analyse in their meditation. They lose the innocence of approach that is so essential and which is retained by the person who starts expecting little or is even highly sceptical.

It could be said that TM is not so much a 'doing' as a 'not-doing'. As such it is very reminiscent of the oriental concepts of the 'wayless-way' and the 'pathless-path', and Maharishi is very much in sympathy with teachers both East and West who have denounced techniques which involve 'doing' of any kind.

Now this does not mean that one should not do anything. The

distinction between effortless meditation and doing nothing-in-particular is a very subtle one, but a very important one. I said earlier that when people complain that meditation is no longer working satisfactorily it is frequently because they have introduced some effort into the practice; but I have occasionally come across people who, having quite correctly understood that TM should be an entirely effortless procedure, have left the actual technique behind and sat down to do nothing but day-dream for twenty minutes twice a day. This is not TM and does not produce the same effects as TM.

People are sometimes suspicious of TM precisely because it is a technique. Enlightenment they say lies in knowledge of oneself and not in techniques. In part this is true: enlightenment does lie in knowledge of oneself, but this does not mean that one must also discover the path to enlightenment for oneself. That would imply that we should not learn from the experience of others. If we had seriously followed this principle in the past then most of us would still be sitting in caves wondering how to make a fire. What Maharishi is trying to do is to show other people how they too can reach a state of profound mental and physical silence.

The beauty of TM is that it allows a person to come to a state of complete stillness and inactivity through using an activity – but an activity which spontaneously reduces all activity including itself. It is this ability of TM to transcend itself as a technique which makes it so effective. In fact any technique which did not finally transcend itself along with all other mental activity could never take the mind to a state of complete silence. But on the other hand any technique which is both effortless at every stage and which eventually transcends even itself must in effect be transcendental meditation – whether it be called Transcendental Meditation or any other name.

Mantras

During TM one experiences a given thought at progressively earlier stages in its development. But not just any thought would be suitable for this: it has to have specific qualities which allow the attention to step down from the normal gross levels of thinking and begin to appreciate the finer underlying levels.

The first requirement is that it should be a thought without meaning. Any thought which has a meaning – and almost every thought does – will hold the attention to the surface levels of thinking. So a thought is chosen which has no meaningful associations. This thought could be derived from any of the senses. It could, for instance, be a meaningless visual image. The tradition from which TM originates holds that the sense of hearing is the most suitable. This may be because we are used to thinking verbally. It may also have relevance to the fact that hearing is the last sense to disappear during the onset of an anaesthetic.

Now not any meaningless sound would do. It is obviously going to be more conducive to meditation if the sound is soothing rather than jarring or agitating. To take an example of the latter, the sound of finger nails scraping down glass may not contain much meaning but for most people it would not have a very soothing quality and would not be a very suitable sound for meditation! The sounds used in meditation are ones which resonate with the nervous system in a soothing harmonious manner.

Until recently many would have scoffed at the idea that the choice of sound was so important. But Western science is now beginning to discover that sounds do indeed have profound effects on living organisms. It has, for example, been found that some bacteria will thrive when certain notes are played and die when subjected to others, and plants will grow better when played the Brandenberg Concertos than when subjected to heavy rock music.[4] Recently it has been found that certain algae displayed genetic-like mutations after being subjected to the sound of a certain sledge hammer – and that only that particular sledge hammer vibration would have the effect.[5] Roberto Assagioli, an Italian psychologist of whom I shall have more to say later, bases much of his work on the belief that music can both cause disease and cure it.[6] And the work of Hans Jenny and others has shown how specific vibratory patterns in time can produce intricate three-dimensional patterns in space which are often very reminiscent of simple life forms.[7] So the suggestion that specific sounds can have particular effects on the individual does not appear to be so far-fetched.

The sounds which are used in TM are called *mantras* and are taken from the ancient Vedic tradition of India which has always recognized the intimate relationship between sound and form. The long-term effects of these sounds are just as important as their effects within meditation, and mantras are traditionally divided into two categories, recluse mantras and 'householder' mantras.

The recluse mantras have the general effect of supporting a withdrawn, recluse way of life. The householder mantras on the other hand support the way of life of a person engaged in worldly affairs.

Unfortunately this distinction has often become very muddled and recluse mantras have been given to active 'householders'. When the original teachings became distorted and lost it was always the householder practices which were lost first: the recluse practices were not so widely disseminated and remained in a purer form. Thus when at some later date a person wished to take up meditation he naturally turned to the monks and anchorites for instruction, they being the only ones to have preserved some remnants of the original. But they invariably gave out their own reclusive practices with the result that the meditation led to a withdrawal from activity. This seemingly confirmed the idea that a recluse life was the only path to enlightenment.

Just how important it is to have the correct type of mantra is revealed by those cases in which people have decided to teach themselves 'TM'. Some 'friend' may have described the technique – even though the technique is not easily described in words – and the enthusiastic aspirants then chose some mantra for themselves, usually from some book or other. They then began 'TM' – or so they thought. Within a short time they were puzzled to find the qualities of their lives slowly deteriorating and the desire to engage in normal activities decreasing. This was not at all what they expected of TM. Faced with this disappointment some gave up the whole idea of meditation, although others sought correct instruction and began to gain better results.

One very important distinction between TM and other practices involving mantras is the way in which the sound is used. Nearly all other practices which make use of mantras involve a constant repetition of the sound, either out loud as a verbal chant or as a subvocal repetition. In India this procedure is often called *mantra-japa* ('Japa' meaning a 'constant repetition') and the intention is to keep up a continuous repetition of the sound, often with the aim of filling the mind with the *idea* of the devotional object, usually some deity, in the hope of gaining some spiritual union.

It is possible that many of these practices arose from misunderstandings and distortions of TM-like practices. If, for example, we look back to the teachings of Shankara, one of the principal sources of contemporary Hindu practices, we find him clearly contradicting repetitious practices when he declares that 'deliverance is not achieved by repeating the words "Brahman", but by directly experiencing Brahman . . .'.[8] Sadly Shankara's teachings have now been turned upside down and most of his modern 'followers' indulge in the unending repetition of 'Brahman' or some similar word.

All such practices bind the attention to the gross surface levels of the mind and do not allow experience of the subtler levels of thought nor of the field of pure consciousness beyond all thought. In TM the mantra has no associations and, more importantly, is not chanted – either verbally or mentally. The mantra is not so much an object for the attention to be focused on as a vehicle on which the attention rests and which leads it down to the subtler levels of thinking. This is brought about by the passive rather than active nature of the technique, the meaninglessness of the chosen sound, and the greater charm of the finer levels which allow the attention to be spontaneously drawn within.

Personal Guidance

Unfortunately the actual technique of TM cannot be written down; it can only be taught through practice and with personal guidance. I say 'unfortunately' for Maharishi's professed aim is to spread TM as fast as possible, and he would be the first to seize upon any chance of speeding its propagation. But it is also Maharishi's aim to spread *TM*; to ensure that it is TM which is taught and not something else.

He explains fully this need for personal guidance in *The Science of Being*:[9]

The practice of transcendental meditation has to be imparted by personal instruction. It cannot be imparted through a book, because the teacher must not only show the aspirant how to experience the subtle states of thinking but should also be responsible for checking his experiences as he proceeds on that path.

Experiences vary from man to man. Therefore it is not practical to record all the possible experiences. Nor is it to the advantage of the beginner to know in advance all that it is possible for him to experience.

. . . The moment one begins to experience the subtle states

of thought, one finds oneself drifting towards increasingly abstract states of experience. It takes a while for the beginner to be able to pinpoint his experience of subtle states of thought, even with the help of a personal teacher. For this reason it is of no practical value to describe in writing the details of the practice. The practice of transcendental meditation must always be taught by expert masters of meditation, who have been trained to impart it accurately as well as to check experience.

The Psychophysiology of Meditation

5

There is a difficulty which bedevils nearly all attempts to measure subjects during TM. The very act of measuring people disturbs them both physiologically and psychologically, making the meditation shallower than normal.

I have known of researchers asking subjects to sit and meditate while laden down with tubes and wires, with recording devices clicking and buzzing away close by, and with technicians scurrying around. It is hardly surprising that under these conditions only slight changes are recorded. This does not discredit TM: it only shows that under such intrusive conditions TM yields less significant data.

It is fairly easy to eliminate these physical sources of disturbance by making the apparatus and experimenters less obtrusive, but there is still the far more persistent problem of psychological disturbance. Just the knowledge that one is being measured can upset the very delicate practice of TM. This can happen in two ways.

Firstly, the practice of TM is an entirely innocent and effortless process. The meditators remain absorbed in the enjoyable nature of their experience and usually do not even notice that the body and mind are both becoming very still. But in an experimental situation they inevitably become a little more aware of the changes taking place in themselves. This slight shift of attitude, small as it may be, will interfere with the practice to some extent. Subjects from several experiments on TM have reported that meditation was not as deep as normal during experimentation.

Breathing may be one of the easiest physiological parameters to measure during meditation but it is also the most easily disturbed. One of the first doctors to conduct research on TM reported that it took more than two months of daily meditation in the experimental situation to accustom the subject to the apparatus. Only then did he begin to record the very slow, shallow patterns of breathing characteristic of meditation.

The second difficulty is that a subject would quite understandably, like to produce good results. I am not suggesting that they start consciously trying to produce good results – any meditator knows how futile and disastrous that would be – but deep inside there arises a slight eagerness for a 'good' meditation. With this faintest degree of anticipation they lose the all-important innocence of approach and the practice immediately loses its effectiveness.

As far as the experiments during meditation are concerned one seems to be approaching the psychological equivalent of Heisenberg's Uncertainty Principle. The closer the investigation the greater the disturbance and the less actually known about the state the subject would have been in if unobserved. Nevertheless the experiments to date do reveal some very interesting changes and suggest that the body may well be passing into a unique state during TM.

Metabolic Activity

The overall rate at which the body consumes energy is measured by the *metabolic rate*. The more active we are the more energy we use and the higher, therefore, the metabolic rate. It is usually assumed that there is a lower limit to metabolic activity, called the basal metabolic rate which can be thought of as the minimum energy necessary to keep the body 'ticking over' when sitting or lying still. In deep sleep the rate can fall to about 10 per cent below the basal level but much below this has generally been considered very unusual and even abnormal for human beings.

Since oxygen is one of our prime energy sources the metabolic rate is reflected in the rate and depth of our breathing. So, when early TM meditators noticed their breathing becoming very slow and shallow they naturally assumed a considerable reduction in their metabolic rate.

The first objective analysis of these changes was carried out in 1965 in London. Dr John Allison measured the rate of breathing and found that it changed from the customary dozen or so breaths per minute of normal rest to an average of six breaths per minute during TM.[1] This is very low, though not abnormally so – one could achieve this without meditating by taking very deep breaths; what was particularly striking was that the six or so breaths per minute of the meditator were so shallow as to be hardly detectable. This meant that the meditator was not compensating for his slowed breathing by taking in more air each breath; on the contrary he was taking in far less air each breath. A respiratory physiologist estimated that such a breathing pattern was consistent with a drop in metabolic rate of around 75 per cent below the basal level. He commented that anyone who did that for twenty minutes should, by all accounts, be dead: but the subject was very much alive!

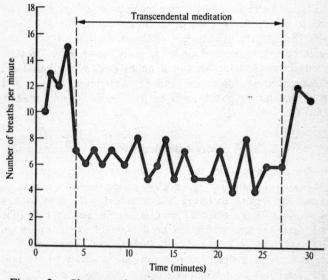

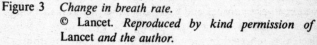

Figure 3   *Change in breath rate.*
© Lancet. *Reproduced by kind permission of* Lancet *and the author.*

The implication that oxygen consumption was decreasing was confirmed in 1970 by Dr Keith Wallace in America. Wallace measured the oxygen consumption directly and found that during TM there was an average fall in consumption of 16 per cent below the basal level.[2] The reason that his subjects did not show as slow or shallow a breathing as Allison's was probably because the apparatus was more disturbing and little time was allowed for the subjects to get used to the experimental situation.

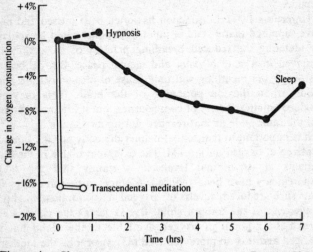

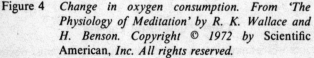

Figure 4   *Change in oxygen consumption. From 'The Physiology of Meditation' by R. K. Wallace and H. Benson. Copyright © 1972 by* Scientific American, *Inc. All rights reserved.*

Wallace also studied several other physiological variables. He found that the production of carbon dioxide – which results from the combustion of oxygen – decreased by the same amount as oxygen consumption. Thus less oxygen was being used up by the body and this suggests that the reduced breathing was the consequence of a reduced need for oxygen. This hypothesis is supported by two other observations. First, there was no compensatory over-breathing after meditation, i.e. the body did not have to make up for any lack of oxygen. And second, measurements of the gases dissolved in the blood showed normal levels of oxygen and carbon dioxide.

When we are very active the carbon dioxide level increases and the body compensates for this by increasing the rate and depth of breathing. Conversely, when the carbon dioxide level falls below the optimum breathing slows down. Wallace's findings show the optimum levels of both gases being maintained throughout TM. The reduced rate and depth of breathing must therefore be a *result* of reduced metabolic activity. If it were the *cause* there would be a deficit of oxygen in the blood and a build-up of carbon dioxide.

Unfortunately this distinction has often been missed and many have supposed that a state of inner tranquillity could be achieved by imitating the reduced breathing patterns of those they had observed in a state of calm and mental peace. But deliberately restricting the breathing will only cause oxygen starvation and a mild carbon dioxide poisoning of the brain. This may well produce an altered state of consciousness but it is almost certainly not the same state as that reached during meditation.

It is important to realize that neither the body nor the brain are deprived of oxygen during TM. The oxygen available in the blood remains at its normal level; it is simply that the body's requirements have been reduced. Mothers-to-be sometimes fear that such reduced levels of oxygen consumption might be dangerous for the unborn child. But as far as the child is concerned the amount of oxygen available in the blood has not changed and it is no more deprived of oxygen than the mother is.

Other Physiological Changes

Reduced breathing and oxygen consumption is the most obvious change to take place during TM but it is by no means the only change. The results of several other research projects suggest that TM affects nearly every aspect of the body's physiology.

Along with the reduction in breathing there is a decrease in heart rate of about 5 beats per minute[3] and a decrease in cardiac output (the amount of blood pumped out by the heart) of about 25 per cent.[4] These changes show that the work load of the heart is being reduced. Blood pressure also decreases, especially in hypertensive people,[5] and this is related to the reduction in stress which TM brings. These changes have been found to carry over into ordinary life showing that people are more relaxed during the day as a result of meditation.[6]

Analysis of the blood itself shows that a chemical called blood lactate, produced during strenuous physical activity and also associated with anxiety states, is eliminated from the system much more rapidly during transcendental meditation.[7]

Studies of brain activity with the EEG (electroencephalogram) show a relaxed but alert state of mental functioning. They have also revealed fascinating changes relating to the co-ordination of the two halves of the brain and I shall look at these in more detail shortly. Interesting changes in the electrical activity of the skin indicate a general decrease in anxiety and corresponding increase in stability and adaptability.[8] Many of these effects have been found to occur right from the very first session of meditation.

Besides these physiological experiments there are also studies which show a general improvement in health, decrease in insomnia, relief from asthma, decreased use of drugs (both prescribed and non-prescribed), faster reaction time, sharper perception, improved mind-body co-ordination, fuller development of personality, growth of creativity and intelligence, and improved interpersonal relationships. These studies and others will be discussed later in the book where they are more relevant.

Research into TM is expanding at such a rate that any information given in this book may well have been superseded by the time it reaches the reader. All the studies have been put together in a book of collected papers and I recommend anyone who wants further details of the research to refer to it and its future editions.[9]

A Fourth State of Consciousness

It has been claimed that the physiological research into TM demonstrates the existence of a fourth state of consciousness distinct from waking, dreaming and deep sleep, i.e. transcendental consciousness. But this I think is stretching the present results a little too far. The research is still very much in its infancy. Most of the studies have been of an exploratory nature and few have included adequate control groups. The results to date simply give a degree of objective support to the meditators' personal claims that they are reaching a state of profound rest. This does not necessarily mean that meditators are not reaching transcendental consciousness: it only reflects the difficulty in measuring people in this state.

Besides the experimental difficulties discussed earlier there is also the difficulty of pin-pointing a particular stage of meditation. The process of TM is a continually changing series of states. One does not dive into transcendental consciousness and remain there for the duration of the twenty minutes meditation. There is repeated movement between the subtler and grosser levels of thought. The present measurements concerning oxygen consumption, blood chemistry, blood pressure and heart rate do not depict the deepest states of meditation but represent the time-average of a person who is varying between deep and shallow states. And for just this reason they are all the more interesting. They suggest that the deepest states of meditation involve physiological changes far more profound than those so far observed.

Meditators have often reported that during the deepest states of TM the breathing dies away completely and preliminary research with more sophisticated apparatus at Maharishi European Research University in Switzerland has now confirmed this. It has been found that during those periods when the subject reported a clear experience of transcendental consciousness the breathing had indeed come to a standstill. Such periods usually lasted for between thirty seconds and one minute and occurred quite spontaneously without any attempt to hold the breath. Further experiments suggest the breathing can die away for even longer periods – up to ten minutes at a time – if so this would imply a considerably reduced metabolism and would be a major discovery for Western science.

Although such low states of metabolism go far beyond the experience of Western physiology, we should not immediately discount them; a healthy scepticism should be balanced by an equally healthy open-mindedness. Furthermore, because the claims of meditators do indeed go beyond our present Western understanding of what is possible, beyond the current physiological paradigm, experiments in this field will need to be more convincingly designed and more strictly controlled than experiments investigating more orthodox phenomena if they are to pass the sceptical scrutiny of the scientific establishment.

Yoga and Zen

The yogic teachings of the East have always held that the deepest state of meditation, the state of *samadhi,* or 'stilled mind' is also a state of complete physical stillness; a state of suspended animation – but a conscious one.

Scientific investigations into the claims of yogis have suffered the same difficulties as the research into TM. Additionally they have been hampered by the vast variety of techniques employed, making any degree of uniformity difficult to achieve, and by the physical difficulty of getting delicate apparatus up to mountain retreats where many of the more adept practitioners live. Nevertheless the experiments that have been conducted generally reveal the same trend towards decreased metabolism as found in TM. Similar changes have also been found in Zen monks in Japan.

It is significant that although the physiological effects of Yoga and Zen are in general similar to TM, it often takes many years, even a lifetime, of practice at these techniques to achieve states which are reached after only a year or two with TM. Maharishi never claims that TM is the only way to a full inner development; he readily accepts that there are many practices which eventually lead to the same state. He does however maintain that TM is the fastest way. In that most other practices teach some control or mental concentration they are, he claims, opposed to the mind's natural tendency to move towards greater satisfaction and are therefore not only arduous but circuitous routes to the goal.

A second difference is that most of the yogis and Zen masters studied in experiments tended to be recluses whereas the subjects in the TM experiments were all active people engaged in normal everyday lives. This supports Maharishi's claim that renunciation and retirement from the world are not prerequisites to meditation, and that the technique of TM is particularly suitable to the 'householder'.

Biofeedback?

In recent years it has been demonstrated that it is possible to produce many physiological changes previously thought to be beyond individual control. The subject 'learns' to control blood pressure, skin resistance or EEG activity not by deliberately trying to change them but by attending to information 'fed back' from monitoring instruments. The technique is known as 'biofeedback'. All the subject does is to try to find a mental state resulting in the correct physiological change. Since many of the changes which can be induced by such techniques are similar to those found in meditation it has been suggested that biofeedback might be a short cut to these states. Initially this suspicion was supported by the finding that the correct mental attitude for biofeedback was usually similar to that of meditation – 'a detached non-anxious, merely expectant' attitude.[10] But more recent work suggests that far from being a short cut to these states it may not even be a route at all.

Firstly, biofeedback falls down in that whilst most subjects find that they can produce one, or perhaps two, physiological changes by this method, it is not possible to produce a large number of changes in an integrated fashion as occurs with TM. And secondly, with TM no attempt is made to produce any physiological changes. They usually occur without the person being aware of them and come as the effects rather than the cause of a settling down of mental activity.

Self-hypnosis?

It is sometimes suggested that TM might be nothing more than self-hypnosis. Leaving aside the rather cynical suggestion that through self-hypnosis a person can fool himself into believing almost anything, it is reasonable to note that self-hypnosis, involving the use of repetitious phrases or images, is often used as an aid to relaxation: could not TM be based on similar principles and having a similar effect?

The answer, I believe, is 'No'. On the first point the physiology of hypnosis is generally different from that of TM. Even when a subject is given the hypnotic suggestion to relax completely it is found that despite muscular relaxation the metabolism does not change significantly, if anything it rises slightly (see Figure 4, p. 55). Furthermore, EEG recordings from the brain of a hypnotized subject usually show a waking pattern of activity (unless the subject is deliberately sent to sleep in which case he will show sleeping patterns) whereas with TM the EEG patterns are different from both waking states and sleep states. These and other physiological differences argue against TM being just some form of self-hypnosis.

Concerning the superficial similarity of the mantra to a hypnotic rhythm it should be remembered that the use of the mantra in TM is not one of *continual* repetition. Such incessant repetition of sounds is known to have strange effects on perception but this does not satisfactorily explain the experience of TM.

It is interesting that such theories about the mantra are generally put forward by non-meditators. One could argue that they had not therefore become biased towards Maharishi's explanation of the process. But I think it is more likely that they had not personally experienced, and therefore not fully understood, the important difference between continuous forms of repetition (such as in the Indian *mantra-japa* mentioned earlier) and the non-directed, passive awareness of the mantra which occurs in TM. If TM were just a matter of hypnotizing oneself with a repetitious phrase it would surely be more effective to make a steady subvocal repetition of the mantra in order that the nervous system habituate as easily and quickly as possible? But, as anyone who practises TM will verify, such constant repetition does not readily lead to a state of restful alertness.

EEG and Brain Synchrony

The electroencephalogram (EEG) detects the minute electrical changes occurring over the scalp as a result of activity within the brain. The patterns which are recorded can be analysed according to their component frequencies and the different frequencies can be correlated with different types of mental activity.

When, for example, the attention is sharply focused on some mental task there is a broad spectrum of activity ranging from 2 or 3 cps (cycles per second) to 30 or 40 cps. This is called desynchronized activity. When the attention is not concentrated on anything in particular and the brain is, so to speak, free-wheeling most people show what is called alpha-activity. This consists of a predominance of waves in the 8 to 10 cps waveband, particularly at the back of the head. When a person is in deep sleep his brain shows a predominance of very slow activity of the order of 1 and 2 cps called delta-activity.

The EEG is still a very crude measurement of brain functioning. All that is being detected is the overall pattern of activity of millions of neurons. It is rather like hanging a microphone above a large city and recording the traffic noise. You might be able to tell whether it was rush hour or the middle of the night, or whether the traffic lights were changing in synchrony, but that is about all. Nevertheless, crude as it is, the EEG is the most convenient technique available for assessing the general activity of the brain and relating it to different states of consciousness.

During TM there is found to be an abundance of alpha-activity indicating, not surprisingly, that the attention is unfocused and relaxed. This activity tends to be slower than normal (about 8 cps rather than 9 or 10 cps) and of larger amplitude.[11] It also spreads forward from the rear of the brain where it is usually found, to cover the whole of the scalp and at the same time appears to become synchronized in the sense that the waves from different areas of the scalp take the same form. In order to understand the significance of this synchronization it is necessary to know a little more about the functioning of the brain.

It has long been known that most nerves from the right side of the body end up on the left side of the brain and most from the left side of the body on the right side of the brain. So when you touch something with your right hand it is the left side of the brain which controls the movement and registers the sensation.

There are, however, many other ways in which the two halves of the brain differ in their functions. Various experiments over the last twenty years have shown that the major control of verbal, linguistic and rational functions appears to take place in the left hemisphere, while spatial relationships, image recognition, and aesthetic appreciation are largely controlled by the right hemisphere.[12]

Most of the functions associated with the left side of the brain involve a sequential or linear type of processing (i.e. one after the other) while most of the right side functions would appear to necessitate a simultaneous or parallel mode of processing. Speech and writing, for example, involve the analysis of an idea into a linear chain of words and phonemes which are then spoken or written one after the other, whereas the judgment of a spatial relationship requires the simultaneous appreciation of several factors and their synthesis into a whole.* Recent work in England has confirmed this hypothesis showing that the left side of the

---

* Reading and writing do not have to be so linear. Techniques of speed reading seem to be using the right hemisphere as much, if not more, than the left. Most of us learnt to read by first vocalizing and then subvocalizing the words. This leaves the process firmly implanted in the left hemisphere. Speed readers seem to break this habit, and can take in several lines at once *visually* rather than one word at a time *verbally*. With writing there are techniques such as Tony Buzan's organic patterning of information which use non-linear, multi-dimensional forms of display, encouraging right hemisphere activity along with that of the left (Tony Buzan, *Use Your Head,* BBC Publications, London, 1974).

brain is better at functioning in a sequential manner while the right tends to operate more in a simultaneous manner.[13]

It used to be thought that the left hemisphere was the dominant or major hemisphere, but it now appears that neither side is fundamentally more dominant than the other. It is more a question of which functions we lay emphasis upon. It has been found that if a person is asked to perform some essentially linear task such as writing a letter, then the right side of the brain becomes relatively inactive, showing a higher proportion of alpha-activity, leaving the attention focused in the left. If, conversely, the subject is asked to draw a picture then the left passes into a state of comparative inactivity and the right concentrates on the problem. What is probably happening is that the half of the brain not directly concerned with the given task is being shut off in order to reduce the level of interference in the other half. In comparing the EEG patterns of different professional groups it has been found that people such as lawyers who concentrate upon analytic thinking show a left-hemisphere dominance whereas artists show a right-hemisphere dominance.

Our society lays greater emphasis on verbal and rational abilities with the result that the left has come to be regarded as the more important half. In school we were taught the three R's (reading, 'riting and 'rithmetic) – all left hemisphere functions – and those associated with the right were largely untouched. So it is not that the left is intrinsically more dominant, only that our emphasis on the left has caused it to become dominant in that most people use this mode for the major part of the day.

Robert Ornstein has suggested that one of the functions of meditative practices is to correct this by establishing a state of balance between the left and right hemispheres. In the case of TM it certainly looks as if this may be the case.

What is particularly interesting in TM is the manner in which the alpha-activity builds up. Detailed analysis by Dr Bernard Glueck revealed that the alpha-activity built up first in the left hemisphere and then in the right,[14] suggesting that the active analytical mode was giving way to the receptive synthetic mode which was then itself being reduced. This relates very closely to the technique of TM.

There are two fundamental aspects to TM: the mantra and the technique of using it. Both together turn out to be conducive to a shift towards right hemisphere activity.

The mantra is meaningless and has no verbal associations. It does not therefore encourage the linguistic thinking normally associated with the left hemisphere. Furthermore in using the mantra one does not make any attempt at subvocal repetition, which would again be a left hemisphere activity.

The technique of TM is very much a technique of not-doing, a passive awareness; one has the attitude of letting it happen rather than making it happen. There is no intellectual analysis of experiences. Consequently the rational analytic processes usually associated with the left hemisphere are not particularly encouraged. Thus the initial effect of TM can be seen to be one of allowing the attention to shift more towards the right hemisphere.

But TM is more than just a turn to right hemisphere activity – if it were only that it would be little different from sitting down and listening to some good music. TM is a transcending of both types of mental activity. But it would appear that to start the process off one first has to reduce the more predominant, active mode of thought and *then* allow the other mode to decrease as well, until both come to a relaxed state. This is borne out by Glueck's work mentioned above and by Dr Jean-Paul Banquet, working at Harvard.

Banquet found that as a person passed deeper into meditation there was a progressive 'synchronization' of the EEG patterns. He uses the word synchronization here in a slightly different way from which it is commonly used in EEG work. Usually one speaks of a synchronization of the activity of groups of cells, and it is this synchronization which gives rise to strong frequency components like the alpha-wave. Banquet extends the use of the word to cover the synchronization of activity from completely different areas of the brain – a much rarer phenomenon. In this type of synchrony not only are groups of cells displaying synchronous activity (i.e. alpha-activity) but all the alpha-activity of the cortex is of the same frequency and in phase.

He found that during TM this synchronization appeared first between the front and rear of the head and then between the left and right hemisphere. It was particularly striking in occasional bursts of faster brain activity (20 cps). Just what this indicates is still unclear but it is interesting that they usually occurred at moments when subjects felt themselves to be in a particularly deep state of meditation.[15]

Because the right hemisphere is usually less active than the left its energy output is less. Mark Westcott, working in England, found that during TM the relative energy outputs of the two halves were equalized. This state of balance continued after meditation as well. In fact the regular meditators started off the experiment with higher levels of balance indicating that the effects were lasting throughout the day. The controls who sat and merely 'relaxed' not only started off with lower levels of balance but the power ratio actually dropped during the experiment suggesting that they were using their left hemispheres in order to make themselves relax, rather than allowing it to happen.[16]

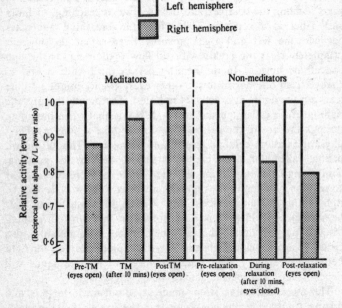

Figure 5   *Equalization of activity levels in left and right halves of brain during and after TM.*

Work at the Maharishi European Research University in Switzerland using specially designed EEG and computer equipment and applying techniques originally developed for the analysis of radar signals has investigated this synchronization more deeply. Two of their most significant findings are that these patterns of brain activity occur right from the very first meditation session, and that the actual pattern of activity is sufficient to distinguish TM from any other known state of consciousness.[17]

The implication of the EEG synchronization is that the meditator does not have to suppress one side of his brain in order to attend to the messages coming from the other half, but can use both halves simultaneously. He can begin to live that long sought for synthesis of reason and intuition, art and science, and the union of Eastern and Western thought, a possibility which I shall return to in Chapter 13.

It may well be that Western science is now rediscovering something which has been known to the East for hundreds of years. Among the complex and diverse Tantric teachings of India and Tibet is a common claim that the breathing alternates between the left and right nostrils. Even when the nose is completely clear the breath will still flow predominantly through one of the nostrils. In the healthy person the breath is said to change from one nostril to the other every twenty minutes (some texts put the figure at exactly 24 minutes). The breath through the right nostril is called the sun breath. It is said that when breathing through this nostril the person should undertake actions involving physical exertion, combat, speech and discussion. The left nostril breath, called the moon breath, is said to be best for painting, composing, listening to music, etc. There is therefore a clear correlation between the left nostril and what we now believe to be right hemisphere activities and the right nostril and left hemisphere activities. This does not mean that when breathing through the left nostril the right hemisphere is dominant – this clearly is not the case: only that there is a predisposition for right hemisphere activity. The actual hemisphere in dominance still depends upon the specific activity being engaged in.

The most interesting claim made by the Tantric texts is that during transcendental consciousness the breath flows equally through both nostrils. This clearly parallels the recent finding that the two hemispheres are in balance during the deeper phases of meditation. Moreover it is written that the perfect individual maintains a state of balanced breath throughout the day. This we shall see later corresponds to the fully developed person who is able to maintain the inner stillness of meditation along with all activity, and represents a fifth state of consciousness.

The Relief of Stress

6

All men, especially the busy, secular as well as the religious should be taught this meditation for it is a refuge to which one can retreat when faced with stressful situations.

from Francisco Osuna (c. 1000 AD)

When any object is subjected to a load it may become deformed in some way. If on removing the load the object resumes its original shape it is said to be elastic; if it remains deformed it is called plastic. Thus an elastic band is so called because it will return to its original shape when released. But if you were to stretch it too far then it might remain permanently stretched to some extent. When this occurs it is said to have exceeded its limit of elasticity.

A similar phenomenon takes place with the human body. When it is put under some load the physiology may be changed in a number of different ways. If the changes are only slight the body will be able to return to what is known as the state of 'homeostatic balance': a state in which all the variables are in mutual equilibrium. But if the variables are displaced too far they may exceed the 'limit of homeostatic tolerance': they will not return to the ideal norm but stay slightly displaced. We could say that the physiology has ceased to be perfectly elastic and has remained a little 'stretched'. The overloading experience has left a physiological scar, and the body is said to have accumulated stress. (If we were to follow the physicists' definition then we should say that the body has accumulated strain. Stress is the load displacing the variables while strain is the effect. The biological sciences are however looser than the physical sciences in this respect and often refer to the effect as a stress. Since Maharishi also uses stress in this looser sense it will be less confusing, even if less pedantic, if I use the word 'stress' to refer to the physiological changes occurring within the organism in response to some external load.)

There are many factors which can give rise to human stress. At the physical level it is produced by electric shock, intense heat or cold, physical wounds, loud noises, malnutrition, lack of sleep, physical exhaustion, drugs, etc. On the psychological level the mere threat of any of these can be a stress. The loss of personal or social esteem, the deflation of the ego, and anything which upsets or threatens to upset one's sense of identity will likewise be a source of stress. Demanding jobs, jobs which do not demand enough, responsibilities that one cannot cope with, extreme competition, overcrowding, conflicting personal and social goals, continual adaptation to opposing social pressures, and mental fatigue are also common forms of stress.

It is now thought by many psychologists that change itself can be a stress. It has been observed that a large proportion of illnesses occur during or immediately after significant changes in a person's life. The death of a close friend or loved one, changing jobs and moving house all correlate highly with illness and stress.[1]

As stress continues to build up the perception becomes duller and less sensitive with the result that the effects of further stress become less noticeable and only the heavier overloads reach consciousness. Hardly noticing the damage being incurred, the heavily stressed person charges into situations from which a less stressed, more sensitive individual would quickly withdraw. And the more stressed that a person becomes the weaker the body becomes and the less it is able to cope with further overloads. We become trapped in a vicious circle — or rather a vicious spiral — winding ourselves up until, like a weak elastic band which has been stretched too far, too often, we snap! We break down, mentally and physically.

The Flight-Fight Response

Physical evolution is, by our standards of time, a very slow process. The human body is developing no faster today than it did a million years ago. But our minds, our knowledge of the world, and our ability to manipulate the environment are changing far more rapidly. In these fields humanity has progressed more in the last few hundred years than it did in all of its preceeding million years taken together. As a consequence we are now living in a twentieth-century environment, with (it is hoped) twentieth-century minds, yet with bodies that have not changed significantly since the stone age.

There is one physiological mechanism in particular which is something of a hangover from the past. It was first recognized in 1929 by an American physiologist called Walter Cannon who named it the 'Flight-Fight Response'. As its name suggests it is a preparation for fleeing or fighting and is invoked whenever there is a threat of danger. The effect is an immediate mustering of all the body's resources in preparation for intense activity.

The response is said to be both integrated and stereotyped: integrated in that all, or nearly all, the organs of the body are involved, each modifying their functioning so as to be of the greatest value in the impending activity; and stereotyped in that a very wide variety of stimuli will all elicit this same basic response – in fact it can be triggered by almost any form of threat, psychological as well as physical.

Much of the brain's control of the body is affected by the discharge of hormones. These are chemical messengers which travel round the body activating or inactivating various organs. Whenever there is a threat of danger specific hormones are released in abundance into the bloodstream. Their effect is to temporarily change the functioning of the whole body. The heart speeds up, blood pressure rises, the lungs take in more oxygen, the muscles become tense, fats and sugars are released into the blood to provide more energy, and the body begins to cool itself through perspiration. At the same time digestion, sexual activities and other processes which will not be needed come to a halt. In short the organism becomes instantly mobilized.

Several thousand years ago when one was completely at the mercy of the surroundings, this flight-fight response was undoubtedly very useful. If you met with some wild animal then your very survival might depend on the ability instantly to prepare yourself for activity. You either had to flee, or, if cornered, fight the animal. You could not just stand there. Today, however, the response has lost much of its survival value. Urban man seldom encounters situations where he has either to run for his life or fight to the death, and the response has become more of a handicap than an advantage.

Imagine that you are walking down a street and a car suddenly speeds by very close. You feel startled and alarmed. It makes you 'jump', but only mentally. What has happened physiologically is that the speeding car has signified possible danger and set off the flight-fight response. Your heart beats faster, blood pressure increases, you sweat a little, and your muscles tense. But you do not run away, nor do you fight the car. You continue walking down the street and only gradually does the reaction subside.

If you think that pedestrians get a raw deal, pause for a moment to consider the driver of a car. Experiments have shown that the city driver is in a continual state of physiological arousal. When overtaking another vehicle, for instance, the heart rate may rise to 150 or 160 beats per minute, blood pressure increases, the palms sweat and the muscles tense, as one prepares oneself for no greater activity than a slight movement of the wrists and ankle. Half an hour in city traffic will usually leave a person in a state of hyperarousal from which it may take several hours to recover.

But it is not only physical dangers which will produce this response. Any threat to one's sense of identity will invoke the same response. If you are insulted, for example, then the blood pressure will again rise, the heart starts pounding, the muscles tense, and the face flush perhaps. You feel as if you could hit the person – but usually you restrain yourself and try to 'simmer down'.

Most of us probably regard it as almost a matter of definition that a stress is something 'distressful' and unpleasant. But pleasant stimuli can also be a source of stress if they overload the nervous system. To win the football pools, for example, would almost certainly be a pleasant experience but it might also produce a similar adverse physiological reaction to those of an unpleasant experience. Most of us have had such excitement at some time. Often we describe the event by saying that 'the heart leapt with joy'. But it is this very 'leaping' of the physiological processes that culminates in stress. Lennart Levi, an eminent stress researcher from the Karolinski Institute in Stockholm, has supported this view by showing that amusing and laughter-provoking films elicit the same kind of physiological reaction characteristic of stress as do aggressive or horror films.[2]

A milder form of the flight-fight reaction known as the 'alerting response' occurs every time there is some major or significant change in the surroundings. A sudden noise, for example, will make the ears 'prick up', the head turn, and the eyes focus in the direction of the sound. One is ready, should there be any danger, to go into a full blown flight-fight reaction.

In every case the flight-fight response prepares the body for action, yet almost invariably we do not act and do not play out the reaction to its intended end. We remain doing whatever it was that we were doing, perhaps just sitting at a desk, yet with a body prepared and yearning for action. The tense muscles are not used, the fats and sugars in the blood are not consumed, and the physiology stays displaced. After a quarter of an hour or so you may feel that you are back to normal. But do not be deceived. Although the hormonal changes which started the response may not last very long it may well be an hour or more before the body has completely returned to normal.

If this just happens occasionally then perhaps there is little harm, but when it happens continually the situation is very different. Imagine this reaction setting in every fifteen minutes. Not only do you never play out the reaction but you never even recover from one alert before the next one sets in. A state of *continual* physiological arousal and tension results. Blood pressure remains high, the blood-chemistry stays changed, the muscles continue to be tense and we feel 'wound up'.

This permanent imbalance leads to many functional disturbances in the body. Layer upon layer of fat is deposited on the walls of the arteries choking them and precipitating heart failure. The natural balance of acids in the stomach is upset and it begins literally to digest itself resulting in peptic ulcers. Skin disorders such as eczema result from the abnormal chemical secretions in the skin. The lungs, kidneys, bladder, reproductive system, muscles, eyes and brain are all susceptible to similar damage.

Nor is the damage purely physical. As stress accumulates there is a general loss of vitality. The continuous over-stimulation and physiological hyper-arousal raises the level of background activity in the mind, effectively raising the threshold for conscious experience. What was before a quiet level of conscious thought is submerged by the increased mental noise and disappears from the conscious mind. Thinking becomes less clear, less resourceful and less efficient. We feel dull, 'under the weather', or 'off colour'. The body is sluggish to respond and our actions become inept and ineffective.

One might suppose that the remedy would be to engage in vigorous exercise every time that the reaction was aroused. Undoubtedly the problem of stress has been made worse by our tendency to lead more sedentary lives, but exercise alone will not solve the problem. In many cases of alarm such action would be most inappropriate. Our society does not condone the person who starts a fight at the slightest provocation. The city driver could hardly jump out of the car and run for his life every time another car came too close. And the aspiring executive who did fifty press-ups every time a phone call or news bulletin threatened his career would probably lose his job anyway.

The pace of life today is such that there is just not enough time to allow the body to readjust. Indeed, as time goes on the pace of life speeds up subjecting us to more and more change, and, if we fail to adapt, to more and more stress. Fifteen years hence the pace of life will probably be double what it is now, and the level of stress many times higher. It is therefore imperative that we find a way to adapt faster and cope with the stress as soon as possible.

Rest – The Release of Stress

What is particularly novel in Maharishi's teaching on stress is his clear insistence that the accumulation of stress can be reversed; that given the chance the body will automatically dissolve accumulated physical tensions and return towards the optimum homeostatic balance. And, claims Maharishi, the condition which allows this reversal to take place is simply the condition of deep rest.

When in physics a load is applied to an object the work done by the load produces some structural change in the object and this change represents an increase in potential energy. When the physical system is 'relaxed' this energy is converted back into kinetic energy – hence the effectiveness of an elastic band as a catapult. What Maharishi is saying is that the same principles apply to human physiology.

When stress is being accumulated abnormal activity produces some physical change in the organism, representing a gain in potential energy. Work has had to be done against the body's natural tendency to return to a state of homeostatic equilibrium. When stress is being dissolved the reverse takes place. The energy stored in the stress is released resulting in some temporary increase of activity in the organism.

This activity could take many forms depending on the stress that is being released. In many cases it will not even be noticed. Sometimes the dissolution of the stress may produce some increase in brain activity. In this case the change would be experienced as some random thought or mental image suddenly popping up into the mind.

Now one might expect that in this situation the thought which appeared would be closely related to the original stressful experience. But this is not the case. What determines the meaning and content of a thought is the present state of the brain. All the dissolving stress has done is to increase temporarily the mental activity: it does not by itself determine the thought which will be generated. It may, however, determine in a very general way the type of thought that occurred.

If, for example, a stress had been caused by some strong visual experience then this will probably have left some permanent traces in the associated areas of the nervous system. On being dissolved there will therefore be some increased activity in these areas and, provided that it reached consciousness, this would give rise to a visual experience. But the overall state of the brain will have changed considerably over the period between the inception and the dissolution of the stress and so the actual content, meaning and details of the present experience will almost certainly bear little relationship to the original stress.

It is probable that similar processes are happening during normal sleep, our nightly dreams signifying the release of some tension somewhere in the system. Maharishi believes that since TM provides a much deeper form of rest than is normally gained during sleep it is able to dissolve more deeply rooted stresses. But TM should not be seen as a replacement for sleep. Although many people do find that as a result of practising TM they do not need as much sleep as before, this is not the prime intention of TM. To give the body this extra rest at the expense of sleep would be counter-productive. The real value of TM lies in its ability to restore the balance between rest and activity and thereby enrich all aspects of life.

People often wonder whether the total elimination of stress would be beneficial. Una Kroll, for example, in her appraisal of TM feels that a fully relaxed person would not be able to do well in examinations, interviews or public speaking. She argues[3]: 'It is only under the stimulus of the audience that the speaker really comes alive.' Her difficulty would seem to stem from two different uses of the word 'stress'. The physicist talks of stress as the pressure being applied, whereas the biologist talks of it as the physiological reaction to this pressure. Una Kroll is saying that we all need pressure to draw out the best in us, and with this I would certainly agree – if the audience is not demanding, the exam of no consequence, or the interview unimportant there would be little incentive to apply oneself wholeheartedly to the task. But this should not be confused with stress in the sense of physiological damage which is invariably an impediment to effective thought and action. From my own experience it is only when one is calm and rested that one can think clearly, draw deeply upon one's knowledge and experience, and present it in a coherent and comprehensive manner.

What is necessary is not physiological stress but the ability to respond effectively to a demanding situation without simultaneously driving the body into a state of imbalance. In the physicist's terms we need the stress without the strain. So the release of physiological tension which TM provides, far from being a handicap in these situations, would be a distinct advantage.

Another point which should be made clear is that a stress is not the same as a memory. When the body throws off some stress it is simply throwing off the undesirable side-effects arising from an inability in the past to cope with a certain experience. We in no way lose the memory of that experience or all that we have learnt from it.

The Stay and Play Response

The flight-fight response is controlled by what is known as the sympathetic nervous system. Complementing this is the parasympathetic nervous system which when activated promotes the conservation of energy. It facilitates digestive processes, reduces heart rate and lowers blood pressure. Ideally the body should be balanced between sympathetic and parasympathetic activity, changing from one to the other as the situation demands. Unfortunately the person who is in a permanent state of tension remains overbalanced in the direction of sympathetic arousal. TM appears to redress this balance by eliciting a parasympathetic response – what Dr Benson from the Harvard Medical School refers to as a 'relaxation response'. It lowers heart rate, blood pressure, muscle tension, etc., and appears to be the exact opposite of the flight-fight response.

Whereas the flight-fight response is brought on by fear the relaxation response characteristic of meditation is brought on by the increasing enjoyment experienced as the mind settles down into quieter levels of thinking. This has led Dr Orme-Johnson to dub it the 'stay and play' response.

Orme-Johnson studied the rate of occurrence of small electrical changes in the skin known as the galvanic skin response (GSR). These fluctuations occur most frequently when a person is startled in some way and accompany the flight-fight response. He found that when he repeatedly made a subject 'jump' by sounding a loud tone, those who practised TM quickly habituated (i.e. the skin response ceased to occur) while the non-meditators continued to react each time they heard the sound.[4] This suggested that they had gained some greater resilience to stress. It also indicated that the meditator might be becoming more stable both in himself and in his interactions with others. Previously it had been found that people who displayed a high frequency of spontaneous GSRs tended to be introverted, unstable, anxious and prone to mental and physical illness. Conversely those in whom these fluctuations were relatively fewer tended to be more stable – both physiologically and emotionally – better able to relate to the surroundings, and more mature.

Dr Denver Daniels working at Exeter University has taken this work further. He studied the GSR response of meditators and non-meditators subjected to unpleasant noises – the sound of finger nails scraping down a blackboard. This was a large-scale study involving some 200 subjects of which one third were regular TM meditators. The 120 or so non-meditators showed the expected sudden drop in GSR, slowly returning to normal over a period of about five minutes. The meditators on the other hand recovered much more quickly, and the longer they had been practising TM the faster the recovery. In many who had been meditating for several years there was no reaction whatsoever to the unpleasant noise. This was not because they had not heard it – they reported that it was indeed a most unpleasant noise – but they were no longer showing the same adverse physiological reaction to it, i.e. the flight-fight reaction was no longer being evoked.[5]

This work suggests that those practising TM were indeed increasing their resistance to stress. Furthermore, it suggests that meditators were able to adapt faster to a changing environment. In his book *Future Shock* Alvin Toffler argues that the pace of life is continually speeding up and that man is rapidly approaching the state where he can no longer adapt fast enough to the ever increasing changes in his environment. What man needs, concludes Toffler, is to find some means by which he can increase his adaptability. These experiments suggest that TM may well be a way.

Health, Creativity and Intelligence

7

The so-called normal man, the one we may term the 'healthy Philistine', is only a fraction of what he could be.

William James

Over two thousand years ago Plato wrote that: 'The cure of the part should not be attempted without the treatment of the whole ... and therefore if the head and body are to be well, you must begin by curing the mind: that is the first thing.' Western medicine has progressed considerably since Plato. We know how to cut the body open and adjust its parts when it goes wrong; how and where most diseases attack us; and how to stave off these attacks with drugs of one kind or another.

But despite all these advances we are only just beginning to appreciate the root causes of many of these disorders and still tend to regard the body more as a machine than an organism. In this respect we appear to have progressed very little since Plato's time.

When we fall ill we are often more concerned with removing the symptoms of the problem than its root cause. Once we 'feel' well again we consider ourselves no longer in need of any care. But the physical symptoms which we are so keen to eliminate are generally only the tip of the iceberg. Cutting off its top is no solution for the iceberg immediately bobs up to reveal more of itself. Submerging the iceberg will keep it out of sight so long as you keep it down, but as soon as you let it go it will come bobbing up again. Rather than just trying to remove or suppress the physical symptoms, medicine should be equally concerned with treating the root cause of the disorders.

Now what is the root cause? A decade ago doctors were cautiously proposing that perhaps 50 per cent of all disorders were caused by stress. This figure grew rapidly and in 1972 Peter Blythe started his book *Stress Disease* with the statement 'Authoritative medical opinion in the United States and Britain has gone on record to the effect that up to 70 per cent of all patients currently being treated by doctors in general practice are suffering from conditions which have their origins in unrelieved stress.' Two years later Dr Elmer Green speaking at a conference on health in London remarked that[1] 'even stuffy doctors are now agreeing that 80 per cent of all problems are psychosomatic.' Some less 'stuffy' doctors would suggest that the figure is probably higher still.

We saw in the last chapter how stress could be a major factor in the incidence of peptic ulcers, high blood pressure, coronary problems, etc., and most of us would also accept that many of our incidental aches and pains are also a product of stress. But what about infectious diseases, these surely are not caused by stress but by bacteria and viruses? That is true, but the body's susceptibility to bacterial or viral attack depends upon the person's overall health; the less stressed person is less likely to fall ill in the first place and better able to cope with any illnesses that do occur. There is now mounting evidence that even the incidence of many forms of cancer is closely related to the patient's emotional state; frequently it has been found that the appearance of the disease follows a serious emotional loss occurring six to eighteen months earlier.[2]

Just in terms of the stress relief which TM provides we should therefore expect a general improvement in health amongst meditators. It is getting to the root cause of many disorders and, by treating the mind and body together as an integrated unit, is fulfilling the Platonic ideal of medicine. Meditators have often reported that they feel healthier and some preliminary surveys are beginning to substantiate these claims, showing not only a general improvement in health but a corresponding decrease in the use of tranquillizers and other medicinal drugs.[3]

TM and Psychotherapy

It is not only physical health that is improved. A New York psychiatrist who started using TM as an adjunct to conventional psychotherapy reported that:[4]

[those] who have persevered with TM have shown a much faster rate of improvement in the course of psychotherapy. With several this improvement has been dramatic, even spectacular. Some have been relieved of symptoms that had never been helped by psychotherapy. With two such patients this relief and general improvement, increase in ego-strength, general productivity at work and happiness in living have continued with greatly decreased hours of psychotherapy. With every patient who has been faithful in TM, the improvement has been at least twice the expected rate (as judged by previous experience with the patient). Sometimes it seems to be at least ten times the expected rate. Sometimes when a patient complains about not moving at a satisfactory rate I find that the patient has stopped TM. When TM is again undertaken, movement picks up again.

Dr Bernard Glueck from the Hartford Institute of Living in Connecticut has been using TM for some time in his treatment of schizophrenia. His findings so far are very encouraging. He gave a third of his group TM, a third biofeedback training and a third a standard relaxation technique. His provisional results show TM to be the most effective of the three, most of the meditating patients being able to cut down considerably on conventional medication. TM had the advantage over biofeedback of not requiring elaborate and expensive equipment. With the biofeedback patients he found that positive results were only obtained so long as they had access to the EEG and computer: they could not relax on their own as the TM subjects could.

Dr Harold Bloomfield, who has also used TM as part of his psychiatric practice, notes several other advantages of TM over drugs and therapists. TM is exclusively under the control of the patient. If he gets better it is not due to a pill or a therapist but to his own natural regenerative processes. In addition TM saves time both for the doctor and for the patient.[5]

Two particular interesting cases in which TM appears to have brought about remarkable personal changes are described by

Daniel Goleman in the *Journal of Transpersonal Psychology*.[6] The first involved a woman in her late forties who had obviously suffered a great degree of distress over her mother's death, to which she had never grown fully accustomed. During one meditation much of this latent sadness, which had been locked up within, flowed out. Afterwards she not only regained many of the happy memories of her childhood which previously had been suppressed, but she also began to see people 'as though for the first time ... like all the grey cardboard figures came to life'. She continued:

> Had you asked me yesterday, I would have felt my percep-
> tion was excellent, but I have been perceiving people
> through learned responses ... not *seeing* them. All that is
> different now ... when I saw my daughters' faces I really
> saw them like I hadn't ever before, and they knew, they
> responded.

In view of the stressed conditions in which many of us live it is particularly interesting to note that she did not realize beforehand that she was not functioning to her full capacity. Until the 'doors of perception' are cleansed there is little awareness of the grey fog through which everything is seen, and it comes as a surprise to many, although a pleasant surprise, to discover that awareness can be sharper, richer and more lively.

In the previous chapter we saw that the actual form of the stress dissolution process bears little relation to the original stressful experience. This is clearly illustrated in the case of this woman. Although she experienced some of the feelings connected with her mother's death, she did not relive that past experience. Psychoanalytic approaches to mental health often attempt to eliminate the stressful effects of past experience by bringing the forgotten or repressed experiences back into consciousness. This is in sharp contrast to TM where there is never any attempt to delve into the past. In this respect Maharishi is going against the predominant psychoanalytic view which holds that only a full awareness of the original cause will allow the person to cope with the stress.

This difference between TM and conventional psychotherapy is important for Maharishi. If one deliberately relives the experience there is the danger that the conscious recall of the experience might itself result in further stress. By innocently allowing the tension to flow out without going through the original disturbance the meditator is not adversely affected by the process.

The second case which Goleman quotes in his article is particularly remarkable in that it involves the normalization of a physical deformity. It concerns a girl of twenty-two, who reports:

> I had very crooked teeth when I was a child. My teeth are so big for my jaw they had to pull eight teeth. When my second teeth came in I started to notice my jaws didn't match. For several months while I meditated I would feel my jaw pulling around, always to the right. It got more and more intense, and then the other day there was a very strong and painful pull, a large 'Crack!' and my jaw moved over. When it happened I was so amazed, it was so intense, but I didn't stop meditating, I knew what was happening. When I looked in the mirror, my teeth were aligned.
>
> Now my mouth muscles are more relaxed; when I smile now it feels different.

I know of a similar case concerning a young man who had broken his elbow in a motor accident two years previously. Although it had mended fairly well he could not completely bend his arm out straight. His doctors told him this was a fairly common occurrence resulting from the way the bone had reset. They added that it was impossible to do anything about it and he would have to put up with it as a permanent disability. However, two years later, during meditation he suddenly had an intense pain in the elbow very similar to the pain of the accident. At the same time his hand became paralysed again. A surgeon who examined him during this episode confirmed that the paralysis was of the same form as that which would be caused by an injury to the nerve at the elbow. Two days later the pain had disappeared and so had the restriction of the elbow. He was now able to straighten his arm as fully as anyone else.

Most people would be prepared to accept that some forms of mental and emotional damage are reversible, but the idea that physical structural damage could also be reversible is astonishing. Many doctors would doubt whether such changes are possible without major surgery let alone concede that they could occur spontaneously as they did in these cases.

Of course, experiences such as these do not happen every time one meditates, they happen only occasionally, but even their occasional occurrence is of profound import for medical science. If it could be substantiated that such reversibility were possible on a much wider scale it would herald a revolution not only in medical practice but in our whole understanding of the human organism.

The Expansion of the Mind

William James, one of the fathers of twentieth-century psychology, recorded that:

> most people live, whether physically, intellectually or morally, in a very restricted circle of their potential being. They make use of a very small portion of their possible consciousness ... much like a man, who, out of his whole bodily organism, should get into the habit of using and moving only his little finger.

Many other psychologists have expressed similar views, saying that most of us use only 10 per cent of our full potential. Whether the figure is 10 per cent or not is questionable – 10 per cent is probably a generous overestimate – but whatever the figure is, it is certainly small.

In Maharishi's model of the mind we are only aware of the surface levels of mental activity. Mental stresses maintain the background neural activity at a high level, preventing one from being aware of the quieter underlying levels of thinking. In terms of the pond analogy, the effects of stress are like mud in the water. The bubble is seen only at the surface because the water below is murky. But if the water were to become clearer we could begin to see it rising up from the depths of the pond. As the nervous system becomes freer from stress the background of mental 'chatter' decreases and ordinary thoughts are appreciated at earlier and earlier stages in their development, not only during meditation but in daily activity as well. The proportion of mental activity which reaches consciousness increases until, when the system is completely free from stress, the whole of mental activity is open to consciousness. Maharishi refers to this as 'an expansion of the conscious capacity of the mind'.

This expansion of the conscious mind does not mean that one actually experiences one's mind becoming larger or anything like that: it is simply that the finer levels of thinking are now open to

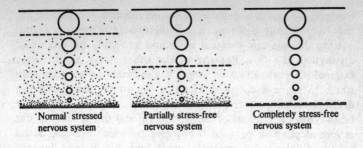

'Normal' stressed nervous system

Partially stress-free nervous system

Completely stress-free nervous system

‐ ‐ ‐ ‐ Effective threshold for conscious experience

Figure 6   *Expansion of conscious capacity of the mind: lowering of effective threshold for conscious experience with progressive dissolution of stress.*

the awareness and one begins to make more use of these in normal thinking. What one actually experiences is thinking becoming clearer, faster and more effective.

Maharishi talks of thinking at these subtler levels being more powerful. He is not suggesting that mental activity becomes more intense – that would clearly contradict the notion of subtler thought levels: what he is saying is that thinking at subtler levels has more potential and is more effective. We might liken the situation to driving with the car radio on. When speeding down the motorway the noise of the engine and the wind necessitate turning the radio up full and what we hear is only the general outline of the music, the rest is either distorted or drowned out. When we slow down we can turn the radio down and we then find that many of the subtleties of the music become apparent. Similarly with thinking, at quieter levels of activity much of the subtlety of thought is revealed and thinking becomes far richer, and when translated into action that much more effective.

The reduction in background noise also has a marked effect on perception and activity. The brain might be considered as an immensely complex decision-making system. Each neuron is receiving signals from hundreds, perhaps thousands, of other cells. Some of these pulses may be meaningful signals or they may be unwanted 'noise'. One job of the brain is to sort out the signals from the noise in order that it can decide how best to respond. The more noise there is the harder will this task be. To take a specific example, we can in a quiet room distinguish two notes which are only very slightly different. But if there were a pneumatic drill outside the window most of us would probably be unable to distinguish the two. Because of the other noise, in this case external noise, the brain no longer has sufficient information with which to make a decision. The two 'sound the same'. Similar decision-making processes govern nearly every process in the brain. Thus the fineness of our perception and the delicacy of our actions depend in part on the degree to which we can detect minute differences in internal signals, and this in turn depends upon the amount of noise in the system.

In addition to the personal reports of many meditators several different lines of psychological research indicate that there is a general increased sensitivity amongst meditators. Graham,[7] Pirot,[8] and Brown et al.[9] have all found significant improvements in perception. Shaw and Kolb[10] found that the reaction time of meditators was faster than non-meditators, and Blasdell[11] found that TM subjects were more accurate in complex eye-hand co-ordination tasks. In fact, since nearly everything we do is mediated by the ability of the nervous system to make fine discriminations one would expect a decrease in neural noise to lead to some improvement in nearly every field of activity.

Intelligence

The sharper perception, clearer thinking and more efficient action that is claimed to come with the practice of TM might be expected to lead to an increase in intelligence. Maharishi claims that this is indeed the case, but when he uses the word intelligence he is using it in a special sense. He defines intelligence as that which gives order and direction to change. So when he talks of a person becoming more intelligent he means that thinking and action are becoming more orderly. Thus, as far as Maharishi is concerned, the more intelligent person is he who is better able to order his perceptual data into meaningful form and direct his activity in a more effective direction.

This concept is, in fact, in keeping with modern approaches to the study of intelligence which are now moving away from the idea of intelligence as a fixed constant such as IQ and looking at it more in terms of a person's ability to learn as a result of experience.

Although there is not the space here to discuss the matter fully, several lines of research suggest that TM results in an increase in both the speed and capacity of information-processing in the brain, changes which we might expect to lead to an increase in intelligence.[12] Tests in Holland have given further support to this contention. Measuring a factor known as the 'intelligence growth rate' it was found that meditating schoolchildren increased significantly compared with a similar non-meditating control group.[13]

Maharishi sees an increased orderliness of thinking to be the result of an increased orderliness in brain activity (illustrated by the increase in synchrony and coherence of the EEG patterns), and claims that this orderliness is itself a direct consequence of giving the nervous system deep rest. He writes:[14]

> This rule of 'intelligence through rest' seems to be analogous to a very general law of nature discovered by the science of physics to apply to all natural systems.
>
> This law, the third law of thermodynamics, states that entropy (disorder) decreases when temperature (activity) decreases and that the condition of zero entropy, perfect orderliness, coincides with a temperature of absolute zero (absolutely no activity). In fact, the region near absolute zero temperature in physical systems is closely connected with a strong tendency towards wave coherence and synchrony and is exemplified in the onset of superfluidity and superconductivity near absolute zero temperature when activity is minimum. This suggests a striking analogy to the synchrony of brain waves induced by the very deep rest of TM. If we define for the purpose of comparison a 'mental temperature', corresponding to the level of mental and neurophysiological activity, and systematically reduce this through the technique of TM, we perceive a class of tendencies in the human mind that reminds us of the third law as seen in the realm of basic physics. This quantum mechanical analogy suggests that orderliness in the brain and in thinking is natural to man. TM accomplishes this orderliness by providing an opportunity for the mind to follow the natural tendency of the most general patterns of nature.

This idea that the tendency towards increased orderliness is a natural impulse of life was also recognized by the physicist Erwin

Schrödinger. 'Life,' he wrote,[15] 'feeds upon negative entropy.' If an organism's total entropy were to increase then it would pass into a state of molecular disorder characteristic of death. A creature stays alive because it is able to 'drink' order from its environment and remain in a highly ordered state. Following Maharishi, we could say that life was therefore the expression of intelligence in Nature, and that by reducing mental activity TM enables the individual to drink more fully of orderliness and of life itself.

Creativity

Creativity is generally thought of as the ability to produce novel and original change and usually involves some association or synthesis of previously unassociated concepts. Newton, watching an apple fall, made an association between the motion of the apple and the orbit of the moon and created his theory of gravity. Shakespeare set private love against public duty in *Anthony and Cleopatra* and Cézanne brought the diverse elements of a setting and their underlying oneness together in his paintings.

Many creative people, both scientists and artists alike, have noted that creative thinking most frequently takes place when the mind is in a quiet relaxed state. Kekulé, for instance, solved the problem of the shape of the benzene molecule – a problem which was baffling many chemists of his day – whilst idly day-dreaming in front of his fire. And Coleridge, as every schoolboy knows, composed the Kubla Khan while in a dream.

In terms of Maharishi's model of the mind the dream state corresponds to a subtler level of thinking. Subtler levels of thought are by definition less structured and less well-defined than the grosser levels of thought and the more the boundaries dissolve the more chance there is of making cross-connections. The associations made in such states have still to be put in a more concrete form so the creative person tends to be someone who can alternate between the deeper states of reverie and the surface waking state.

In so far as TM takes the attention to deeper levels of the mind than usually reached during dreaming it affords the possibility of making more fundamental and further reaching cross-connections. It is a common experience that on coming out of meditation one often finds the solution to some problem that had been on the mind for a long time. No attempt is made during meditation to find solutions to problems – that would almost certainly keep the attention on the surface levels of thought and out of meditation: the association is made quite spontaneously and without conscious direction.

Moreover, by expanding the conscious capacity of the mind, TM allows one to retain an awareness of the deeper levels of thought while in the waking state. So creative thought begins to become a more general feature of life, occurring throughout the waking state as well as in states of deep reverie.

We could also look at the creative process in terms of the two hemispheres of the brain. There is some evidence that creative thought is associated with the right side of the brain. Yet the creative person must still make full use of the left side as well. An intuitive insight is no good if it cannot be formulated and communicated. The creative person is thus one who can both make spontaneous cross-connections and then develop a verbal or symbolic expression of that synthesis. This integration is enhanced by the type of brain synchrony observed during TM, and the fact that this continues after meditation again suggests that TM should lead to a general increase in creativity. This hypothesis has been borne out in tests of meditators which do indeed show higher creativity.[16]

With regard to artistic creativity in particular it has sometimes been suggested that any reduction in stress would lead to a reduction in creativity. It is said that many great works of art have been created by people under considerable stress and that this stress was necessary for their creativity. If all stress were to be released there would no longer be any incentive for artistic expression.

In answering this objection Maharishi concedes that some 'spur' is needed in order for an artist to create – all activity needs a spur or incentive – but, he says, it is not necessary that this spur be one of stress. If all stress is eliminated then any incentive for creative activity will be able to flow forth that much more freely.

In essence he is making the same distinction between stress as pressure and stress as physiological damage that I pointed out in the previous chapter. The artist needs stress in the sense of pressure, but not in the sense of physiological disorders. If the artist's nervous system is not strong enough to cope with the demands made of it then the pressure needed for creative work may well result in some physiological damage. Maharishi's point is that although such physiological stress may, for most artists, be an inevitable consequence of their work it is not a necessary prerequisite for it. Creativity depends upon having a heightened awareness, an openness of mind, and the ability to resolve inner discords through a creative synthesis. These are all abilities which a reduction in physiological stress would enhance.

Water the Root!

Maharishi maintains that most problems arise as a result of stress, and that TM by releasing stress is effectively getting to the root of all problems. This should not be taken to imply that TM by itself will instantly solve everything. Many problems are the result of very real physical difficulties and these will only be resolved by action of some kind on the physical level. Maharishi's point is that merely attending to the surface symptoms of the problem without simultaneously tending to the root of the problem, will never offer a complete solution.

Maharishi likens the process of meditation to that of a gardener tending a sick bush. The leaves of the bush may be withering, changing colour, or ailing in some other way, but if the gardener were to tend only to these surface symptoms of the problem he would not get very far. The solution that any competent gardener would take is simply to supply the correct nourishment to the root and let nature take care of the whole process in her own efficient way.

Much of our time we spend tending to the leaves rather than the root of our problems. We see countless difficulties around us: some personal, others social, political, economic, educational or environmental. Faced with such an abundance of problems the common reaction is to pick out the most urgent or least difficult one and charge ahead at finding a solution. But more often then not this is only eliminating the symptoms of a much deeper problem. We would be much more effective if simultaneously we were to attend to the root of the problem, and in many cases the root is individual stress.

Maharishi sums this up with the phrase, 'Water the root to enjoy the fruit'. But notice how he says '... *to* enjoy the fruit'. He does not merely remark '... *and* enjoy the fruit', which would make the enjoyment something of a side-effect. He emphasizes that the ultimate purpose of meditation lies not in the experience of finer levels of thinking, the rest, the release of stress or the development of Creative Intelligence, but in the enjoyment which naturally follows as a result of all these. It is this personal fulfilment which makes it all worth while.

Part Two

Part One looked briefly at the historical origins of TM and the growth of Maharishi's movement in the world today. We considered the technique itself, how it allows one to experience quieter levels of the normal thinking process and why it is so important that no effort or control enters into the practice. We then saw what the observable effects of TM were: how the brain was beginning to function more efficiently and how the body was coming to a deep state of rest, dissolving stress and tension built up in the past. This section ended by looking at the implications of this for health and individual development.

Now I want to turn and consider the effects that these changes in physiology and brain functioning have on the way in which we perceive and appreciate both ourselves and the world around us. Part Two will be looking at the different states of consciousness to which TM can lead and how these help the individual integrate with the world around him and start living a life of fulfilment. In this section of the book many of Maharishi's points are illustrated with similar points from other teachings, past and present, and the closing chapters of this section look at the type of distortions which have crept into such teachings in the past and how Maharishi is today setting the teaching on a much firmer basis through the establishment of the Maharishi International University.

The Fourth State of Consciousness

8

Look, it cannot be seen - it is beyond form
Listen, it cannot be heard - it is beyond sound
Grasp, it cannot be held - it is intangible

Tao-Te-Ching

Throughout the practice of Transcendental Meditation one is wide awake. Even when one transcends the finest level of mental activity and arrives at the state of restful alertness one still remains conscious. In this state of quiet all mental activity has died away. Consciousness has ceased to vibrate and there is no longer anything to be conscious of. The normal thinking activity of the mind has been transcended, and for this reason the state is known as *transcendental consciousness*.

But although consciousness has ceased to vibrate it has not ceased to exist: it simply does not take on a specific form. The state is not therefore one of unconsciousness so much as un-manifest or pure consciousness. Since consciousness itself remains, the subject of all experience, the experiencer, also remains. Thus we might also call the state one of pure self. But this pure self is not, as we shall see later in this chapter, the ego, or any other form of individual identity, for all these 'selves' are concepts or con-structs of the mind, products of mental activity, and as such they die when mental activity dies. The pure self is fundamental to all

93

experience. Being the very basis of experience, it continues to exist even though there may no longer be anything to experience. In order to distinguish these two uses of the word 'self' I shall follow the practice of referring to the individual empirical self as the self, and to the pure self, the qualityless subject of all experience, as the Self with a capital 'S'.

The Fourth State of Consciousness

The state of transcendental consciousness is quite distinct from the three commonly encountered states of consciousness, waking, dreaming and deep sleep. We may allocate these three major states of consciousness to the squares of a simple 2 x 2 matrix, each square being uniquely specified by two parameters: (1) whether or not the subject is awake; and (2) whether or not the subject is aware of anything. When we do this then transcendental consciousness fits very neatly into the fourth square of the table.

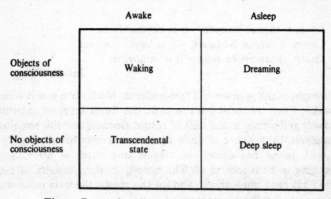

Figure 7   *A fourth major state of consciousness.*

This classification of the states of consciousness is, of course, only a very generalized one. Besides the many shades of consciousness within the waking, dreaming and deep sleep states there are also the borderline regions where one state emerges into the other. Nevertheless, this scheme is useful as a very general basis for distinguishing the transcendental state from each of the other three.

We can gain some insight into the relationship of these four states of consciousness by likening them to the different ways in which we can see a cinema screen. In this analogy the cinema projector corresponds to the brain projecting images onto the 'screen of the mind'. According to what is happening in the 'projector' many different scenes can be perceived on the 'screen'.

If the cinema projector were to be connected to some outside broadcast camera then we would see on the screen various real-life situations as they occurred. This corresponds to the ordinary waking state of consciousness in which we are more or less directly aware of the outside world.

If a film of some kind is being shown by the projector, then whatever appears on the screen, whether it be a replay of past events, a thriller, a cartoon, or merely abstract images, will usually bear little relation to what is happening outside the theatre. This corresponds to the dreaming state of consciousness in which memories and fantasies enter our awareness.

When the projector is switched off, leaving everything in darkness, the situation is similar to deep sleep when we have no awareness of anything.

The fourth possibility, corresponding to the transcendental state, occurs when the projector is switched on, but with no film in it. The screen is lit, but there are no images on it: one is awake but there are no objects of experience.

Normally we do not see the screen itself, we only see the images which are being projected on to it. But the screen is still there. Similarly the Self, the screen of the mind, never ceases to exist – without it there could be no experience – but it is usually overshadowed by experience; by the mental images falling upon it.

In TM the intensity of mental activity is reduced until, disappearing completely, only the unchanging screen of pure awareness is left. One is now left in the silent state of pure awareness: wide awake yet completely still.

Infinity and Nothingness

What has effectively happened in transcendental consciousness is that the object of experience and the subject of experience have become the same. The Self has become aware of the Self. In normal experience there is an object of experience, a subject of experience (the Self) and the interaction of the two, which gives rise to the experience. But when consciousness becomes conscious of consciousness, as is happening here, there is no longer any distinction between object and subject and no longer any interaction. Experience as we normally know it ceases. This is why, when the state is first encountered, it often seems to be one of emptiness. The state is nevertheless a very fulfilling one. It is often described as a state of silent joy, and it is this joy which attracts the attention within during TM.

The Upanishads abound with descriptions of the state. Perhaps the clearest is the following taken from the Manduyka Upanishad:[1]

This state is not subjective experience, nor objective experience, nor experience intermediate between these two, nor is it a negative condition which is neither consciousness or unconsciousness. It is not the knowledge of the senses, nor is it relative knowledge, nor yet inferential knowledge. Beyond the senses, beyond the understanding, beyond all expression, is The Fourth State of Consciousness. It is pure unitary consciousness, wherein awareness of the world and of multiplicity is completely obliterated.

In the West particularly lucid descriptions are to be found in the writings of Plotinus, a mystic-philosopher living in the third century AD:[2]

In this seeing we neither distinguish nor are there two ... Only in separation is there duality. This is why the vision baffles telling; for how can a man bring back tidings of the Supreme as detached when he has seen it as one with himself ... Beholder was one with behold ... he is become the unity, having no diversity either in relation to himself or anything else ... reason is in abeyance and intellection, and even the very self, caught away ... in perfect stillness, all the being calmed ... there is a communion with the self restored to its purity.

In the present century we find Krishnamurti saying:[3]

There is a transcendent spontaneity of life, a creative reality which reveals itself as immanent only when the perceiver's mind is in a state of alert passivity ...

In the ordinary state we have observer and the observed, we have duality – and where there's duality there's conflict.

In the transcendental state the observer and the observed become one. There is no longer duality, there's bliss. The thinker and the thought are one.

Descriptions of the state are to be found in all of the major religious traditions of the world. It is the Void of Buddhism the *Samadhi* (still mind) of Hinduism; the *Ming* (Self-knowledge) of Zen; the *Tso-wang* (sitting with no thoughts) of Taoist traditions; and the *Fana* ('passing away') of Sufism. It is the *En-Sof* ('Infinity') of Judaeism, the *Fund* of the individual, described by mediaeval mystics; and the state of *Quies* referred to by the Desert Fathers of early Christianity.

Such descriptions are not limited to the mystical and religious traditions: some of the finest descriptions of the state are to be found in the great poets. Wordsworth referred to it as 'a happy stillness of the mind . . . a wise passiveness'. In his famous poem *Tintern Abbey* he describes a brief but clear moment of transcendental consciousness:

– that serene and blessed mood,
In which the affections gently lead us on,
Until, the breath of this corporeal frame,
And even the motion of our human blood,
Almost suspended, we are laid asleep
In body, and become a living soul.

And Tennyson employing a meditation technique similar to TM reached a state sounding very much like transcendental consciousness as this extract from *The Ancient Sage* indicates:

More than once when I
Sat all alone, revolving in myself
The word that is the symbol of myself,
The mortal limit of the Self was loosed,
And passed into the nameless, as a cloud
Melts into heaven.

The Peace Which Passeth All Understanding

Most of us tend to associate consciousness so intimately with an object of consciousness that the idea of consciousness without an object seems self-contradictory. One might expect that if all mental activity had ceased then consciousness would also cease. But that would merely amount to a state of deep sleep or coma. Thousands of mystics the world over have testified that in the transcendental state one is very much awake and alert. Far from being a state of sleep they acclaim it to be one of true wakefulness alongside which our everyday waking state pales to one of semi-sleep. So how are we to conceive of a state in which there is nothing to be conscious of and yet consciousness itself remains?

The answer is probably that we cannot. In trying to understand any new phenomena we naturally try to relate it to what has already been experienced and understood. But when the new material lies beyond the range of our previous experiences this process is not so fruitful. To try to conceive of transcendental consciousness is like a congenitally blind man trying to imagine what colour is. However painstakingly we may describe our visual experiences he will only be able to comprehend them in terms of his previous experiences – tone, taste, touch, etc. It is only when we find a way of giving him the actual *experience* of seeing that he is able to fully appreciate our descriptions and know what 'colour' really means. Similarly, in attempting to understand transcendental consciousness we inevitably try to make it fit with those aspects of thinking with which we are already familiar, i.e. we form concepts of the state. But the state of transcendental consciousness, being beyond all mental activity, is, quite literally, beyond conception.

One sometimes hears it said that the aim of meditation is successively to eliminate all thoughts until one is left 'thinking of nothing'. But thinking of nothing is unfortunately still thinking of something and cannot therefore be a state of transcendental consciousness. Thinking about the state can only create an image of the state, not the experience itself, and such practices are no more than idol worship of a subtle kind.

In transcendental consciousness one quite literally 'hasn't the faintest idea' – neither of the state itself nor of anything else. If you *think* that you are in the state then you can be pretty sure that you are not, for it lies beyond thought. Being beyond the active mind the state lies beyond any possibility of being perceived by the senses, conceived of by the mind, understood by the intellect, or felt by the emotions. The sixteenth-century Spanish mystic, St John of the Cross, describing this feature (or perhaps we should say non-feature) of the state, said:[4]

> We receive this mystical knowledge ... in none of the kinds of images, in none of the sensible representations which our mind makes use of in other circumstances. Accordingly in this knowledge, since the senses and imagination are not employed, we get neither form nor impression, nor can we give any account or furnish any likeness, although the mysterious and sweet tasting wisdom comes here so directly to the innermost parts of the soul.

Because it has none of the usual qualities of thought any attempt to describe the state becomes a contradiction. To say anything at all about the attributeless it is to give it some attribute – even to say that it is attributeless is to give it the attribute of attributelessness. Perhaps we should, like the Buddha, remain silent on the subject, but this is of little help to most people. Yet to take the opposite course and say that it has the particular quality 'A', immediately demands the qualification that it is also 'not-A'. Conversely, to deny that it has the quality 'A' immediately demands the qualification 'nor is it not-A'. Dionysius wrote in his *Mystical Theology* that: 'nor can any affirmation or negation apply to it'. But equally, enjoying the paradox, we could say that the opposite is also true and that all affirmations and negations may apply to it.

Some philosophers, finding the notion of pure consciousness to be so self-contradictory, have rejected any possibility of its existence. A few have even gone so far as to remark that it is merely that state which inclines one to speak rubbish. But the fact that descriptions of the state appear to be paradoxical does not necessarily invalidate the state: it may merely reflect the weakness of our language and the limitations of a solely rational approach to the study of consciousness. It is not therefore surprising that those who depend almost entirely on logical arguments and the structure of their own language in their quest for truth should find descriptions of mystical experience a little hard to accept. But to deny its existence is like a blind man denying the possibility of light – to other blind people his arguments may seem plausible and even laudable, but to the person who can see they are empty and pathetic.

The Pure Self

The state of transcendental consciousness has been referred to as the true Self. This does not mean to imply that all other concepts of the self are necessarily wrong. Many of the philosophical, psychological and sociological concepts of personal identity may be quite valid personal attributes. But the pure Self is quite separate from all these concepts and images.

When psychologists talk of the self or ego they may be referring to any one of a number of different concepts. These include the self image we put on to other people, the self we see ourselves as, the self we would like to be seen as, our personalities, unconscious characteristics of our thinking, our sense of unity as an individual person, and many others. But these are all concerned with particular attributes of the individual and are not therefore the same as the pure attributeless Self.

The same could be said of sociological conceptions of the self. For example, the view that our conception of self is conditioned by our social environment may well be true, but here one is talking of a different self from the pure Self which underlies *all* experience, including the conditioned self.

We all have various *ideas* of what we are and how we see ourselves. We talk of ourselves referring to 'my body', 'my mind', 'my experiences', 'my personality', 'my ego', etc. But these are all objects of experience, things that I think I am: they are not the pure Self, the 'I' that thinks and is the subject of all experience.

The pure Self might be thought of as the beam of consciousness shining out from within, and, by taking form, giving rise to everything we are aware of. To look for the pure Self is like taking a torch to look for the source of light, all that we find are a variety of objects giving form to the light. This is why the philosopher Hume's search for his self was bound to failure from the start. In a now famous passage he wrote:[5]

> I always stumble on some particular perception or other, of heat or cold, light or shade, love or hatred, pain or pleasure. I never can catch *myself* at any time without a perception, and can never observe anything but the perception.

But it would be very wrong to conclude that there was no such thing as the self. The very fact that we are conscious shows that a subject of consciousness exists just as the very fact that light is reflected from other objects allowing us to see shows that somewhere there is a source of light.

The only way to know the pure Self is by systematically reducing the impact of sensory experience until only the Self remains. This is what happens in transcendental consciousness. In this state there is no longer any experience of 'I am this' or 'I am that'. There is not even the *experience* of 'I am'. It is simply a state of is-ness or pure Being. It is a field which lies beyond individual consciousness and for precisely this reason there is an absence of individuality. If there is any feeling of identity it is one of universality: an at-one-ness with the whole of creation. The boundaries which usually serve to distinguish one self from another having dissolved, there is no longer any effective means of distinction. One begins to experience that, at the most fundamental level, 'we are all one and the same', and that the pure Self is a Universal Self which, shining through different nervous systems, takes on the form of an individual consciousness and individual self. In the words of the psychologist Carl Rogers: 'the deeper that we go into ourselves as particular and unique, seeking for our own individual identity, the more that we find the whole human species.'[6]

The Absolute

Along with most Eastern traditions and many Western ones Maharishi holds that there is an Absolute basis not only to all conscious minds but to everything in existence. He refers to this Absolute as the field of pure creative intelligence. In Chapter 3 we saw how every thought possesses the qualities of creativity and intelligence and how the source of thought may be thought of as a field of pure creative intelligence. What he is now saying is that the same could be said of everything that exists.

Nothing we experience is permanent but is subject to ceaseless change. Old forms disintegrate and new patterns and structures are created. This ceaseless activity Maharishi refers to as the principle of creativity. But the changes do not occur at random: objects move subject to well-defined mathematical laws; organisms direct their chemical changes so as to preserve a certain orderliness; and the whole of human learning can be seen as the attempt to find order beneath continual change. This underlying orderliness is what Maharishi refers to as the principle of intelligence. If everything in the relative world displays these principles of creativity and intelligence then the absolute of which they are formed must itself be a field of pure creative intelligence.

Maharishi therefore sees two aspects to existence; there is the unmanifest field of pure creative intelligence, the absolute aspect; and there are all the various manifestations which we experience, the relative aspects. The absolute aspect can never be detected by the senses or by science. Both are concerned with detecting events, i.e. changes in the world, and the Absolute, by definition, is unchanging. Its existence cannot therefore be proved or disproved in the same way that events in the relative world can. All that we can detect and measure are the forms which it takes. In much the same way we can never see pure light. Whenever we see light we see particular colours and particular boundaries – the various forms which light takes – but pure light without colour or form remains essentially unknowable.

The idea that everything we observe is relative, that there is no absolute which can be defined or measured, is also found in Einstein's Special Theory of Relativity. This proposes that space and time are not absolute. What I perceive as space and time will only be the same as what you perceive as space and time if we happen to be travelling together at the same velocity. There is no absolute space or absolute time, only a space-time continuum which, when observed, manifests as a particular perception of relative space and relative time. Similarly Einstein's famous equation, $E = mc^2$, shows that matter and energy are, like space and time, interchangeable and not absolute entities.

The idea of an underlying oneness to all creation can also be seen from a consideration of the fine structure of matter. As one passes from the everyday perception of an object through the microscopic levels of molecules and on to the level of sub-atomic particles there is a tendency away from diversity towards oneness. The infinite variety of objects that we perceive around us is constructed out of various combinations of several million different molecules. These in turn are formed by specific combinations of a hundred different atoms, which are themselves particular combinations of just a few sub-atomic particles. We are moving away from diversity towards sameness.

As we inquire further into the nature of these sub-atomic particles even the concept of particle begins to disappear. Discrete solid objects dissolve into infinite waves extending throughout space-time and representing only tendencies to exist rather than individual existences. The idea of an isolated particle no longer has any meaning. At this level all that exists is a relationship between the observer and his observation; the distinction between 'I' and the World fades. In short, the further we continue to divide and separate the physical world the more we find ourselves being thrown back to the idea of Oneness and inseparability.

It is sometimes assumed, particularly in certain Indian philosophies, that if everything in creation is ultimately the same then the complex diversity which we observe around us is somehow unreal and illusory. But it is not an either-or situation. It is not that, the Absolute being real, the relative world of phenomena must be unreal: both are very real. On one level of reality this book is a book; on another level it is also an organized mass of wood fibre; it is also a vast collection of molecules; and from another point of view it is just pure creative intelligence. None of these different views destroys the validity of any other view, they are all different perspectives of reality and are all just as real as each other.

Although it is not possible to experience the Absolute in the same way that everything else is experienced, i.e. as a sensory experience, it is possible to know it through personal participation with it. This is what is achieved in TM as the boundaries of awareness dissolve, and one comes to experience pure Being beyond its manifold expressions. Thus the pure Self experienced in meditation as well as being a Universal Self, the basis of all minds, is also the basis of all creation. This is the central theme of the Upanishads:[7]

What is within us is also without.
What is without us is also within.

A statement remarkably similar to one found in the alleged sayings of Christ in The Gospel According to Thomas:[8] 'The Kingdom is within you and it is without you.' And Plotinus, ever lucid and concise, wrote:[9]

Each being contains in itself the whole intelligible world. Therefore All is everywhere. Each is there All and All is each. Man as he now is has ceased to be the All. But when he ceases to be an individual, he raises himself again and penetrates the whole world.

The Fifth State of Consciousness

9

Before enlightenment chop wood and carry water;
After enlightenment chop wood and carry water.

Zen aphorism

By definition the fourth state of consciousness, transcendental consciousness, is the deepest state which can be reached during meditation and in this respect it could be said to be the goal of meditation itself. It is not, however, the sole or final aim of the practice. There are several 'higher' states of consciousness which develop as a result of regular contact with transcendental consciousness.

I shall use the word 'higher' to refer to states of consciousness in which the normal perceptions of the waking, dreaming and deep sleep states of consciousness have been added to in some way or another. The unmodified waking, dreaming and deep sleep states I shall call the 'ordinary' states of consciousness. Transcendental consciousness, being a state of pure consciousness, is therefore neither an ordinary nor a higher state of consciousness. It is in a unique category of its own.

The first of the higher states of consciousness, the fifth state of consciousness, is defined as that state in which transcendental consciousness is maintained along with each of the three ordinary states of consciousness. This state is quite distinct from the four states we have previously encountered.

The most important thing to notice about it is that pure consciousness is now maintained not just in the deepest states of meditation but twenty-four hours a day, even in the deepest sleep. This does not mean that there is any additional mental activity taking place – waking, dreaming and deep sleep continue just as before – but along with each of the three ordinary states there is also the awareness of the unchanging field of pure consciousness deep within.

Before the dawn of the fifth state of consciousness the finer levels of thinking and the source of thought itself could only be experienced by withdrawing from activity. One had to temporarily retire from the world of change. But in the fifth state the unchanging basis of the mind can be experienced along with the changing surface levels of thought. This corresponds to the full expansion of the conscious mind which we looked at in Chapter 7. Thinking now embraces all strata of mental activity and on this account Maharishi calls it *cosmic* consciousness.

The importance of this fifth state of consciousness lies in the fact that a person now retains an awareness of the true Self throughout all activity and I shall consider the consequences of this in the next chapter; here I shall be concerned with how the state develops.

The Development of Cosmic Consciousness

Maharishi has always maintained that to every state of consciousness there is a corresponding state of physical activity in the body and that it is only by producing a profound change in physiology and brain functioning that one can ever produce a profound and lasting change in consciousness. If there is no corresponding change from the physical side then any perceived mental change will only be a mood superimposed on the waking state. Thus there are two complementary ways in which one may consider the development of the fifth state of consciousness.

One can look at it either from a consideration of the changes occurring within the body (in terms of the effects of releasing stress), or one may consider the parallel changes which are taking place in the mind (the process of 'infusion' of pure consciousness into the awareness).

1. As the Purification of the Nervous System

It will be recalled that one of the premises of Maharishi's teaching is that we are usually only conscious of the surface levels of mental activity. What prevents us from being aware of the subtler levels of thinking, and of the field of pure consciousness itself, is the existence of stress in the nervous system. The fifth state of consciousness is only reached when all accumulated stress has been dissolved.

Since it is a permanent state of consciousness the individual must be *permanently* free from stress. It is one thing temporarily to free the nervous system from the effects of stress and so have a passing 'flash' of the fifth state. It is quite another thing to completely rid the nervous system of stress so that no more is ever accumulated.

One might think that the quickest way to develop the state would be to sit down and meditate continually, day in and day out, until all the stresses had been dissolved. Even though you might temporarily relieve the body of all accumulated stresses by continual meditation, the body would still be susceptible to further experiential overloads and the first burden that the senses encountered would result in stress being accumulated once again. The pure awareness would begin to fade and you would soon find yourself returning to the ordinary waking state.

Activity as well as meditation is fundamental to the development of the fifth state of consciousness. Maharishi teaches that after some stress has been dissolved by meditation the nervous system, by which he means the whole organism, must be 'exercised' in order that it may adjust to its new style of functioning. Activity allows the body to recover from the impairment the stress produced and to return towards normal. The fifth state comes about when, through the regular alternation of rest and activity, the nervous system has both released all its accumulated tensions and simultaneously developed a resilience to any further stress.

The fact that people in this state of consciousness no longer accumulate stress does not mean that they are in any way less aware – it is very likely that they will be more fully aware: it is simply that a strong experience will not have the same adverse physiological effects on them. Maharishi likens this to the difference between drawing a line on stone and drawing a line on water. The line drawn on stone leaves a permanent scratch on the surface which is only removed with difficulty; the line drawn on water is the same line, but it leaves no permanent trace. In cosmic consciousness an experience is like a line drawn on water; the experience is perceived but the nervous system is no longer 'scratched' by it.

It is important to realize that the state is not one of sensitivity and fragility where the slightest intrusion of stress must be continually guarded against: it is a state of complete composure in the face of all adversity, when nothing can overshadow the experience of pure awareness. When asked for a test of cosmic consciousness, Maharishi once replied: 'The ability to stand in the middle of Manhattan and still maintain the experience of the Self'.

2. As the Infusion of Pure Consciousness into the Surface Mind

On returning from a deep meditation to the surface levels of mental activity one usually finds that some of the qualities of the transcendental state have, so to speak, been drawn up into the conscious mind. One experiences this as a sense of wholeness, fullness and stability; an awareness of silence and peace deep within. This Maharishi refers to as the infusion of pure consciousness, or pure Being, into the conscious mind.

At first one may find that these qualities are only present when one is still fairly deep in meditation and that as one returns to the surface they fade away. Later one may find that they are there immediately after meditation but that they quickly fade again as soon as one engages in any sort of activity. It might be concluded that activity should be avoided, or that if one did act then one should try to remain detached from it in order to preserve the state of pure consciousness, as long as possible. But this is not the case. Maharishi repeatedly emphasizes that it is only by allowing the experience of pure awareness to fade away through activity that the nervous system can be 'cultured' to a state where it can continue to maintain pure awareness in all activity.

He frequently likens this process of infusion to the dyeing of cloth using the old vegetable dyes common in rural India. When the cloth is dyed, two processes are necessary. First the cloth is dipped into the dye becoming strongly coloured. But then, since the dyes are not fast, one has to leave it in the sun to fade. After fading it must be again dipped in the dye and again left to fade. The process is repeated, dipping and fading, dipping and fading, each time the colour becoming a little stronger, until eventually the cloth is so fully dyed that it now no longer fades, even when left in the brightest of suns.

The alternation of rest and activity with TM can be seen to be a similar process: during meditation the awareness is 'dipped' into pure consciousness and the mind returns 'dyed' with the qualities of pure consciousness; after meditation these qualities are 'faded' by activity. This process is repeated day by day until ultimately the mind is so permanently 'dyed' with pure consciousness that even the strongest experience will not overshadow it.

It is important to note that, having dipped the cloth in the dye, nothing more is to be gained by leaving it there. Likewise, having 'dipped' the attention in pure consciousness nothing more is to be gained by staying within. It is the regular alternation of dipping and fading that is important rather than the dipping itself.

We could bring these two descriptions of the growth of cosmic consciousness together by likening the human nervous system to a crystal. A crystal sparkles and shines as if it were a source of light itself, and the quality of the sparkle depends very much on the purity of the crystal. If there are irregularities and disorders in its structure then it becomes dull and ceases to sparkle so brilliantly. Similarly the human being can shine and sparkle with life from within but if there are irregularities, that is stresses, in the system then we too become dull. We cease to reflect pure consciousness in its fullest values.

The practice of TM might therefore be considered as a polishing of the 'reflector of consciousness' (the nervous system) so that pure consciousness begins to shine out brighter from within. When ultimately all the stresses have been dissolved then pure consciousness shines out in its full brilliance.

On the Importance of Being Active

By 'activity' Maharishi means any process, physical or mental, in which the attention is directed out towards the senses rather than in towards finer levels of thinking. In effect this means anything other than meditation. So when he says that the way to progress is to 'meditate and act' he is emphasizing the value of getting on with things rather than wallowing in post-meditative bliss. He does not mean that after meditation you should sprint round the block or do a hundred press-ups; but that you should engage yourself wholeheartedly in your normal daily activities. In this respect, an Oxford don philosophizing in his leather armchair is as much engaged in activity as a labourer digging the road. What is important is that whatever you are doing you should be thoroughly involved in it and not try to maintain a sense of detachment. Only in this way will you begin to infuse the effects of meditation into your everyday life.

There is no need to modify one's daily life in order to get the most out of meditation. In fact, deliberately holding on to the peaceful feeling that persists after meditation only retards the development of cosmic consciousness. Whatever it is one is trying to hold on to, being an idea or image in the mind, could not itself be pure consciousness. It is the effects of contact with pure consciousness that are experienced on the surface of the mind; pure consciousness itself remains silent and unchanging.

People who try to remain detached from activity in an attempt to maintain pure awareness lose out in all ways. Firstly, they only maintain an idea or image of the Self. Secondly, the real process of infusion is hindered. And thirdly, their half-hearted activity is less effective than that of a fully committed man. Rather than progressing they stagnate.

Not only is activity vital for the development of higher states of consciousness, it continues to remain an important characteristic of life when the higher state has been reached – a fact well exemplified in the lives of many enlightened men, including Maharishi's. As the Zen aphorism puts it: 'Before enlightenment, chop wood and carry water; After enlightenment, chop wood and carry water.'

The Gentle Dawn

One important aspect of the growth to the fifth state of consciousness is its naturalness and gentleness. One rarely awakes to find oneself suddenly enlightened. One gradually begins to maintain more and more of pure awareness for longer and longer periods of time until ultimately it is there as an all-time, permanent reality. In this respect the gentle rise to cosmic consciousness is like the gentle change from night to day.

As the dawn breaks the intensity of the light increases ten-millionfold, but the change is so smooth and gradual that we hardly notice it. We do not usually observe the light itself increasing: all we notice is that gradually our vision is becoming clearer. Similarly, with the dawning of cosmic consciousness, the gradual brightening of awareness is not itself noticed. If people notice anything it is that their perception is now clearer, their action more effective and the whole of life richer and more enjoyable than it was before.

A smooth continual change is always much harder to notice than an abrupt or intermittent change, and many meditators do not notice the change in themselves although their friends who only see them intermittently often see it very clearly.

It is important that the change is accomplished in such a gentle and unobtrusive manner. Just as a sudden increase in light may be temporarily blinding, so a sudden change from the 'darkness' of the ordinary waking state to the 'full light' of cosmic consciousness might be too much to take. By allowing this new level of consciousness to grow in a very natural manner it is integrated harmoniously into one's life.

On first hearing of the idea of cosmic consciousness people frequently try to interpret it in terms of additional experiences at the conscious level of thinking. They think they will start to have wonderful visions or some other extraordinary experiences. But cosmic consciousness is just becoming more truly oneself; becoming the Self. As Anthony Campbell remarks in his book *The Seven States of Consciousness*, rather than undergoing an extraordinary experience one feels as if one is becoming more and more normal.

Maharishi takes this idea of normality a stage further. For him the fifth state of consciousness is the 'normal' state of consciousness. The fact that most people are living in a state of stress and mental dullness does not mean that such states are either natural or necessary. As far as Maharishi is concerned they are 'subnormal' states. Given the chance the body will throw off stress and purify itself – what Maharishi refers to as the normalization of the nervous system. It is in this respect that he sees the stress-free state as the normal and natural state of life. His aim is to make the fifth state of consciousness the 'normal' state of consciousness both in his sense of the word normal and in its everyday sense.

Self-Realization

10

Whoever dieth before his death, getteth relieved of a world of sorrows.

Mohammed

In the fifth state of consciousness the pure Self has become a permanent feature of the awareness and for this reason the state is often known as one of permanent Self-realization. An awareness of the pure Self does not, however, involve any loss of individual self or ego. These continue to function very much as before but added to these individual attributes is a silent awareness of the attributeless Self, the pure 'I', underlying them. This results in a profound and permanent change in personal identity and it is this which makes cosmic consciousness so significant and valuable.

Before Self-realization a person derives his sense of identity from his interaction with the world around. Reduced to its simplest level this interaction is a cycle of action, impression and desire. Every sensory experience leaves some impression in the brain. On the basis of this impression and other past impressions (i.e. memories) we make decisions. This gives rise to various desires and we try to fulfil, and thereby reduce, these desires through appropriate action. The action changes the environment producing new sensory experiences, these in turn giving rise to further desires and action. So the cycle continues.

In engineering terms it is a simple feedback loop and through it we are able continually to adjust to and interact with our environment.

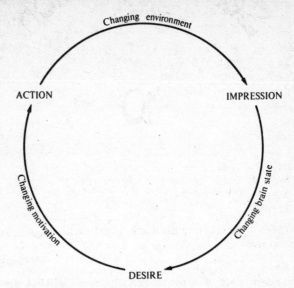

Figure 8   *The cycle of action-impression-desire.*

The continuance of the cycle also provides the organism with a biological identity. It comes to know itself as a semi-autonomous creature interacting with its environment and the sense of individuality which this provides ensures that the organism will strive to stay alive.

Unfortunately the person who is unaware of the pure Self must also rely upon this biological function for a sense of psychological identity and personal existence. Thus we often find ourselves acting not out of some biological need but out of a psychological need – the need to reinforce our sense of personal identity. Indeed, without such continual feedback most of us would die psychologically (literally cease to be) as surely as we would die physically if deprived of food or oxygen.

When changes in the outside world threaten this derived sense of identity we are forced to reaffirm our selves. This may happen in a number of ways. We may filter experience so as only to see what we want to see, we may suppress memories of experiences which threaten our identity or we may find ourselves desiring and acting only for the good of our self-image. How often have we found ourselves defending a point of view not because we really believe it but purely to defend our identity with that point of view? Or when criticized in some way, we may feel psychologically 'hurt'. Ideally we should tend to the cause of the criticism but more often the injured ego demands that it be healed and made to feel strong again. We may do this by retaliating with another criticism, by making attempts to justify ourselves and so save our sense of identity, or, possibly, by pretending to ourselves that we have not even heard it. The net result is that a great deal of psychological and physical energy is wasted on activities which are not only unnecessary and inappropriate, but often damaging to ourselves and our environment.

Now the search for a stable identity is not itself wrong. It is in fact a very basic drive. Indeed, when we recall that the pure Self is experienced as bliss we can see that the search for a stable identity is but another manifestation of the same drive which earlier we saw as the search for greater satisfaction. When there is no awareness of the true Self within, one must seek to derive a permanent and stable identity from the outer world – a world where only change exists – and such a derived identity, being continually at the mercy of events, must be continually reaffirmed. But as a person grows towards cosmic consciousness and gains a greater awareness of the Self the amount of energy and effort which he spends on maintaining his derived sense of identity decreases. When he reaches cosmic consciousness he knows the Self to be a permanent feature of life. From this platform of utter stability he remains unshaken by changes in the outer world. He no longer needs to act and experience in order to derive and maintain a sense of identity. Action now springs not from the demands of the ego but from the demands of the whole situation. This, as we shall see in Chapter 15, is the beginning of true altruism.

Freedom from Bondage

Maharishi continually emphasizes that the enlightened man gains *freedom from bondage* to the cycle of action-impression-desire: he does not have to break or destroy the cycle itself. The Self-realized man* still acts and the fruits of his actions still affect his body and his mind, but since his identity is now derived from the inner Self changes in the outer world are no longer threatening. But as a physical organism he is still as subject to the law of physics as anyone or anything else.

Confusion frequently arises over this distinction and it is closely bound up with the confusion over free-will and determinism.

Looking at the universe from a physical point of view it appears that everything that happens is controlled by the laws of physics and just has to happen that way, i.e. everything is completely predetermined. Yet looking at the world from a subjective point of view, we often experience that we choose the way we will act, i.e. we have free-will. It is commonly thought that these two statements are irreconcilable and it is concluded that the experience of free-will may be only an illusion, that physics may not after all be completely deterministic, or that the mind is somehow able to contravene the laws of physics.

I personally cannot support such an absolutist either-or approach. It may well be that the deterministic and the libertarian interpretations of reality are just two different views of reality which arise from taking different stands with respect to the self. The deterministic view treats the self as an object, the recipient of actions, whereas the libertarian point of view treats the self as a subject, the agent of actions. These two views represent two very fundamental polarities. It is not therefore surprising that the conclusions which they engender are also diametrically opposite.

A similar situation is encountered in quantum physics. It is found that under certain conditions light behaves as waves and under other conditions as particles. At first this contradictory behaviour was very confusing. Niels Bohr, however, suggested that it should be seen in terms of complementarity, and that whether a phenomenon is interpreted as a wave or as a particle depends ultimately upon the way in which the phenomena is observed. Similarly, whether the universe appears to be completely predetermined or open to modification by human free-will depends upon the way in which one observes the situation. From the outside, human beings are as predetermined as the rest of the universe: from the inside, we experience free-will.

---

* All that is said here and in later chapters of the Self-realized man and the enlightened man is of course equally true of the Self-realized and enlightened woman.

The question as to which is right or as to how the two can be reconciled arises from the attempt to transfer terms from one frame of reference to the other. The concept of free-will refers to a subjective experience: it cannot be applied to the physical world where it is meaningless. Similarly, determinism is a concept which arises from an understanding of the physical world and has no relevance to subjective experience. It is not a question of which view is right and which is wrong: both are right relative to the frame of reference from which they arose.

Before the state of Self-realization is gained only the bounded individual self is known and this one self is forced to play two contradictory roles. Firstly, it has to maintain a sense of individuality and personal freedom; yet this same self, being derived from the external world, must also suffer the ups and downs of that world, i.e. it is also deterministic. One is forced to try and fit two mutually contradictory perspectives of the world into one frame of reference. This inevitably results in confusion and paradox. But for the self-realized man there is no conflict. The individual self is still as bound as ever – all his actions, including his thoughts, are still subject to deterministic laws: but the pure Self is completely free. In this way the paradox has been resolved – or rather dissolved.

Thus the enlightened person does not gain freedom from the deterministic cycle of action, impression and desire, but freedom from psychological bondage to this cycle. 'It is not,' writes Maharishi,[1] 'the action or its fruits which bind a man; rather it is the inability to maintain freedom which becomes a means of bondage.' Unfortunately this point is too often missed. It is frequently held that in order to escape from bondage to the cycle the cycle itself must be stopped or broken in some way, and various techniques have grown up with the intention of doing just this.

When action has been seen to be at fault, people have tried to modify or reduce their activity in the hope that they would thereby reduce their bondage to the world. Others, believing experience to be at fault, have advocated sensory control and withdrawal in order that further desires may not be stimulated – that one may not be led into temptation. And others, thinking that desires were the cause of bondage and suffering have sought to eliminate all desires. But all these approaches deliberately disrupt the natural biological feedback processes and can have a disastrous effect on daily life. Moreover it is doubtful whether, by themselves, such practices could ever lead to true Self-realization, which, by definition, is the ability to live the real Self *along with* the natural processes of action, experience and desire.

The Still Point of a Turning World

Self-realization does not entail awareness of the Self at the expense of the self. The action-impression-desire cycle continues and with it the sense of individual identity. All that goes to make up a unique individual is still there; the enlightened man retains his character, personality, memories, etc. The path to Self-realization is not therefore one of self-abnegation, self-subordination or self-elimination; it is one of expansion of awareness to include the pure Self along with the individual self.

One might liken the Self to the hub of the revolving wheel of life. Individual ego, memories, images, experiences, desires, thoughts, etc., continually revolve around the pure Self. The Self, being at the centre, never changes. In Self-realization the wheel has not stopped, it continues to revolve much as before, but one has now also become aware of the centre of the wheel, and one now draws one's identity not from the spinning rim of the wheel but from its still centre.

The state of Self-realization is brought about in TM by allowing the attention repeatedly to retire from the cycle of action-impression-desire into transcendental consciousness. No attempt is made to break the cycle, but, by allowing the mind to settle down, activity, experience and desire all spontaneously decrease. The cycle temporarily dies away. In transcendental consciousness only the Self remains. Then through activity the awareness of the pure Self is integrated into daily life.

Returning to the cinema analogy of Chapter 8 we could say that now both the screen and the film are known separately. But knowing the screen for what it really is in no way destroys the film. What maintains the individual identity of the film is the coherence and continuity of its images and this is not lost when the screen is discovered. In the waking state one identifies with the continuity of experience, i.e. the images falling upon the screen of the mind, whereas in the fifth state of consciousness one knows oneself to be pure consciousness: the screen itself. The continuity of experience does not cease; it continues, but it is no longer mistaken for the screen, the pure Self.

When people try to understand this new state of consciousness they inevitably do so in terms of previously encountered states and frequently conclude that it must involve some kind of separation between the mind and body, or between the ego and the mind. But this is not the case. Self-realization is a clear separation between the silent attributeless Self and *all* activity, mental and physical; a separation between the Self on the one hand and the body, senses, mind, intellect, emotions, *and* ego on the other.

Non-Attachment

Because the sense of identity is no longer derived from nor conditioned by the ego, mind, senses or body, the state of Self-realization is often referred to as one of non-attachment. Unfortunately the real meaning of non-attachment has frequently been misunderstood resulting in a rejection of all material possessions and anything else which gave one pleasure, with the intention that the individual would no longer be 'attached' to the outside world. But this only creates an image or mood of non-attachment and eventually leads to the most bizarre forms of hypocrisy. Non-attachment has nothing to do with the avoidance of action or pleasure. It is the ability to act and enjoy in freedom without being bound to the process for a sense of identity. As it says so clearly in the Bhagavad Gita:

> Not by refraining from action does a man achieve freedom
> from action;
> Nor by mere renunciation does he attain supreme perfection.
> Not even for a moment can a man be without action;
> For all are helplessly driven to action by the forces born of
> Nature.
> He who withdraws himself from actions, but ponders on
> their pleasures in his heart,
> He is deceiving himself, and can only be called a hypocrite.
>
> (III: 4-6)

Attachment arises when the sense of identity is drawn from experience and action. If, for example, a man partly draws his sense of identity from his car then he is said to be attached to it and if his car were to go, his identity would suffer. Non-attachment occurs when the identity is drawn from the pure Self. This does not mean that the Self-realized man would cease to care about the outer world or become insensible to its ups and downs: but, being grounded in the Self, his identity or sense of personal existence is not shaken by changes in the outer world.

It is in this sense that Maharishi talks of the absence of suffering. The Self-realized man can still incur great emotional loss – indeed, his emotions will probably be much richer than the ordinary man's – but being no longer bound to his experience for his sense of identity, *he,* as the unchanging Self, can no longer be shaken by outer change and is, therefore, beyond the very possibility of suffering. Any losses are borne with grace and fortitude without the need to heal an injured ego.

Suffering, concludes Maharishi, is born of a false identification with experience. This does not mean that personal suffering is in any way unreal. For the person whose awareness does not pass beyond the surface levels of existence suffering is very real, and any talk of it not being so is clearly ridiculous. But for the Self-realized man there is the additional reality of a level of life which lies beyond pleasure and pain, and at this level there is no suffering.

Nor will the Self-realized man be insensible to the suffering of others. He is beyond personal suffering, it is true, but from this unshakeable stand he will be more sensitive to the plight of others and better able to help them. As Maharishi remarks:[2]

> A happy man would be able to see the unhappiness of others much more than an unhappy man. An unhappy man is busy suffering himself, he has no time to see the suffering of others. Compassion is not awake in an unhappy, miserable mind. But compassion and kindness are awake in a man who is happy, who is peaceful.

And looking back over history we find that many of the great mystics devoted their lives to alleviating the suffering of others – indeed, it is one of the commonly accepted characteristics of a saint that he should have given himself 'selflessly' to the benefaction of mankind.

It is sometimes held that, since it is the ego ('the illusory self') which is at the root of suffering, the ego must die. If this means that the false identification with the ego must cease then it is, with a qualification or two, acceptable: but if it means that the individual ego must be destroyed, as some contemporary Buddhists appear to believe, then it is clearly untenable. (I say 'contemporary'

Buddhists because it is possible that the original teachings of the Buddha were much closer to those of Maharishi in this respect. Sidney Spencer, for example, argues that there is considerable evidence that the Buddha did teach of an attributeless pure Self very close to that of the Upanishads.[3])

Those who adhere to this latter interpretation teach that all suffering involves 'I': 'I want this', 'I have not got that', etc., and *therefore* the 'I' must go. But this is a denial of the changing self rather than an affirmation of the changeless Self and the path then becomes one of self-destruction rather than Self-discovery – an approach which can only result in self-deceit. Unless a person first establishes an identity with the pure Self any attempt to rid himself of an illusory identity will only result in the creation of a new sense of identity and the replacement of one illusion by another.

Transcending Desire

When suffering is thought to result from the 'craving of I', then it is taught that in order to eliminate suffering one must first eliminate all desires. Maharishi strongly disagrees with this. It is not, he says, desires themselves which lead to suffering but one's inability to fulfil them. Unfulfilled desires are the cause of suffering and unhappiness.

He teaches that the way to get rid of unfulfilled desires is not to try to banish or subjugate the desires themselves but to effectively fulfil them by achieving the goal of all desires. This is not to say that one must actually fulfil all possible desires. Some desires may conflict with those of other people. Others may not be in the best interests of the rest of society or the planet as a whole. And some may even be physically impossible – though whether the mind can directly affect physical reality is another question (see chapter 15).

The source of many desires is the search for a stable identity. When the pure Self has become a permanently established feature of the awareness one has effectively achieved the goal of these desires and the desires themselves no longer arise. In this way one has achieved the goal of these desires without actually having to fulfil each individually.

Of course not all desires are on the level of ego-maintenance: many of them are a natural part of the cycle of action-impression-desire. The basic desire for food, for example, is a natural biological one (although it may in the case of compulsive eaters also reflect some abnormal psychological need). It would be very wrong to try to eliminate such necessary drives, and it would be equally wrong to try to eliminate many of man's 'higher' desires for the health and welfare of his community and surroundings. All these natural desires continue to arise in the mind of the Self-realized man, but with one important difference: they do not give rise to craving.

We have seen that every thought starts from the subtlest levels of the mind and rising up to the surface levels of thinking develops into a fully fledged idea. It is only when the impulse has reached the grosser levels of thinking that it takes the form of a desire. Before this it is merely an incentive for action without craving. The person whose attention is confined to the grosser levels of thinking, only appreciates an incentive for action when it has already become a desire; all his actions start from the level of desire. With the coming of Self-realization one experiences the whole range and depth of thinking and is able to appreciate an impulse before it has become strong enough to be a desire. One's thoughts are translated into action without first expressing themselves as desires, and without the craving and suffering which goes with them.[4]

So we can begin to understand why Maharishi says that the enlightened man has no desires as such and why the state is described as one of personal fulfilment. But it is important to realize that the absence of desire is the *result* of gaining fulfilment: to try to eliminate all desires *in order to* rise towards fulfilment is to put the cart before the horse.

Right Action

When Maharishi says that the Self-realized man acts according to the needs of the situation rather than the needs of the ego he is not saying anything specific about his actions. He is not saying that the Self-realized man will do this or that, nor even that he should do this or that: only that his actions will spontaneously be more effective and more suited to the overall situation. But do not misunderstand the nature of this spontaneity. It is not that actions themselves occur any more spontaneously – the actions of the enlightened man are probably no more and no less premeditated than those of his unenlightened fellows – but that whatever actions he decides to undertake will, without any additional deliberation, be more appropriate and more fruitful.

The full effects of any action are unfathomable: they are so far-reaching, both in space and time, that it is beyond the scope of any mind to follow them all through. Moreover, even if we could know the full effects of any action this by itself would not dictate whether that action was right or wrong. We must still decide upon the correct ethic by which to evaluate the effects, and in this task reason alone is insufficient.

When it comes down to making a decision we simply act as we feel is best. What Maharishi is saying is that the way we *feel* will spontaneously change as we raise our level of consciousness. We might think of this as the growth of intuition – and in the final analysis it is intuition which is at the basis of all our moral laws however they may subsequently be rationalized and codified. But intuitive feelings of right and wrong are not of course always correct. The degree to which they are right or wrong will depend upon one's clarity of mind. Moreover, one's intuitive responses must still be analysed in the cold light of day and here the synthesis of intuition and reason that develops with meditation becomes of increasing importance.

Many people find it alarming that Maharishi lays down no moral precepts or codes of behaviour. Meditation may make a man act more efficiently but what, they ask, is to prevent him from channelling this activity in undesirable directions? Indeed, since the Self-realized man has, in transcending the individual self, transcended the element of personal fear upon which many of our laws depend, what is there to stop him becoming a wanton criminal?

Maharishi's answer is that, in transcending the individual self, the Self-realized man has transcended the very roots of immoral and criminal action, for these stem from the need to maintain a derived sense of identity. His motivations have changed and he simply would not want to engage in such actions. What one begins to notice as one continues with meditation is that one is refraining from 'wrong' action, not because one has been told it is wrong or because of the fear of punishment, but because it *feels* wrong.

I do not mean to suggest that anyone who meditates is necessarily more moral than someone who does not – this is clearly not the case: only that the growth of awareness will be accompanied by a spontaneous tendency to act in a more 'life-supporting' manner. The actual moral standing of any particular individual will depend upon where they started from and their speed of personal growth.

The fact that Maharishi never speaks of evil, only of good, could be taken to indicate that he ignores the presence of evil: but this is not the case. He is merely looking at what we would call negative or evil actions from a different point of view. He believes that all actions have the same final goal – union with the fundamental ground of all existence, the Self or Absolute. The most egocentric and selfish actions are only manifestations of the search for the true Self and ultimate fulfilment. In this respect Maharishi sees all action to be for progress and fulfilment. He likens the situation to a man trying to row a flimsy boat across a river. In mid-stream he may encounter a log and be forced, by the frailty of his craft, to turn back temporarily in order to avoid the obstacle, but he is turning back *in order that he may continue towards the other side*. Looking at his manoeuvre out of context, he would seem to be rowing the wrong way, but seen as part of the whole journey it is, under the circumstances, the only possible course of action for him. Someone in a more rugged boat might be able to sail straight ahead ploughing the obstacle aside. Likewise, apparently negative actions can be seen as the attempts of a weak man to cope as best he can with the obstacles which crop up in his journey across the river of life.

But even though the Self-realized man may act more in harmony with his surroundings, Maharishi makes it clear that one can never judge another's state of consciousness by his actions alone. The only criterion of his state of consciousness is an internal one: is Self-awareness established as a permanent reality independent of experience? All that we, as external observers, can know of a Self-realized man is on the level of his words and actions and these are no sure indication of his inner state of consciousness. In the words of the Tao-Te-Ching:[5]

> The ancient masters were subtle, mysterious, profound, responsive,
> The depth of their knowledge is unfathomable.
> Because it is unfathomable,
> All we can do is describe their appearance.

Higher States of Consciousness

11

As a man is, so he sees.

William Blake

Until now my concern with higher states of consciousness has been limited to the fifth state of consciousness, but Maharishi speaks of several higher states of consciousness beyond this. At first this might seem surprising for does not the fifth state of consciousness involve the full expansion of the mind, an awareness of all levels of mental activity from the gross level right down to the silence of the transcendental state? What more could there be?

By definition the fifth state is that state in which the transcendental state is permanently maintained along with waking, dreaming and deep sleep. There is full inner development along with ordinary daily awareness. But, although the subject of experience, the Self, has become fully known, the perception of objects in the outer world remains much as before. It is this which now begins to develop.

Earlier I suggested that the pure Self, the oneness within, also underlies the whole phenomenal creation. In the normal waking state one only sees the surface levels of life both within and

123

without. During TM one experiences the subtler underlying levels of thinking and then, transcending these, gains an awareness of the pure Self within. In the further development beyond the fifth state, one begins to experience the finer underlying levels of objects in the outside world until finally one appreciates the Absolute in everything that is perceived, both within and without.

The Sixth State of Consciousness

The first stage of this development is what Maharishi has defined as the sixth state of consciousness. He says that in this state the perception of objects has been refined to the state where one can be aware of the finest levels of relative existence but the perception has not yet been so refined as to take in the absolute value as well.

When he claims that one becomes aware of the finer levels of existence, he does not mean to imply that one actually sees molecules, electrons or anything like that. These only represent the finer levels of an object in terms of its gross physical structure, i.e. as it would appear under a microscope. Maharishi seems to be talking more of the structure of perception than the physical structure of the object, and as far as perception is concerned the finest level of creation is one of pure light.

This is not such a novel idea; similar views are often expressed by both artists and theoretical physicists. What Maharishi is saying is that in the sixth state of consciousness this knowledge becomes a living reality. The perception has developed, or as he puts it, 'been refined', to the point where one is personally aware of this finest level of creation. Everything is seen as if composed of and pervaded by pure light. He refers to this as a state of glorified cosmic consciousness.

There is abundant testimony to such an experience in the writings of poets, mystics and 'visionaries' throughout the ages. Wordsworth would appear to be describing such an experience in his *Ode: Intimations of Immortality from Recollections of Early Childhood*:

> There was a time when meadow, grove and stream,
> The earth, and every common sight,
> To me did seem
> Apparelled in celestial light.

And in 'Il Paradiso' of his *Divine Comedy* Dante wrote of:[1]

> the Eternal Light ... my sight becoming pure was entering more and more through the beam of the lofty light which is itself true ... In its depth I saw that it contained, bound by one volume, that which is scattered in leaves throughout the universe. Substances and accidents and their relations as it were bound together in such a way that what I tell of is a simple light.

Amongst the mystics we find Jacob Böhme writing that:[2]

> [this light] is the true spiritual angelic world of divine joy which stands hidden within this visible world.

And St Augustine noted that:[3]

> It was not the common light which all flesh can see, nor was it greater yet of the same kind, as if the light of day were to grow brighter and brighter and flood all space. It was not like this, but different: altogether different from all such things.

It is in Walt Whitman's words a 'light rare, untellable, lighting the very light – beyond all signs, descriptions and languages'.[4]

As with cosmic consciousness and all higher states of consciousness, it should be made clear that nothing is lost in the development of this state of consciousness. The ordinary gross levels of perception are there just as before, but *added to them* is the perception of the finer levels of creation. A chair is still a chair, but subtler values of the chair, which previously lay beyond perception, now reach awareness.

This heightened perception of the relative world comes from a more intimate appreciation of the Absolute. In the fifth state of consciousness the Absolute was known only on the subjective level of experience as the pure Self. Now, in the sixth state of consciousness, the awareness of the Absolute begins to overflow into one's perception of the objective world. The world begins to appear suffused with the light of the Self, and objects which previously were only appreciated impersonally now begin to take on personal qualities – qualities which one could, if one were so inclined, describe as Divine.

The Seventh State of Consciousness

William Blake wrote in *The Marriage of Heaven and Hell*: 'If the doors of perception were cleansed everything will appear to man as it is, infinite.' Such a state of full perception represents the next level of consciousness, what Maharishi sometimes calls the state of 'unity consciousness' or more often just 'Unity', and which mystics have termed the state of enlightenment.

In the sixth state of consciousness the doors of perception were only partially cleansed, in this seventh state the perception has become refined to the point where one becomes directly aware of the Absolute basis of the outer world. Both the subject of perception and the object of perception are appreciated in their fullest values, as manifestations of the transcendental absolute field of life. Everything, both within and without, is now appreciated in terms of the pure Self.

Meister Eckhart was clearly describing this state when he wrote that:[5]

> All that man has here externally in multiplicity is intrinsically One.
> Here all blades of grass, wood and stone, all things are One.
> This is the deepest depth, and thereby am I completely captivated.

And, according to the alleged Gospel of Thomas, Christ said: 'Cleave a piece of wood and I am there; lift up a stone and you will find me there.'[6] A statement which might easily be interpreted as a description of unity consciousness.

It is important to note that the diversity of creation is not lost in this experience of oneness. 'Here', in the state of Unity, all blades of grass, wood and stone are still perceived as blades of grass, wood and stone, but added to this surface awareness is an appreciation of their underlying unity and common essence. The phenomenal world does not dissolve into some kind of qualityless grey fog. The relative world of infinite diversity continues to exist, but is now experienced as co-existing with its absolute basis.

This co-existence of relative and Absolute reflects Maharishi's teaching that the relative world of phenomena is just as real as its absolute basis. I mentioned earlier how the idea has sometimes arisen that if the Absolute is real then the relative must be an illusion. In some systems of Indian philosophy this is known as the doctrine of *maya*. But Maharishi insists that it is not the relative world of phenomena that is an illusion – it is very real: the illusion lies in the question of a relationship between the two; in the question 'How does the Absolute become all this?' The Absolute and the relative are two different perspectives of reality and as such neither can be explained in terms of the other. The relative cannot be accounted for in terms of the Absolute, nor can the Absolute be understood in terms of the relative.

Imagine you have in your hand a cylindrical block. Looked at from the side it will appear as a square: looked at from the end it will appear as a circle. Fortunately we are able to integrate these partial two-dimensional perspectives of the object in the more comprehensive three-dimensional concept of a cylinder and we

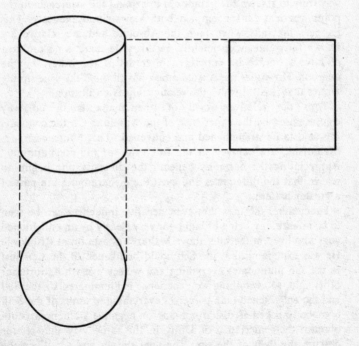

Figure 9   *Two partial and potentially conflicting perspectives of a cylinder.*

find no conflict between the two views. But if we did not have this broader perceptual framework and had to relate everything in a two-dimensional frame of reference we would be faced with an object which appeared sometimes as a square and sometimes as a circle. In this situation the only way to resolve the apparent paradox would be to try and explain one in terms of the other and if this failed declare that one or other must be an illusion. This is the sort of situation that the person in the waking state faces with respect to the Absolute and the relative. They are two different perspectives of reality, but since the awareness cannot encompass both simultaneously a paradox arises, and it cannot be resolved by simply accommodating one perspective within the other.

It is not that the relative is an illusion, as many Eastern philosophers have tried to say, nor that the Absolute is unreal, as many Western thinkers have suggested. Both are real, and the only way truly to resolve the paradox is to expand the awareness to the point where it can encompass both views simultaneously. This happens in Unity when both the Absolute and the relative are known fully and independently. In this state there is no problem of how is one to be explained in terms of the other. To the question 'How does the Absolute become all this?' the sage simply replies that it is 'Maya' – the relationship is an illusion.

Thus the relative world of phenomena is in no way compromised by the experience of the Absolute. On the contrary, it is said to be strengthened and enlivened. 'The differences,' says Maharishi, 'are enjoyed in the full value of infinite harmony.' Appreciating the harmony beneath the diversity one begins to realize that the differences and even the disharmonies are part of a greater pattern.

I remember the idea that even negative influences can be seen to be in harmony being brought out very clearly by an enlightened yogi who lived in the hills above Maharishi's ashram at Rishikesh. He was explaining that the Self could be likened to the sun: just as the sun illuminates everything and we see everything in terms of its light, so everything we experience is illuminated by the Self and the enlightened man perceives everything in terms of the Self. Somebody asked if disharmonious or negative influences could obscure the experience of Unity in the same way that clouds obscure the light of the sun. The yogi simply replied: 'Even the clouds are illuminated by the sun!'

But it is important to realize that the state of Unity is not a mere understanding that 'all is One': it is a state of consciousness in which a person experiences his essential unity with the rest of the world. A mere intellectual understanding of this fact cannot by itself give the immediate knowledge which comes from personal experience. Although many philosophers have at various times dwelt upon the idea of an underlying unity one would not guess from reading their analyses and arguments that the actual experience of the state was a most enjoyable and fulfilling one. Indeed, some have even suggested that it would be an unpleasant experience. Yet, nearly all the great mystics have made very clear that this state of union is a state of peace and fulfilment. Maharishi himself writes:[7]

Every perception, the sound of every word, the touch of every little particle and the smell of whatever may be, brings a tidal wave from the ocean of eternal bliss. Every rising thought, word or action is a rising of the tide of bliss.

In every static or dynamic state of existence the divine glory of the unmanifested is found dancing in the manifested field of life. The Absolute dances in the field of the relative. Eternity pervades every moment of transitory existence.

State of consciousness	Awareness of self		Awareness of other objects		
	Individual self	Pure Self	Relative level		Absolute level
			Gross	Subtle	
Deep sleep	—	—	—	—	—
Dreaming	?	—	?	—	—
Waking	✓	—	✓	—	—
Transcendental state	—	✓	—	—	—
Fifth state (cosmic consciousness)	✓	✓	✓	—	—
Sixth state	✓	✓	✓	✓	—
Seventh state (unity)	✓	✓	✓	✓	✓

Figure 10 *The seven states of consciousness.*

First, Know Thyself

The growth of awareness which TM brings occurs in an orderly fashion. One starts off from the ordinary, everyday waking state in which there is only a partial appreciation of the objects of experience and the subject of experience. Through regular meditation one gains contact with transcendental consciousness and through activity stabilizes this awareness, bringing about the fifth state of consciousness. On the basis of this full subjective development one then gains a full awareness of the object of experience. Thus the direction of development is from the inner to the outer. This is very important.

As the mind becomes clearer and the awareness of the Self stronger there is much less chance of a strong experience overshadowing the Self. When the fifth state is reached then, by definition, the Self is so established that no experience can overshadow it. As one continues from the fifth to the seventh state one encounters experiences which, from all descriptions, are quite remarkable but the Self being fully established ought not to be obscured by them. If on the other hand one were to deliberately encourage these experiences of refined perception without having first stabilized the Self then there is the danger that they would completely obscure any Self-awareness there might be. Such practices would certainly lead to a welter of most remarkable and sensational experiences, but because they tended to overshadow the Self it is questionable whether they would also lead to a state of full enlightenment.

Another important consequence of developing the states in this order is that the whole process is entirely natural and effortless at every step. We saw in Chapter 4 how, having taken the correct start and let go, the process of meditation takes place quite spontaneously without any control or coercion on the part of the individual. The same principle applies at every stage of development. From the fourth to the fifth state of consciousness the formula is 'meditate and act': meditate regularly and effortlessly and then carry on with the rest of one's life as normal. Then, without any restraints or artificial control of mood, one gently and spontaneously rises to cosmic consciousness. The further development from the fifth state through the sixth to the seventh state of consciousness is likewise said to be effortless and spontaneous.

In practice, the development does not occur in such well-defined stages as the above description would imply. One state can begin to develop on the basis of the partial establishment of the states which underlie it, and so one may have some experience of a higher state before the preceding states have become fully stabilized. This also implies that having reached one state of consciousness the next will already be partially developed. Thus the sixth state will appear to dawn more rapidly than the fifth and the seventh more rapidly still. Maharishi sees this phenomenon as an example of a more general principle: the principle that any development or evolution speeds up as it progresses – a theme which I shall return to in the final chapter.

Removing the Mystery from Mysticism

In many instances I have illustrated parallels between Maharishi's teachings and those of the mystics, but this does not make TM in any way mysterious. Mysticism has very little to do with mystery – indeed, the revelation experienced by the mystic could be said to remove much of the mystery from his world. It is true that mystery and mysticism both come from the same greek root *muo*, meaning to close the eyes and lips and become silent, but whereas a 'mystery' is a lack of knowledge frequently resulting from the silence of others, 'mysticism' is a fullness of knowledge brought about by personally retiring from the world into a state of inner silence. Any mystery there may be in mysticism is merely the consequence of an imperfect understanding and insufficient experience of these states.

Sidney Spencer in his excellent study of this field[8] has described mysticism as 'an immediate contact with the Transcendant'; TM clearly satisfies this criterion. Other scholars, such as William James, Walter Stace, Rudolph Otto, F. C. Happold, Marguenita Laski, Evelyn Underhill and Aldous Huxley, who have also studied the teachings and writings of mystics in some detail have tried to establish more specific characteristics of the experience. Examining their conclusions one finds half a dozen commonly recurring themes: a feeling of at-oneness with the whole of creation; a greater and more profound knowledge of the cosmos; the feeling that this knowledge is somehow more real than other knowledge; an experience of joy and fulfilment; a sense of blessedness and contact with the divine; and an alleged ineffability (an inability to describe the experience in words). These characteristics are also common to the higher states of consciousness which develop through TM, as I have tried to illustrate in this and previous chapters.

Several of these commentators have also pointed out that mystical experience would seem to underlie all religious experience. Happold writes that mysticism is 'the raw material of all religions' and William James said similarly that 'personal religious experience has its root and center in mystical states of consciousness.' Thus TM could be thought of as the core of religious practice. But this does not make TM itself a religion. Maharishi is always at great pains to point out that TM is simply a technique for bringing the body and mind to a state of quiet. No faith or belief is necessary. Indeed one could meditate quite happily (and many people do) without accepting any of the theory that Maharishi puts forward.

It could be argued that the religious traditions are all concerned with raising the individual's level of consciousness in the same way that TM is and that they must have involved similar techniques to TM. But however similar the original practices may have been they have inevitably been distorted over the ages to an unknown extent and most of what remains today is largely on the level of ritual and faith. It is very much as if a major oil shortage had forced private cars to be discarded and their real function to be forgotten. Many books on cars and driving might survive and various sects might be found ardently reading out passages of incomprehensible material to each other, studying the road maps, and ritually manipulating the controls. But, ignorant of the fact that there was an engine under the bonnet which, given the correct fuel, could make all their dreams come true, their only solace would be the hope that the spirit of Henry Ford might look kindly upon them and bless them with 'a journey'. Some, remembering that the car itself was supposed to move, might develop techniques by which to push it physically down the road, and after much strenuous effort a small journey might indeed be completed. But, without knowledge of the all-important fuel any suggestion that so heavy an object could move of its own accord would be treated with scorn if not as heresy.

The fuel of religion is the practice which, by its simplicity and effectiveness, allows the man-in-the-street to realize the goals spoken of by the teacher. When this is lost all that remains is a dry and often meaningless intellectual understanding. In the search for meaning the teachings become progressively distorted until very little of the original remains. Countless numbers are left straining at misconceptions, fruitlessly trying to understand what is already a misunderstanding, and more often than not they end up doing the opposite of what was originally intended. So, if today we find a vast array of apparently different techniques and doctrines it may not necessarily be because the original practices were very different: it may well be the result of different cultural and political forces distorting the original in different directions. As William Law remarked in the eighteenth century:[9]

> There is not one way for the Jew, another for a Christian, and a third for the Heathen; No; God is one, human nature is one, salvation is one and the Way is one.

But, as the Tao-Te-Ching had already warned:[10]

> When the Way is lost, there is goodness,
> When goodness is lost, there is kindness,
> When kindness is lost, there is justice,
> When justice is lost, there is ritual,
> Now ritual is the husk of faith and loyalty, the beginning of
>   confusion.

As far as India is concerned, Maharishi believes that techniques very similar to TM can be found described in the ancient Sanskrit verses of the Vedas. Most contemporary translations of these texts treat them on the level of mythological tales and hymns to various Indian deities. But this, he says, is the shallowest level of interpretation: the Vedas can also be understood at much deeper and far richer levels and when properly interpreted they can be seen to contain precise instructions for meditation which are remarkably similar to the technique of TM in the present day.

Traditionally the Vedas were always chanted and handed down as an oral tradition. This is because much of their value lies in the actual sounds of the words which compose them. When written down – or, worse still, when translated – the key to their knowledge is lost; the Vedas are interpreted only on the level of their surface meaning and their true significance is missed.

Ancient Sanskrit was a very compact and concise language In its written form many redundant words were omitted and the actual meaning of a given phrase depended very much on its context. If the Vedas were concerned with the realization of higher states of consciousness, then it is important that every statement be understood within this context. But if the commentator is not himself in a higher state he is lacking the most fundamental clue to their interpretation. He must base his rendering on the 'traditional' view, thus preserving and supporting the current misconceptions. A faithful commentary of these texts can only be undertaken by one who is living at the same level of consciousness as that from which the texts originated. In India such a person is called a 'rishi' meaning 'seer', and the title 'Maharishi' means 'great seer'. And Maharishi is himself working on a new commentary of the Vedas with the intention of bringing back to the world a wisdom that has been lost for many centuries.

Maharishi believes that since the time of the Vedas this knowledge has been lost and found many times. As far as India is concerned it has recurred principally in the Bhagavad Gita, the teachings of Buddha, and those of Shankara. He goes into this cycle of loss and revival in some depth in his introduction to the Bhagavad Gita and I highly recommend it for anyone interested in this topic.[11]

Whether or not the same cycles of loss and revival have taken place in the West is difficult to say – one would need both the original biblical texts and an enlightened scholar before one could undertake a similar analysis of the Judeo-Christian tradition. Nevertheless it is interesting to note that in the more esoteric Christian traditions one finds descriptions of techniques which sound intriguingly similar to TM.

But I think it would be a mistake to become too involved in what may or may not have happened in the past. What to me is important is that one has, in TM, the possibility of raising one's own state of consciousness, now. Maharishi has alluded to himself as an engineer sent to repair a road that has, with the passage of time, fallen into disrepair and disuse. In this case, what is important is not to study the holes in the old road or wonder who else may have walked down it in ages past, but to travel on down it ourselves.

Some Psychological Perspectives

12

To the psychologist the religious propensities of man must be at least as interesting as any other of the facts pertaining to his mental constitution.

William James

Psychology had its roots in philosophy and set out, as its name implies, to be the study of the mind. In its eagerness to appear as a natural science rather than a speculative study it adopted the methodology and techniques of physiology and physics. This led to the development of psychophysics (the physics of perception) and to the establishment of the powerful behaviourist approach which maintained that all that could be objectively studied was the observable behaviour of an organism. Powerful as it was, the behaviourist approach had many shortcomings, in particular it failed to take subjective experience into account.

The first major alternative to behaviourism came with Jean Martin Charcot and the study of the unconscious mind. This was taken up by his pupil Sigmund Freud and subsequently by researchers such as Carl Jung, Alfred Adler and Theodore Reik, to form the basis of the various schools of psychotherapy and psychoanalysis. This approach was certainly more concerned with mental experience – or in most cases with what was not actually experienced – but it tended to focus on those who were mentally sick or psychologically deficient in some way or another.

A steadily growing dissatisfaction with both the experimental-behaviourist approach and the psychoanalytic schools led to the emergence of many splinter groups. In the fifties and sixties these began to coalesce into a third force in psychology, known as Humanistic Psychology. This included psychologists such as Carl Rogers, Rollo May, Erich Fromm and writers such as Herbert Marcuse and Norman Brown, but the greatest single figure in the movement was Abraham Maslow.

Maslow turned away from the study of mentally sick people towards the study of the mentally healthy – the healthiest people that he could find. The people he investigated were all composed, stable, integrated members of society. They all displayed a degree of what he called 'self-actualization': 'the actualization of potential, capacities, and talents, as fulfilment of mission, as a fuller knowledge of and acceptance of the person's own intrinsic nature, as an unceasing trend towards unity, integration or synergy within the person'.[1]

Maslow's studies showed that self-actualizers had a clearer perception of reality, were more creative and spontaneous in their daily life, showed an increased acceptance of self, and were centred on problems external to themselves rather than on the task of ego-maintenance. They had a strong sense of identity with humanity as a whole and were consequently capable of deeper personal relationships without having to bother about social status. They also tended to be optimists rather than pessimists, not dwelling on the negative but seeing the positive possibilities and utilizing them to their fullest. For the self-actualizer, life was meaningful and worth while.

There are obviously many parallels between Maslow's 'self-actualizer' and someone developing towards Maharishi's fifth state of consciousness. Apart from the obvious semantic similarity between self-actualization and Self-realization, most of the characteristics of self-actualizers are also those which Maharishi claims for the Self-realized man. These similarities are borne out by psychological tests on meditators. Questionnaires have been developed to test the degree to which a person is a 'self-actualizer'. One such test (Shostram's Personal Orientation Inventory) was given to a group of university students before learning TM and then again two months later. The results were compared with those of a control group who were given the same test but did not start TM. Bearing in mind the caution with which one should approach all questionnaire studies the results are none the less interesting. Compared to the control group, the meditating subjects showed a significant movement in the direction of self-actualization – and this within only two months of TM.[2] This tendency has been confirmed by other tests,[3] and is supported by several studies which show a movement away from neuroticism,[4] depression,[5] and anxiety[6] towards a state of increased psychological health.

Of Peaks and Plateaux

One of Maslow's most interesting findings was that self-actualizers tended to have a high frequency of 'Peak-experiences'. These he described as 'moments of great awe ... pure, positive happiness, when all doubts, all fears, all inhibitions, all weaknesses were left behind', in which one felt 'one was the world, pleased with it, really belonging to it, instead of being outside looking in ... the feeling that they had really seen the ultimate truth, the essence of things. ...'[7]

The existence of such experiences was not, of course, a new discovery: mystics, poets and other 'gifted' people had often reported them. But Maslow found that their occurrence was not limited to any particular group of people; they occurred just as much among businessmen, industrialists, managers, educators and political people as among the professionally 'religious', the poets, musicians, and others who were supposed to have such experiences.

One might ask whether peak experiences are related to any of Maharishi's higher states of consciousness? Clearly a peak experience is not the same as transcendental consciousness for in a peak experience one is usually enraptured by something whereas in pure transcendental consciousness there is no object of awareness. There remains the possibility that a peak experience may be a temporary glimpse of cosmic consciousness. In a few cases the descriptions of peak experiences do sound remarkably similar, but in general the term is used to cover such a wide range of experience – almost any ecstatic experience could count as a peak experience – that it would be extremely dangerous to equate the two.

If there is any trace of higher states of consciousness in Maslow's work it is probably to be found in the 'plateau experience' with which he became very involved in the later years of his life. Plateau experiences were something like continuous peak experiences but without the suddenness or excitement of the peak experience. He describes a plateau experience as a 'witnessing, an appreciating, what one might call a serene, cognitive blissfulness'.[8] Unfortunately, Maslow died shortly after he began work on the plateau experience and it is impossible to tell from the descriptions he did give whether or not they do represent glimpses of Maharishi's fifth state of consciousness.

Even though it may not be possible to equate peak and plateau experiences with higher states of consciousness, the fact that TM leads to an increase in self-actualization would lead us to expect that the growth towards a higher state of consciousness would be accompanied by a higher frequency of these experiences.

Metapathology

Alan Watts points out in *Psychotherapy East and West* that Western therapeutic techniques tend to concentrate only on those with very dramatic or peculiar disturbances, the most unfortunate sufferers in our society, whereas the Eastern approaches to therapy are concerned with improving the lot of everyone. What we regard as normal is in fact far below man's full potential, it is in effect a state of psychological impoverishment. This impoverishment, he writes, is the origin and breeding-ground of much mental disease.

Carl Jung appears to have held similar views. He felt that all men had a fundamental need for inner development and an understanding of the meaning and significance of life. The lack of satisfaction of this need was, he believed, the root of many of man's 'neuro-psychic' disorders.

Maslow saw a similar relationship between psychological health and self-actualization. He believed that human needs were arranged in a hierarchical structure. Needs lower down the hierarchy, such as the need for food and oxygen, dominate until a sufficient level of satisfaction is reached and then the next level of need emerges. The fourth need is for group esteem which in Western societies usually appears as the need for material possessions. The fifth level of need is the need for self-actualization, for growth, health and full humanness. Maslow called this a 'metaneed' in contrast to the other more basic needs. In the same way that deprivation of any of the more basic needs leads to physical and mental illness of one kind or another so deprivation of metaneeds leads to what he calls 'metapathology', a state characterized by cynicism, nihilism, hatred, bleakness, disintegration, boredom, hopelessness, insecurity, selfishness, confusion, conflict, depression and boredom – 'a sickness of the soul'. The fact that we see the symptoms of metapathology all around us shows that our society does not yet provide a reliable or effective means of fulfilling metaneeds. One might conclude that what is needed is some form of metatherapy.

Daniel Goleman defines a metatherapy as 'a procedure that accomplishes the major goals of conventional therapy and yet has as its end-state a change far beyond the scope of therapies, therapists, and most personality theorists – an altered state of consciousness'.[9] Transcendental Meditation clearly satisfies these criteria. Goleman himself suggests that just as behaviour therapy and psychoanalysis were the tools of the second force in psychology, and encounter groups the tool of humanistic psychology, so meditation may be the main vehicle for the rapidly emerging fourth school, what is often known as Transpersonal Psychology.

Transpersonal Psychology, as its name implies, is concerned with those aspects of experience which take a person beyond individuality. Its principal studies are 'ecstasy, mystical experience, being, essence, bliss, awe, wonder, self-actualization, self-transcendence, spirit, sacralization of everyday life, oneness, cosmic awareness . . .'.[10] Although it would be a mistake to equate the transpersonal with the transcendental, transpersonal psychology at present represents the closest approach that psychology has made to the study of meditation. This can be seen from the following passage from Roberto Assagioli, one of the principal figures behind this movement:[11]

> The changing *contents* of our consciousness (the sensations, thoughts, feelings, etc.) are one thing, while the 'I', the self, the *centre* of our consciousness is another. From a certain point of view this difference can be compared to that existing between the white lighted area on a cinema screen and the various pictures which are projected upon it.
>
> But the 'man in the street' and even many well-educated

people do not take the trouble to observe themselves and to discriminate; they drift on the surface of the 'mind-stream' and identify themselves with its successive waves, with the changing contents of their consciousness.

Assagioli similarly believes that this mistaken identity results in unnecessary emotional conflicts and desires, leading to misery and suffering, and a society which is continually at loggerheads with itself. It is, he believes, one of the goals of life to be aware of the Self in whatever one is doing.

Thus far he is largely in agreement with Maharishi, but a major difference arises when it comes to the actual techniques used for developing Self-realization. In order to bring about the synthesis of the pure Self with the normal stream of consciousness Assagioli has developed a system of personal development known as 'psychosynthesis'. (He uses this term in contradistinction to psychoanalysis – although, as he himself remarks, much of Jungian analytic psychology embodied synthetic principles.) Psychosynthesis involves a large variety of practices, some of them working on the physical level (e.g. body awareness, dance and music); others working on the psychological level (e.g. self observation, dream analysis, hypnosis). Without doubt many of these techniques do have a significant effect on both physical and mental health and are of great benefit to the individual, but it is not immediately apparent that they will also lead to transcendental consciousness. This difference between Maharishi and Assagioli is reflected in the above quotation where Assagioli appears to be more concerned with *remembering* the Self, 'observing' and 'discriminating' rather than coming to a state of pure Self-awareness. There is always the danger that such practices may cultivate only an idea of the Self as a *content* of consciousness rather than the direct knowledge of it as the *centre* of consciousness.

Chemical Transformations of Consciousness

There is a feeling among some psychologists, and among many non-psychologists, that it is possible to induce mystical experiences by directly changing the brain chemistry. Surprisingly Maharishi agrees with this in principle. Since a higher state of consciousness is dependent upon a specific mode of functioning of the nervous system it should in theory be possible to bring about the necessary modifications in function by a chemical modification of the nervous system. But, he adds, none of the chemicals that we have at our disposal today produce the correct changes – indeed their effects are often in the opposite direction.

From descriptions of higher states of consciousness and drug-induced states one might assume that there was a close similarity. But not all mystical-sounding experiences are necessarily of a mystical nature. When it comes to describing inner states of consciousness our language is very limited and one may often be forced to use the same phrase to describe very different experiences. Thus a mere verbal description of two states is not always sufficient to differentiate them.

To take a specific example, LSD tends to be concentrated in the visual system of the brain. By a process of selective inhibition it increases visual activity resulting in the legendary enhancement of colour and pattern. In effect what was previously random noise in the system is now reaching consciousness. When this is very strong one may well have experiences in which white light seems to pervade all that is seen. Comparing this experience with similar descriptions of mystical states one might easily assume that one had had a mystical experience. But when both states are experienced rather than just described it immediately becomes clear how very different they are.

Similarly it is quite possible for drugs to produce states of consciousness in which the perceiver and the perceived become one. But this is a very different state of unity to that reached in the seventh state of consciousness. In the drug-induced state the union usually arises through a loss of distinction; one loses oneself in the experience. But in the true mystical experience there is no loss of distinction; the perceiver and the perceived remain clearly differentiated. Added to this normal awareness is the awareness of an underlying oneness which transcends all boundaries. Not unity at the expense of some diversity, but unity in addition to all diversity.

Furthermore the drug-induced state is usually of a transient nature. The body soon rids itself of the foreign material and returns to the normal waking state leaving only a memory of another reality, and a memory, however strong, is not the same as a change in consciousness.

On the other hand, drugs have often had the effect of opening a person's awareness to the possibility of some higher state of consciousness – even if they did not actually provide it. In this respect drugs may in some cases have served as a stepping stone, albeit a slippery and treacherous one. But having crossed the stream the stepping stone is finished with: if it is carried on it only becomes an impediment to further progress.

Many people who have been engaged in drug-taking report that after starting TM their drug usage decreases. Several surveys have already been carried out to see how far these claims can be substantiated. The largest survey to date covered 1,862 meditators, and the results indicate a general and dramatic decrease in all types of drug usage, from heroin right through to tobacco.[12]

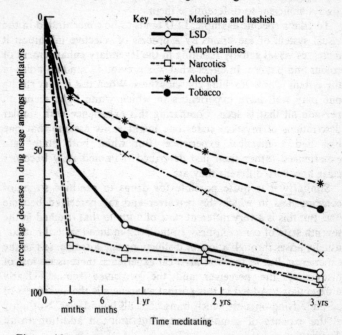

Figure 11 *Decrease in use of non-prescribed drugs in meditators (taken from Benson and Wallace's survey of 1,862 meditators).*

These general tendencies have been confirmed by the several other projects which have been conducted in this field.[13]

Most subjects confirmed that with meditation life became more enjoyable and the need for drugs decreased. One subject reported that he had 'no need for drugs any more for I have found what life is and how I want to live it'. Another that 'life after meditation finally became satisfying'. And a third that 'I didn't try to stop – after a while I just found myself not taking them any more.' Many found the drug experience to be less satisfactory, with such comments as: '[The] drug effect interfered with the good effects of meditation', drugs 'proved temporarily dulling and moody' and 'I have no desire to become disorientated or to be unclear in my thoughts.'[14]

Partly because of the negative side effects of drugs and partly because of their social and political implications the governments of most Western countries make great efforts to eliminate them. This, however, is only eradicating the symptoms of the problem. If the need is still there people will simply find other chemical means to their goals – and probably more dangerous ones at that. If the problem is to be permanently resolved and not just patched up each time that it reappears one must attend to the root of the problem.

A large number of the people now experimenting with drugs of one kind or another are doing so as part of a search for some higher state of consciousness and a more meaningful perspective of reality. The root cause of the problem is not the availability of the drug or the social conditions which promote its use but the absence of any alternative means to raise the level of consciousness. Rather than fruitlessly trying to eliminate drugs themselves governments should be turning their attention to providing more acceptable and less damaging ways of allowing people to fulfil these needs.

The Adulation of Childhood

Because both the mystic and the very young child experience a certain oneness with the world it is sometimes suggested that the mystic may be returning to a state of mental functioning similar to that of early childhood. Psychologists call such a return to an earlier level of functioning 'regression' and have tried to explain mystical experience in terms of this phenomenon. But, as with those who draw parallels between mystical experience and drug experience, the similarity between mystical states and those of regression are very superficial and tend to reflect the inadequacy of our language rather than the similarity of the states.

The mystical state is one of *differentiated union:* the world is known for all its diversity *and* for its essential unity with the Self. With the young child, on the other hand, the state tends to be one of *undifferentiated unity:* the ego has not yet attained any degree of autonomy and the child fails to recognize any distinction between his individual self and the rest of the world. The first is a state of knowledge resulting from a full experience of reality: the second a state of relative ignorance arising from a lack of experience.

It is true that many enlightened men have a certain child-like quality about them, but it is not so much a return to childhood that one is witnessing as a fuller maturity which synthesizes the innocence and openness of childhood with the experience and wisdom of adulthood. Not a circle from unity to diversity and back to unity: but a spiral from unity through diversity to an awareness of unity and diversity together. In most cases mystical experiences have led to a transformation of the individual in the direction of wholeness, health and self-actualization. And the healthier that a person becomes the more optimistic is his attitude, the less self-centred his actions and the more meaningful his life – qualities not usually found in infantile regression.

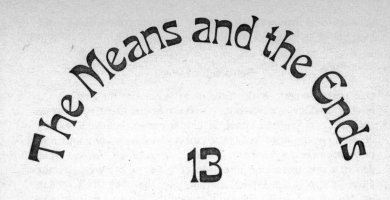

The Means and the Ends

13

> Liberation can be achieved neither by physical postures, nor by speculative philosophy, nor by religious ceremonies, nor by mere learning ... Let people quote the scriptures and sacrifice to the gods, let them perform rituals and worship the deities, but there is no liberation without the realization of one's identity with the Self.
>
> Shankara

A higher state of consciousness is in essence an inner change, but with this inner change come many changes in one's outer life. Observing this people have often sought to cultivate the ways of an enlightened man in the belief that they will thereby raise their own level of consciousness. But this is to confuse the *results* of a changed state of consciousness for its *cause*. It is putting the cart before the horse and in many cases results in a cart with no horse at all.

The way an enlightened man speaks and acts is the result of his inner development, to try and achieve the same state by copying him is rather like a poor man trying to get rich by copying the behaviour of a wealthy man. The wealthy man can buy this or that at will, but the poor man who imitates his style of living ends up further than ever from the goal. A man must first raise his level of consciousness then, *as a result*, he will spontaneously develop the qualities of an enlightened man.

Self-Remembering

One common error is the attempt to remember the Self on the level of thinking. Understanding that the Self-realized man has an awareness of the true inner Self, many have believed that by deliberately trying to 'remember themselves' as a conscious *idea* they will develop this inner awareness. Gurdjieff, for example, declared this to be one intention of his system: 'We copy the effects of consciousness,' he said, 'in order that they will stay with us.' His followers have tried to maintain the experience of the Self by thinking about it, by trying to hold on to an idea of the Self throughout daily activity. But whatever it is that is being remembered, being an idea of some kind, cannot be the true Self. Moreover, the more that one concentrates on any idea the stronger that activity becomes and the more that it overshadows the real Self.

Such practices may well produce a witnessing experience, but it is not the same as that which comes with a higher state of consciousness. In the fifth state of consciousness the Self is a witness to all activity, but the witnessing which these practices lead to is a mental activity in which one is conscious *of* something. 'I am conscious of myself looking at the flower.' 'I am witnessing myself doing this and doing that.' This is not a separation between the pure Self and all activity, physical and mental: only a separation between part of the mind and the rest of experience and activity.

Merely understanding or thinking about an experience will never by itself bring about that experience. It may be true that 'the Self is a witness to all activity', but merely maintaining this as an intellectual idea will never bring about the changes of consciousness which will allow this understanding to become a living reality.

No man ever escaped from a prison, either mental or physical, by thinking about escape or repeating to himself that he was free. It may have given some the encouragement to get down to doing something about it, but by itself it can only result in delusion: a freedom which disappears as soon as one falls asleep and stops thinking about it.

Rather than leading to an integrated and strengthened personality such conscious remembering of one's self divides the attention and weakens the mind. Half the mind is involved in looking after normal activity and sensory experience, and half the mind is involved in self-remembering. Activity suffers because it is not receiving one's full attention, while Self-awareness remains an empty idea. The poor man loses out both ways and ends up further than ever from a state of enlightened fulfilment.

One recent variation of this theme suggests that while eating a meal you should continually remind yourself of every action involved in the process. It is believed that by destroying any enjoyment there might be in eating the person will be left as a mere witness to the act of eating. It certainly does destroy all enjoyment; as the commentator himself remarked, 'By the time you are half way through the meal you've got the screaming meemies.'[1] Even if you were to survive the 'screaming meemies' the process would again leave you witnessing only on the level of thinking, not on the level of pure consciousness. In addition it would not even be an imitation of cosmic consciousness, for the Self-realized man both witnesses *and* enjoys.

Imitations of Immortality

Another common form of imitation is the attempt to copy the words and actions of an enlightened man. This may well seem even more ridiculous, but it is, nevertheless, very widespread. How many people leading a 'good life' are doing so not solely for the joy which it will bring to themselves and to others, but also with the hope that by helping others they will raise their own level of consciousness, or reap some other spiritual reward?

Now I am not suggesting that we should not be helping others, but we should not expect that by doing so we will raise our level of consciousness. Indeed to indulge in 'self-less' behaviour in order to raise one's level of consciousness will usually lead to an identification with one's own sense of goodness. Bondage to experience becomes even stronger and true Self-realization moves yet further away.

Furthermore, how are we to know whether the right action for the enlightened man in one situation will necessarily be the right action for us in our own situation? Out of its true context it may be most inappropriate and damaging, not just to us but to others and our environment as well.

At other times people have tried to copy the physiology of what they take to be an enlightened man, but with little more success and often with disastrous consequences. It may be found that people in higher states of consciousness eat only certain foods and then only in certain quantities – presumably because their physiological needs have changed. But forcing such a diet on an unprepared body will quickly lead to malnutrition. It may well produce an altered state of consciousness but it certainly is not a prerequisite to enlightenment. 'A healthy mind in a healthy body!'

Similar inversions occur with the breathing. It has often been claimed that in the state of *samadhi* (transcendental consciousness) the breath stops completely and for considerable periods of time – a claim which recent experiments appear to be substantiating. But it is pretty certain that were an ordinary man to hold his breath for ten or fifteen minutes he would reach a very different type of *samadhi*!

No enlightened man ever had to control his body, his actions, his words or his thoughts; if they changed they changed as a spontaneous result of the higher state of consciousness. We can only act as we are – it is what we are that must change.

The Four Aspects of Yoga

Although he has himself come from India, Maharishi's teaching differs significantly from contemporary teachings of Yoga. He believes that the plethora of practices which today pass under the title of 'Yoga' are descended from one common source, but as always the passage of time has caused the original teaching to become distorted and misunderstood. Consequently we now have a variety of systems which often bear little obvious relation either to each other or to their origin.

Traditionally the techniques of Yoga are divided into four principal categories: Raja Yoga (which includes Hatha Yoga) means the Royal Yoga and is concerned with various forms of meditation and techniques of purification of the nervous system; Karma Yoga is the path of action; Bhakti Yoga the path of devotion; and Jnana Yoga the path of knowledge. Each of these systems comprises a complex philosophical and metaphysical framework and a wide range of practices. It is therefore impossible to do each justice in such a brief summary. There are also many minor systems of Yoga: some are separate systems in their own right; some are subsystems of the four major systems; and some are eclectic systems which have taken selections of techniques from the other systems. But as far as we are concerned here any practice which achieves the goal of Unity Consciousness may be classed as Yoga.

Maharishi takes the view that the four major systems of Yoga were not originally different paths to enlightenment but represented different aspects of enlightenment. The fully enlightened man is one who maintains transcendental consciousness throughout his activity; he is a Raja Yogi. He no longer identifies with his actions and as a result they are more in accord with the needs of nature; a Karma Yogi. His heart expresses supreme devotion to the whole of creation; a Bhakti Yogi. And he knows as a matter of direct personal experience that the Self is, in essence, identical with the rest of creation; a Jnana Yogi. But when the natural path to Unity was lost all that remained were descriptions of the effects of Yoga. The unenlightened man once again began to copy the effects of consciousness and the four principal consequences of reaching the goal became four different paths to it.

Maharishi cites many instances of how the original yogic teachings appear to have become inverted over the ages and the effects taken for the cause. In many traditions, for example, it is now taught that inner purity is a prerequisite to enlightenment and that one must practise righteous living before even being allowed to meditate. But inner purity and righteous living are the effects of gaining enlightenment. Meditation itself purifies the individual, as a snowplough clears its own way, leaving a clear path behind it as the effect of its action. Trying to purify the system first in order that the 'way to the Self' may be clear is like walking ahead of the snowplough shovelling all the snow out of the way first in order that the snowplough may have a clear run. You may still reach the goal but it is a far more lengthy and arduous procedure, and moreover, it is tragic waste of a most powerful tool.

200 per cent of Life

In the East the ascetic approach to life has been supported by the idea that since 'all this is in truth One' the various forms which the 'all this' takes must be an illusion. The physical world has come to be ignored, or in some cases even despised, and fulfilment has been seen solely in spiritual terms – often with disastrous consequences. Conversely, the apparently successful materialist-behaviourist paradigm has led us in the West to ignore, and sometimes even despise, the possibility of an inner development, with the result that fulfilment has been seen in predominantly material terms – and with equally disastrous consequences.

Maharishi's apparently revolutionary teaching is that inner and outer fulfilment are both possible; that one can live a full spiritual life along with a full material one. It is neither necessary nor advantageous to retire from the material world in order to reap the rewards of an inner development. Nor, conversely, is it possible to fully enjoy the delights of the physical world without an equal inner enrichment. The two support each other. Inner satisfaction enhances outer progress and outer satisfaction enhances inner progress.

To live life in fulfilment, Maharishi emphasizes, is to live 200 per cent of life – 100 per cent inner life plus 100 per cent outer life; a full spiritual life along with a full material life; full appreciation of the Absolute along with full enjoyment of the relative. The fully enlightened man has a fully developed heart and a fully developed mind; love and reason, so often held to be in opposition, are now found co-existing in harmony. The balance between the two 'opposing' modes of thought having been restored thinking is not active *or* receptive but active *and* receptive; intellectual *and* intuitive; scientific *and* artistic; concrete *and* abstract; focal *and* diffuse; – a synthesis of all polarities.

This synthesis is the result of a fundamental change in consciousness. It is not the same as trying to think of opposites simultaneously: that would simply overload the left half of the brain even more heavily. If any success at all were achieved in this direction it would probably only amount to the ability to maintain a 'happy medium' between the opposing ideas. The balancing of opposites experienced by the enlightened man is not a compromise of opposites: it is a true synthesis of opposites in which both are enjoyed to the full and neither is appeased. The enlightened man does not stand midway between a material and a spiritual life: he lives both to the full as aspects of a higher reality – a *dynamic* balancing of opposites.

Roberto Assagioli illustrates this point by the use of a triangle:[2] the two base corners represent the opposing polarities, and their midpoint is the happy medium. The true synthesis is the apex of the triangle; a higher reality encompassing both of the opposites in their fullnesses. Figure 12 shows Assagioli's example of the opposites sympathy and antipathy with their compromise and synthesis.

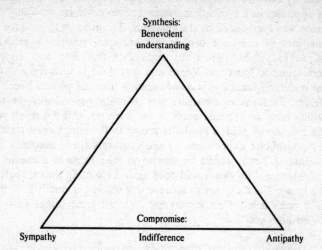

Synthesis:
Benevolent
understanding

Compromise:

Sympathy   Indifference   Antipathy

Figure 12   *Assagioli's triangle demonstrating the difference between compromise and synthesis of opposites. Similar diagrams could be drawn for most other polarities of human thought.*

Nearly all the mystics and religious teachers have made reference to this synthesis of opposites making it one of the hallmarks of mystical experience. The Middle Way of Buddhism is, according to Christmas Humphreys,[3] not 'a weak compromise but a living synthesis, a creative moving forward in which the opposites are consumed, digested and made one'. And, in The Gospel According to St Thomas, we read that:[4]

When you make the two one, and when you make the inner as the outer and the outer as the inner and the above as the below, and when you make the male and the female into a single one ... then you shall enter (the Kingdom).

This male-female symbolism of polarities is also found in Tantric Yoga. In many of the Tantric rituals the female represents the absolute aspect of creation and the male the relative aspect – the active creative principle, which is to be reunited with the passive receptive principle in a symbolic cosmic sexuality. Much of alchemy can also be seen as the attempt to realize the co-existence of opposites in a symbolic manner. In the 'chymical wedding' the union was symbolized by the amalgam. The attempt to produce an amalgam of iron and copper, for example, may seem misconceived today, but when we remember that iron and copper correspond to Mars and Venus and that these in turn represented the male and female aspects of creation then the picture becomes clearer. To form an amalgam was to unite symbolically the opposing male and female poles of the universe, and the result was the creation of gold, a symbolic return to the enlightened state.

As symbolic expressions of the synthesis these accounts are fascinating but it would be unwise to take them as a means to enlightenment for this would once again be putting the cart before the horse. The only way to achieve this union personally is to first raise one's level of consciousness, then 'all these things shall be added unto you'.

The Knower and the Known

14

A University is a place where the universality of the human spirit manifests itself.

Albert Einstein

Contemporary education is frequently criticized because the knowledge which is taught bears little obvious relationship to the students' own experience or to the situations they are likely to encounter when they leave school. This does not necessarily mean that the knowledge taught is wrong – it may be entirely correct – but it is not always entirely relevant or useful. Alvin Toffler points out in *Future Shock* that the curriculum today is more concerned with what was of use yesterday than with what will be of use tomorrow, 'a mindless holdover from the past'.[1]

In most cases our present educational system is concerned with the development of the rational aspect of the mind: the 'intuitive' aspect of the mind remains relatively undeveloped. The result is an impressive collection of facts and highly developed powers of reason but little sense of value. Without a sense of value a person has no way of judging whether or not they are applying their intellect to a good end. Reason will tell them the outcome of their actions but not whether such an outcome is right or wrong. In order to develop a sense of value it is necessary to develop the emotional and intuitive side of the person along with their rationality. This requires the development of a deeper awareness and an integration of both aspects of the mind. By largely ignoring these aspects of the individual contemporary education leaves the development of a sense of value up to the parents, or, if they fail, up to the students themselves. Most parents and students, however, have little idea of how best to achieve such a development and so we turn out people with prodigious powers of reasoning and argument but very little feeling or sense of value. A. N. Whitehead's 'merely well informed man' who 'is the most useless bore on God's earth'.[2]

So often a mere barrage of facts leads not to the development of the mind but to its death. Einstein, recalling his own education, commented: 'One had to cram all this stuff into one's mind, whether one liked it or not. This coercion had such a deterring effect that, after I had passed the final examination, I found the consideration of any scientific problems distasteful for one entire year.'[3]

It is sometimes thought that this can be remedied by making the facts more interesting and relevant. But this alone is not enough. The student's ability to appreciate a fact depends upon the level of his or her awareness. A dull mind may see some item as merely another boring fact, whereas a clear alert mind may see a greater significance in it and be able to relate it to other knowledge. This is the very first point that Aldous Huxley makes in *The Perennial Philosophy:* 'Knowledge is a function of Being. When there is a change in the Being of the knower, there is a corresponding change in the nature and the amount of knowing.'[4] But, as he points out in a later essay,[5] present education refuses to accept increased inner development as either possible or useful. It has become so concerned with filling the mind that it has no time to consider the development of awareness or the direct expansion of the mind.

In an attempt to do something practical about these failing' Maharishi has set up his own unversity, the Maharishi International University (MIU). His intention is to develop the student's awareness along with the assimilation of information. This is achieved by incorporating the study of TM as an integral part of the curriculum. The student at MIU follows similar academic courses as he would at any other university, and added to these is the study and practice of TM.

The motto of MIU is 'Knowledge is structured in consciousness'. This could almost have come straight from Huxley but in fact it comes from the Rig Veda of ancient India. The use of the word 'structure' in this context is sometimes puzzling, especially to the English for whom the word is only used as a noun. Roughly interpreted we might take the phrase to mean that consciousness is the medium in which knowledge takes a form. To know anything at all a man first has to be conscious and the degree to which he is conscious affects the depth of his knowledge. An unconscious man knows nothing; a partially conscious man (one in the waking state) has a partial knowledge of reality; a fully conscious man, a man with full awareness of his own inner nature and of the external world, has a full knowledge of reality. Thus the higher the level of consciousness the more profound the level of knowledge.

Objective and Subjective Knowledge

When we talk of knowledge or truth we are referring to those aspects of the world and of our experience which are unchanging. We know that something is true if under a wide variety of conditions we arrive at the same conclusions. Experience itself is not knowledge because experience consists only of change; all the information supplied by the senses to the brain is concerned with changes in the external world. The process of gaining knowledge is in essence the process of abstracting unchanging features from our ever-changing experience. When we see a tree, for example, the eyes only tell us of continually changing patches of brown and green (continually changing because the eye is never still). But the changes are found to possess a certain order: they have a well-defined boundary and a certain internal structure. The senses do not tell of this, our brains abstract this orderliness and on this basis we arrive at the concept of a tree.

We might say that experience is born of the interaction between the object of perception, 'the thing in itself', and the subject of perception, the transcendental Self. Now although experience itself is always changing the pure subject and the pure object remain invariable – and hence lie beyond sensory experience. The search for knowledge can therefore take either of two possible directions: one may try to discover the invariant nature of the object; or one may try to discover the invariant nature of the subject. These two approaches could be said to represent the objective and the subjective approaches.

In order for knowledge to qualify as truth it must be agreed upon by all people at all times. The objective approach tries to achieve this by eliminating as far as possible the variations introduced by the internal state of the observer. This is the principle of objectivity and is the basis of Western science. The subjective approach, on the other hand, tries to achieve consistency by establishing a state of consciousness which is the same for everyone and unperturbed by changes in the external world. This involves the development of a full awareness of the Self which is maintained throughout all experience, i.e. the development of Self-realization.

The objective and the subjective approaches to knowledge may look very different on the surface but deep down they are remarkably similar. The more that Western science delves into the finer levels of creation the more that statements of the scientist come to resemble those of mystics who have reached the same level of knowledge through a subjective investigation of reality.

On the surface, however, the objective and subjective paths remain very different and in this respect are only partially useful and fulfilling. If knowledge is to be complete then a synthesis of these two approaches is required: a synthesis in which neither approach compromises the other but both coexist together as two separate aspects of a single holistic path of knowledge. Maharishi sees this being achieved through the introduction of TM into the regular curriculum. By gaining greater Self-awareness and inner stability the student at MIU should be able to draw upon subjective experience without interference from the outside world and also be able to examine the outer world without interference from the inside – full subjective stability along with full objective reliability. This is what Maharishi refers to as 'full knowledge'. He does not mean that a man should have a detailed knowledge of every field of life – that is clearly impossible – but that he should have a full knowledge of some specialist field of inquiry along with a full knowledge of his own inner nature.

He believes that 'the natural result of sustained exposure to *full* education is the development of permanently broadened awareness and the establishment of a state of consciousness that expresses the ideals of human strength, compassion, stability, creativity, and fulfilment.'[6]

SCI and Interdisciplinary Studies

The word 'university' is derived from the Latin word *universitas* meaning wholeness or, more literally, 'turned into one'. The early medieval universities tried to achieve this holistic ideal by teaching Theology, Common Law and Mathematics together. But the explosive growth in both the complexity and range of knowledge has since made increasing degrees of specialization a necessity. Such fragmentation is, however, highly artificial. Life does not fall easily into such well-defined compartments as the specialist would like and many of the fields overlap considerably. Indeed, the more one comes to specialize in any particular field the more one begins to find oneself drawing on other widely separated specialist disciplines. The neuro-psychologist, for example, may find that he must call upon such disciplines as biochemistry, quantum physics, physiology, cybernetics and mathematics, as well as possessing the skills of a competent electronic engineer and computer programmer. It is partly as an attempt to fulfil this need for a more general education that there has recently been an expanding interest in interdisciplinary studies.

The predominant approach to interdisciplinary studies has been concerned with trying to establish common domains between the various fields of knowledge. It is easy, for example, to trace links between physics and chemistry, chemistry and physiology physiology and psychology, and on through psychology to sociology, anthropology, comparative religion; philosophy, mathematics, and back again to physics. But this only establishes the surface interrelationships between the different disciplines: not their fundamental basis.

What is common to all the different fields of study is a search for order. Every discipline seeks to discover those aspects of its field which are invariable and by so doing make another contribution to our knowledge of the Universe.

As the tree of knowledge has grown it has branched out in many different directions, and these branches have themselves divided and subdivided into ever more minute fractions of the whole. We have now become so preoccupied with the tips of the branches and the fruits which they bear that the trunk of the tree has been almost entirely obscured and forgotten. So when it comes to studying the interrelationships of the various disciplines we look at them on the level of the leaf, comparing their superficial similarities and interconnections rather than their common underlying basis. Consequently students have come to regard interdisciplinary studies as superficial, and 'general studies' as something of a light relief from the real business of in-depth study.

The approach at MIU is very different. It starts with the Science of Creative Intelligence (SCI), which Maharishi defines as 'the systematic study of the nature, origin, range, and application of creative intelligence in life'. In essence SCI is the study of TM both in theory and in practice. The actual process of meditating becomes an experiment by which theoretical hypotheses about 'the nature, origin, range and application of creative intelligence in individual life' can be tested.

Through the practice of SCI (i.e. TM) the student is gaining a direct personal experience of pure creative intelligence and hence of the basic ordering principle of Nature. He is therefore following the subjective path of knowledge right back to the trunk. But since this is the same trunk from which all the objective branches of knowledge have also sprung he gains a familiarity at a very fundamental level with all fields of study. His awareness being open to 'cosmic intelligence' he begins to feel as if 'in tune' with

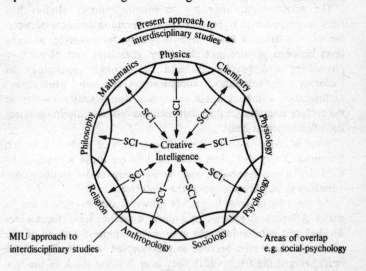

Figure 13 *A selection of different studies showing their relatedness to each other and to SCI, and the corresponding approaches to interdisciplinary studies.*

all the different disciplines, an experience which Maharishi refers to as 'being at home with all the branches of knowledge'.

Now this does not mean that a man who has never studied quantum physics, for example, will spontaneously come by a detailed knowledge of the subject: he will still have to study the subject in depth if he is to gain this sort of information. But when he does study the subject he will find himself 'at home' with it and that much better able to assimilate the detailed facts and theories involved.

In Figure 13 I have depicted a selection of interconnected disciplines as lying around the perimeter of a circle, each discipline merging into the next as, for example, physics merges into chemistry in the field of molecular structure. The present superficial approach to interdisciplinary studies tries to relate one subject to another by seeing the surface interconnections round the perimeter of the circle. If we let the centre of the circle represent the field of pure creative intelligence, the inner core of all these various disciplines, then the Science of Creative Intelligence becomes an interface between the direct experience of transcendental consciousness and the study of specific fields of knowledge. With this basis, all the various disciplines come to be perceived as aspects of a whole.

SCI and Science

In the past the study of states of consciousness has been largely confined to the East with the result that most people in the West have come to regard the whole field as 'oriental' and therefore alien to their own culture. In many cases their study has come to be regarded as positively unscientific, and, in a derogatory sense, mystical. Maharishi has progressively removed the embellishments of the Orient to show that these teachings can be expressed and understood just as satisfactorily, if not more satisfactorily, in Western terms as in Eastern ones. By deliberately referring to the study of creative intelligence as a science, he is trying to make people continually aware that inner development and the evolution of consciousness can be analysed as objectively and rationally as any other subject. Its claims are open to test through personal and public experiment and must be accepted or rejected on this basis.

It might be objected that SCI is not scientific because much of it is concerned with the changes which occur in higher states of consciousness and that only a person who was himself in a higher state could verify the hypotheses. But this criticism could equally be applied to most 'orthodox' sciences. We accept the theories of atomic physics, for example, because they have been borne out by other experts in the field. We do not ask that we all have a billion dollar cyclotron in our back garden, but put our faith in others who are recognized as authorities in the field, accepting that in principle at least we could duplicate the experiments. The results of SCI are also, in principle, duplicatable by anyone. Since the process of TM does not depend on an individual's personality, character or intellectual ability but on the structure of the normal thinking process anyone could meditate and, rising to a higher state of consciousness, test the claims of SCI. If other people in, or on the way to, higher states support Maharishi's propositions then that should be sufficient validation for the layman.

What is important is not the name so much as whether or not it works and is of value. Philosophers of science still argue about whether sociology, for example, is worthy of the title science. Yet, while they continue their deliberations, sociology continues to provide deeper insights into the functioning of individuals within society.

Nor do we need to understand the theoretical frameworks of the subject in order for it to be valuable. Most of us do not know the physical principles which underly the functioning of a simple transistor – indeed, if they were explained to us we would probably refuse to believe them for the theories of quantum physics often appear in direct contradiction to our everyday experience – yet we accept transistors, and the resultant electronic gadgetry not because we understand them but because they work. Likewise, even if some of the concepts behind SCI initially seem to be as far removed from everyday life as quantum theory is, we should still judge its merits on whether or not it works and is useful.

Maharishi International University

The study of creative intelligence is the keystone of study at MIU. At whatever level a student may enter MIU, whether it be from high school or at the Ph.D. level, he takes the same basic introductory course for one year. This starts with a one-month course on SCI, and then, with this basis, he moves on to an interdisciplinary study in which the fundamental principles of twenty or so different subjects are examined in the light of SCI. Now it is obviously impossible for the student to go into a detailed study of each field in so short a time, but the purpose of these courses is only to look at the basic principles of each subject and relate them to the basic principles of SCI – to see the different branches of knowledge not merely as branches, but as branches emanating from a common trunk. It is only after this very broad and basic framework is established that a student begins to specialize in his chosen field. And when he does come to specialize he receives as deep and as rigorous treatment of his field as he would at any other university.

By incorporating Self-knowledge into its educational system, MIU is not just adding subjective knowledge but is paving the way to a better objective knowledge as well. Students at MIU have reported that the study of different disciplines becomes much easier and more interesting and pilot studies carried out on meditating students have supported this claim by showing that there was a significant all-round improvement in academic performance.[7]

One aspect of MIU that might at first seem surprising is the almost total absence of formal vacation periods; apart from a one-month break at the end of the academic year, courses at MIU run continuously. But this is not quite as formidable as it might seem, for the curriculum at MIU includes a month of 'residential vacation' once every three months. During this period students undertake no formal studies, but instead retire to what are called 'forest academies'. These are retreats located well away from the cities and university, and during his stay there the student has a chance to gain a deeper personal experience of Transcendental Meditation. Such periods of rest are intended to accelerate the 'purification of the nervous system', and allow the student to gain sustained experience of the finer levels of thought. The net effect is an enhancement in the rate of personal evolution and the development of consciousness.

As any student knows, the assimilation of knowledge takes place in those moments of complete relaxation when one is not busy studying. By structuring these long periods of deep rest into the course, MIU also gives the student a real chance to digest and order the knowledge he has gained.

Another unique part of the MIU curriculum is the inclusion of extended periods of field-work. A postgraduate student at MIU will probably spend half his time out of the university learning to apply his specialist knowledge in the world, directly experiencing the relationship of his specialist field of study with the needs of society, and learning to apply his understanding in real life. This both crystallizes his knowledge and tests its validity in the context of life in society. Students at MIU should not therefore be complaining that their studies have little relevance to real life.

The reaction from students to the setting up of MIU has been very enthusiastic. Unperturbed by the thought of no vacation, and apparently encouraged by the promise of a 'coherent, unified, progressively illuminating, purposeful', education, 'directly supportive of personal growth' offering 'rapid release of stress, richness of experience, and depth of knowledge',[8] many students who had previously dropped out of the conventional universities are coming back and signing up again. The students, at least, would appear to appreciate that MIU is filling a gap in the present educational system.

MIU has already received official recognition in the United States and has been running regular courses there since 1973. In 1974 it moved from its provisional campus in Santa Barbara, California, to a larger permanent site at Fairfield, Iowa. At the same time research laboratories were set up in New York and Switzerland. In addition Maharishi and the faculty staff have recorded the bulk of the MIU courses on video-tape so that students can take the courses in their own countries at local TM centres. Eventually Maharishi wishes to extend the MIU courses to cover education at the secondary and primary school levels and at the adult level in order that full personal development can 'be made available to all men and women of every age-group, every interest, every background and every degree of educational involvement'.[9]

Transcending all these goals is Maharishi's intention to establish a more permanent foundation for the teaching of TM. MIU he hopes will not only spread the technique widely across the world but also leave behind such a firm understanding of the underlying principles that distortion and misunderstandings will in future find it much harder to creep in.

Part Three

Part One looked at how TM by giving deep rest to the whole organism dissolved deep-rooted stresses resulting in a healthier body and clearer, more alert mind. Part Two showed how, with this increased clarity of mind, one begins to unfold the pure Self underlying all mental activity. This formed the basis of several higher states of consciousness. In transcendental consciousness, reached during meditation when the mind is completely still, one is aware of the pure Self alone. Through the regular alternation of meditation and normal daily activity a stage is reached in which awareness of the pure Self is maintained outside of meditation as well. This is the fifth state of consciousness. Further development entails the gradual refinement of one's perception of the outside world until finally in the seventh state of consciousness one is aware of the Self not only within but in everything around one.

In looking at the value of these higher states of consciousness I have so far only considered their effects on individual experience and action. Now in this final section I want to consider the implications of higher states of consciousness for society as a whole, and their significance for the world today. If humanity is to continue to progress it is essential that man develops a deeper awareness of himself in relation to the rest of nature. Such a development is, I believe, the next major step in evolution and will form the basis of a healthy and integrated society.

This section is a more personal reflection on the role of TM in the world today, and here more than ever any errors or deficiencies must be laid at my door rather than Maharishi's.

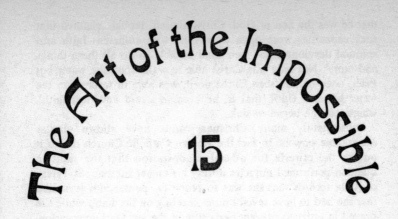

The Art of the Impossible

15

Maharishi has always maintained that once a person's awareness has become established in inner silence then 'anything becomes possible'. We in the West have tended to reduce the 'anything' to our own level of understanding of what may be possible. Thus we might be able to accept that the enlightened person is eternally fulfilled, at one with the rest of creation, and able to act in such a way that he causes suffering to no one. But the idea that the enlightened person can also walk upon water, become invisible or float through the air, appears to contradict the laws of physics and therefore is regarded as impossible.

Throughout history yogis and enlightened sages have repeatedly claimed that as a person achieves a greater clarity of consciousness such seemingly impossible powers do indeed develop. Faculties such as intuition, telepathy, clairvoyancy, knowing the future, mastery over one's own body, and even the rest of nature, are said to develop, as well as walking on water and levitation.

Examples of such apparently impossible abilities are to be found in the spiritual teachings of most cultures. Indeed, the ability to perform such feats is usually taken to be an authentication of a person's enlightenment or sainthood. Christians, for example, often cite Christ's ability to perform miracles as proof that he was the Son of God. Christ himself, though, claimed that such capacities were open to anyone with sufficient faith and spiritual development – 'you shall be able to do all these things and more'. Not only was Christ able to walk upon the water but Peter, once he had seen Christ do it, was able to walk upon the water himself. Until, that is, he became afraid and 'lost faith', whereupon he began to sink.

Subsequently many Christian saints have shown similar remarkable powers. In fact the Roman Catholic Church makes it one of the criteria for official canonization that the saint in question performed miracles during his or her lifetime. St Teresa of Avila records that she was so prone to spontaneous levitation that she had to have several nuns kneeling on her habit while she prayed in order to prevent her rising in the air. On one occasion, while talking with St John of the Cross through the convent grille, both saints became so rapt in spiritual bliss that the convent sister found them 'lifted up into the air in ecstasy; St John holding on to the chair, vainly attempting to struggle with the force which impelled him upwards, St Teresa still on her knees, and also miraculously raised above the ground'.[1]

A similar case of spontaneous levitation occurred with an Italian priest. He likewise became so enraptured during his services that he would fly up into the air, often landing high up on a gallery inside the church.

The Buddha is said to have possessed the powers not only of flying through the air whilst sitting cross-legged, but also of appearing in more than one place at a time, vanishing, and walking upon water. Again, many of the Buddha's monks were also said to have been endowed with such powers, or *siddhis*, as they are called in the East.

Buddhist texts traditionally list eight great *siddhis*:[2]

> Shrinking to the size of an atom.
> Becoming light enough to fly through the air.
> Becoming very heavy.
> Touching distant objects.
> Irresistible will.
> Mastery over one's body and mind.
> Dominion over the elements.
> Instantly fulfilling any desire.

And there were said to be eighty-four *Mahasiddhas*, that is saints and holy-men from various cultures who had successfully mastered all of the eight great *siddhis*.[3]

In ancient India such phenomena, though not frequent occurrences, were always accepted as possible. The Upanishads and Vedic Brahmanas never questioned the supernormal powers of the enlightened sage, they were accepted as natural consequences of an integrated state of consciousness. Similarly in Islam many Sufis were attributed with the ability to heal the sick, know another's feelings, appear in more than one place at a time, walk upon water, etc.

Patanjali's Yoga Sutras

The most complete description of such powers is to be found in Patanjali's *Yoga Sutras*. Patanjali lived in India some 2,000 years ago, and his *Yoga Sutras* are generally taken to be the standard treatise on Yoga philosophy. In the third chapter, entitled 'Powers', Patanjali lists some fifty-two siddhis which come with the growth of enlightenment, and describes specific techniques by which they are developed. In addition to most of those already mentioned Patanjali includes:

> Knowledge of previous births.
> Development of friendliness, compassion, etc.
> Subduing hunger and thirst.
> Intuition.
> Leaving the body at will.
> Radiating a blaze of light.
> Knowledge of the arrangement and motion of the stars.
> Strength of an elephant.
> Understanding the sounds of all creatures.

Although numerous people have read his instructions and many have tried to follow them, extremely few have succeeded in attaining such powers. There are probably two reasons for this failure: first, one has to understand his instructions correctly; and second, one has to be in a very particular state of consciousness in order for them to work at all.

The key to successful development of these powers is a technique which Patanjali called *samyama*. He defines it as the synthesis of three separate abilities: *dharana*, holding the attention still; *dhyana*, allowing the mind to flow continuously on a specific theme; and *samadhi*, being in transcendental consciousness.

The idea of synthesizing these three might at first appear to be somewhat contradictory. If the mind is in *samadhi* then there is complete mental silence with no object of attention, and no possibility, it would seem, of allowing the mind to flow on a given idea. As a result, many attempts to follow Patanjali's instructions have resulted in people trying to do all three together, and the very act of *trying* completely destroys the possibility of samadhi (see chapter 4). Many translations of the *Yoga Sutras* translate the word *samyama* as concentration; but concentration on the powers to be developed seldom, if ever, brings those powers. Thus many people who have tried to follow Patanjali's instructions have failed to achieve the desired results, and have ended up doubting that there was any validity at all in his practices.

Maharishi, through his own insight, has brought out the essence of *samyama*. The technique is extremely simple, so simple as to be almost unbelievable, yet when correctly understood it is extremely profound. Like the technique of TM itself, the simplest things often escape our notice completely, or are dismissed without consideration. Yet if we are to use the mind's own natural potential rather than try to restrain it, the correct techniques will always turn out to be simplicity itself. Rather than consciously trying to integrate the three states of *dharana, dhyana,* and *samadhi,* Maharishi shows that *samyama* is a single technique which automatically contains the essence of these three basic states. The paradox of how to integrate them is resolved, and at the same time any effort disappears. The result is that the practice works.

It works, that is, if the person is in a very specific state of consciousness. It is necessary to be at the borderline between the complete mental stillness of transcendental consciousness and the faintest impulse of a thought. In terms of the bubble diagram referred to in chapter 3, this corresponds to the junction of the bottom of the pond with the water in the pond; the junction of the active mind with the Absolute. Along with many other spiritual teachers Maharishi has frequently claimed that any desire entertained at this level of the mind is spontaneously fulfilled, and that once a person is in this state the techniques described by Patanjali work quite automatically. If one is not in this state then *samyama* itself is not possible and no amount of trying will make it possible. If there is no current then no amount of turning the light switch will light the bulb: but if the power is there a simple flick of the switch produces light.

Maharishi first introduced sidhi* techniques into the TM programme in 1976. As an experiment, he gave Patanjali's instructions to a group of TM teachers and showed them how to perform *samyama* correctly. He was interested to see whether their long experience and depth of meditation were sufficient to make the techniques work. After a three month trial period they were achieving such success that he decided to make the techniques more widely available.

Initially he made them a standard feature of all advanced courses for TM teachers, and has since extended the programme to include anyone who has been practising TM for six months or more. In most cases about 95 per cent of the participants are successful in one or more of the techniques, and many have successfully mastered several of them.

Mechanics of the TM Sidhis

One of the techniques which Patanjali describes leads to 'knowledge of subtle objects or things obstructed from view or placed at a great distance'. TM meditators practising this technique found that they were able to test its effectiveness by telling what had been hidden inside a box, or by 'seeing' the location of objects which they had lost. A business man reported that with this technique he 'knew' what had been happening in the stock market and was able to foretell correctly the market report in the paper. In another case a person could 'see' a friend in another country, and could tell where the friend was sitting, what she was wearing and the layout of the room.

Another of Patanjali's techniques leads to 'knowledge of the bodily system', and many people have reported seeing the internal layout of their organs, often being able to spot areas that were not in perfect health. One person found himself inside his own eye, able to turn around and inspect all the different structures in detail.

Other phenomena produced by the TM Sidhis have included the ability to see into the future, and into the past; subduing hunger and thirst; and increasing perceptual sensitivity. After

* Maharishi spells sidhi with one 'd' when referring specifically to TM Sidhis in order to distinquish the phenomenon from *siddhis* generally.

practising one technique specifically designed to improve hearing, it was found that the subjects' auditory acuity had risen by an average of three decibels. That is to say, the subjects could now hear sounds half as quiet again as their previous minimum level of hearing.[4]

Such apparently 'supernormal' powers are, it has been repeatedly confirmed, the natural consequences of a fully developed awareness – what Maharishi would call the 'normal' state of consciousness – and from this state such powers are 'normal'. It is only our relatively dull state of normality that prevents such experiences occurring more widely. The stress and fatigue we are continually accumulating from our environment stops the mind reaching the requisite state of stillness. And if there is no conscious connection between the normal active level of thinking and the field of transcendental consciousness which is at its base, such powers do not normally emerge. 'There is', as one recent treatise on miracles asserts, 'no order of difficulty in miracles. . . . Miracles are natural. When they do not occur, something has gone wrong.'[5]

In fact many people who have not been practising the TM Sidhi techniques may have at times had some experience of such powers. One may, for example, have suddenly had a very strong feeling about a friend or relative who was away, and known what was happening to them at the time. Or one may have had a dream which accurately foretold what was going to happen. Such experiences are not uncommon, and tend to occur when the mind is in a quiet receptive state. The TM Sidhis are simply techniques which bring out this natural potential of the mind to the full, and make such experiences a more regular occurrence.

The actual mechanics of how the techniques work is still obscure, and the connections between specific instructions and the effects they create often appears to be tenuous. Obviously, there must be much more to the interaction of ideas at a subtle level of the mind than we are currently aware of. The situation is probably rather like that of the early days of yoga. Initially little was known about the internal functioning of the body, and yet it was found that certain postures produced specific improvements in health. It was not known, however, that the postures involved were having a physical effect on certain bodily organs, which in turn were related to the ailment concerned. Thus how certain postures achieved certain beneficial results remained for a long while rather mysterious. Similarly, the effects of the TM Sidhi techniques are only magical or miraculous so long as we do not understand the underlying mental mechanics.

The Flying Sidhi

The most sensational technique and the one that has attracted the most attention is the ability to fly through the air. People practising this technique found that they would suddenly lift up 10 or 20 centimetres and maybe move forward by half a metre, or more – and they would do this while sitting in a full-lotus position, that is with each foot up upon the opposite thigh.

Although the movement appears somewhat like hopping, it is difficult to produce such hops with the legs in this position. Arthur Koestler once observed such hopping taking place in a Buddhist monastery, where the monks rose a metre in the air while sitting in the full-lotus. But he did not connect it with the development of flying techniques, he merely thought it a clever trick.

According to the Shiva Samhita, an ancient Indian text, the ability to fly through the air develops in three phases. First there come changes in breath and sensations of warmth and vibration up and down the spine. Second comes the 'hopping like a frog' experienced by many people practising the TM Sidhis. Finally there comes the ability to stay floating in the air. This stage of 'flying' is still a comparatively rare occurrence. At the time of writing very few, if any, people on current TM courses seem to be experiencing it.

If true levitation does occur – and many spiritual texts claim that it does – it would surely appear to contradict physical laws? Yet in saying that it contradicts the laws of physics we must make clear that it is only contradicting the laws of physics as we now know them. The greatest certainty in modern science is that nothing stays certain for very long. The laws of physics are being continually changed in the light of new data. Ninety-five per cent of physics known fifty years ago has been modified as a result of new experiments, and 80 per cent of the physics of twenty years ago has been likewise surpassed. Therefore to say that something must be impossible because it contradicts the laws of physics as we now know them is myopic arrogance.

If we had no knowledge of the principals of aero-dynamics we would probably feel that it was impossible for a plane to fly through the air. Indeed, only eighty years ago, before people had seen that planes could fly, many did believe it to be impossible. Similarly, how it might be possible to levitate by a simple redirection of conscious attention is not yet understood. Consciousness is almost totally beyond the scope of present-day physics, which at present has nothing to say on the direct interaction of mind and matter.

Yet slowly, the whole of science is beginning to go through a major shift in which consciousness is being taken more and more into account. The first sign of this shift came with the Uncertainty Principle and the finding that the consciousness of an observer played an important role in any physical observation and could not be divorced from it. A whole range of paranormal phenomena, many of them now well authenticated, recently hit hard at the old materialist model. The supernormal powers of the TM Sidhis, as they become increasingly widespread and verifiable, may well be the key to a broader understanding of the world, and one which synthesizes physics and consciousness.

Maharishi, in explaining how the Sidhis work, says that since the field of transcendental consciousness is the same throughout the human race, and is moreover the basis of all relative existence, any impulse of mental activity at this level can directly affect other aspects of creation besides the individual concerned. One might consider individuals as islands emerging from an ocean. Normally we see each individual island as a separate entity and forget that at the level of the seabed everything is one. What Maharishi is suggesting is that the Sidhi techniques are working from the level of the seabed, and thereby affecting all aspects of creation, rather than working at the level of the island. This fundamental level he calls the field of all possibilities. Its essence is simplicity. The state of consciousness required is one of *simple* awareness – a natural state of simple alertness. And it is this simplicity which is the key to directly influencing the rest of creation.

The EEG and the Sidhis

Physiologists at MERU (Maharishi European Research University) have been looking at a number of changes in people practising the TM Sidhi techniques. The most interesting findings have been those in brainwave activity (EEG). In chapter 5 it was mentioned that deep in meditation the left and right sides of the brain begin to show synchronized activity, what has been termed

'EEG Coherence'. Research on people practising the TM Sidhis shows that this coherent phenomenon increases, and covers not only the alpha range but also spreads down into the lower theta range and up into the beta range. The coherence is strongest during the flying technique when it has been found to extend throughout the spectrum of brain activity, from zero right through to 25Hz and higher.[6] (These measurements were during the hopping stage, the floating stage is not yet common enough to allow consistent EEG measurements to be taken in the laboratory.)

This increased coherence correlates with Maharishi's claim that operation of the Sidhis is based upon a more perfect co-ordination of mind and body, and that this co-ordination has its roots in a more integrated brain function. The brain is the interface between the mind and the body, and the more perfect the function of the brain the more faithfully can the body respond to the desires of the mind. The TM Sidhis show just what is possible when the brain is functioning perfectly, and this perfect functioning is borne out in the high coherence level of the EEG activity.

It has also been found that different Sidhis produce different EEG signatures, that is different patterns of coherence. The coherence may start in different areas of the brain according to the precise technique being practised. Maharishi has always insisted that the value of the Sidhi techniques is not in the effects themselves, though of course these may be useful, but in developing subtle aspects of the mind not normally brought into use. Each Sidhi exercises a different aspect of the mind and this is brought out by the fact that the EEG signature is different in each case.

The value of practising the Sidhis may be compared to that of physical exercise. A person who goes into the gymnasium every day and exercises on a trampoline, wooden horse, parallel bars, the weights, etc., finds that over a period of time he is developing all of his muscles and maintaining a state of physical fitness in which he can respond better, faster and more flexibly. Similarly, a person practising the Sidhis is regularly exercising different areas of the mental apparatus, maintaining the mind in a much healthier condition so that in daily life he can draw more fully upon his mental resources.

This is the real value of these techniques.

The supernormal powers resulting from the TM Sidhi techniques should really be seen as a side effect rather than the goal. Transcendental Meditation itself produces some rather interesting side effects, such as the fact that the breathing may often slow down or stop completely. But people do not practise TM *in order to* reduce their breathing dramatically; it is practised for the benefits which follow in daily activity. In the same way the TM Sidhis are not practised for their supernormal powers but for the general development of consciousness and mental flexibility.

Ethics

One question which is often raised is that of ethics, could the powers being developed by these techniques be used for negative or destructive ends?

The traditional view is that this is very unlikely. First, any action performed at this level has immediate effects on the doer. Anyone who tried to misuse such powers would very rapidly find himself reaping his due reward.

Second, and more important, it is very unlikely that a person who was able to master the techniques would be capable of wanting to use them in negative ways. The state of consciousness necessary for successful practice of the Sidhis is one in which the awareness is in tune with the rest of creation, and as we saw in chapter 10, any actions which come from this level must be supportive to the world as a whole. To perform actions which were disruptive to the balance of nature would require that the person involved was no longer in contact with this unifying level of awareness. If he was not in contact with this level of awareness, *samyama* would no longer be possible.

Nearly all the people I have met who practise the TM Sidhis radiate a strong feeling of warmth, love and softness. With this love in their hearts it becomes difficult to harm another person or being. And, perhaps the most significant effect, this love is contagious. Just being around some of these people is enough to make one's own heart swell with warmth and love. And a general expansion of the heart is one thing which the world today surely needs.

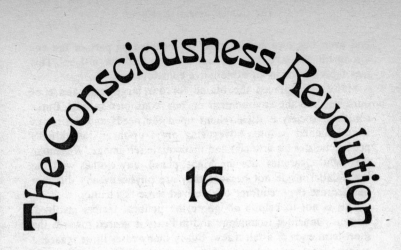

The Consciousness Revolution

16

Love the world as yourself
Then you can truly care for all things

Tao-Te-Ching

Humanity is now facing one of the most crucial periods in its history. This no longer needs to be spelt out: any impartial survey of the situation shows that the problems of over-population, resource depletion and pollution are all very real and rapidly getting worse. But this is not going to be another apocalyptic look at the day of doom, nor a hearty reassurance that science and technology alone will see us through – they won't. If we are to avert the coming disaster some very fundamental changes will be necessary: changes in the way that we relate to ourselves, our bodies and our environment: changes in the demands we make of others and of our planet: changes in our awareness, in our thinking and in our appreciation of the world. In short, changes in ourselves.

We still interact with the world on an 'I versus It' basis: 'me-in-here' versus the 'world-out-there'. This distinction stems from the continual need of the unenlightened person to reaffirm his sense of personal identity. The reaffirmation occurs at the expense of the environment – the not-I – and in this respect other people

175

and even our own bodies must be included as part of the environment. We take from the 'out-there' to feed the 'in-here'. This inevitably results in an exploitative consciousness.

Many have placed the blame for our large-scale abuse of ourselves and the environment on our 'consumer society'. But a consumer society is itself reliant upon the needs and desires of unenlightened people. Advertising preys upon an individual's need to bolster his artificial and inadequate self-image. We smoke the 'right' cigarettes, use the 'right' petrol, buy clothes with the 'right' label inside not because they are physically any different but because they reinforce our derived sense of identity.

This is not to belittle or ignore the political factors involved. Certainly much of technology and industry is geared towards the short-term ends of a select few. But in many cases those regarded as exploiters are only trying to maintain their own sense of identity. Furthermore they are only able to do this at the expense of others because the others too need to reaffirm their sense of identity – you cannot sell someone a car he does not need physically unless he needs it psychologically.

So the cycle continues. Irreplaceable resources are moulded into objects of temporary support for the ego and then, once their psychological value is spent, thrown away as scrap. Acting in the most short-sighted manner we persist in upsetting the delicate and intricate ecological systems on which we are so dependent. If we were to do this to our own bodies we would surely be certified as insane, but when we do it to our environment it is excused in the name of progress.

The root cause is the fact that we do not really appreciate our essential oneness with the rest of the world. We may know it intellectually, but we do not know it as an immediate awareness, as a personal reality. Our immediate awareness is still one of isolated individual selves, what Alan Watts referred to as 'skin-encapsulated egos'.

On one level this distinction is very real and very necessary, but it is not the whole truth. It is a biologically useful model which develops in early childhood and allows the organism to interact with its immediate environment as an autonomous unit. The model itself is not at fault: the fault lies in having to depend totally upon this dualistic awareness. If as a species we are to advance further it is now imperative that we gain an awareness of our essential oneness with creation to balance this sense of separateness. This awareness must come not merely as a change of idea but as a change of consciousness.

A Paradigm Shift

Thomas Kuhn used the word 'paradigm' to denote the basic theoretical model which underlies the main body of a science, and which serves as a framework for understanding new observations.[1] An example of a paradigm in the field of physics is Newtonian Mechanics. Until the end of the nineteenth century it was possible to explain nearly all that was known about the physical interaction of objects in terms of the principles laid down by Newton in the seventeenth century. But there were a few phenomena which could not be satisfactorily explained by Newton's model. By the beginning of the twentieth century the number had grown to the point where it was no longer possible to accept Newtonian Mechanics as the whole truth and a new paradigm was needed. The new model which emerged was formulated in the Theory of Relativity and this shift has been referred to as the Einsteinian Revolution in physics. Examples of other major paradigm changes in science are the Darwinian Revolution in biology, the Freudian Revolution in psychology, and the Copernican Revolution in astronomy.

It is now becoming increasingly apparent that a paradigm shift is needed in the fields of industry, technology, economics and education. The current model which measures its successes in terms of immediate material returns has become most inappropriate in the present global situation.

Willis Harman and a team of researchers at the Stanford Research Institute made a major study of the possible 'future histories' of mankind and concluded that there were only two alternatives which did not end in collective disaster. The first of these was what was referred to as 'friendly fascism' – 'a managed society which rules by a faceless and widely dispersed complex of warfare-welfare-industrial-communications-police bureaucracies with a technocratic ideology'. This more or less amounts to continuing along present lines into an Orwellian 1984 where stability can only be maintained by force. The second alternative was envisioned as an 'evolutionary transformation'. This, the report summarizes, would (1) entail an ecological ethic; (2) place the highest value on self-development; (3) be multivalued, multi-faceted and integrative; (4) involve the balancing and co-ordination of satisfactions rather than trying to satisfy just one narrowly defined field (e.g. economic); (5) convey a holistic sense of perspective or understanding of life; and (6) be experimental, open-minded and evolutionary.[2] This amounts to a major paradigm shift in our whole approach to life. The report concluded that such a shift was the only feasible path for humanity.

But however much we may argue for a shift to a new paradigm it is very unlikely to come about while the individuals concerned are themselves still bound to the old 'I versus It' model. We will not be able to build a non-exploitative, holistic, ecological ethic into our policies unless it is also built into our awareness – built in not just in the sense of being understood but as an immediate awareness. We need to know it organically, at the heart of our being, rather than just cerebrally as part of our reasoning. As well as restructuring our model of the world we must restructure the basic model which governs our thinking and experience of the world.

Identity as a Metaparadigm

The models which underlie thinking and experience are paradigms in much the same way as the models which underlie a particular science are. They determine how sensory perception is to be interpreted, which experiences to accept and which to reject as illusion, and in which direction thinking should be channelled.

Different types of mental experience will involve different models. (To make sense of a simple drawing of a cube, for example, requires the tacit assumption that the lines represent a three-dimensional object.) But underlying all experiences there is one fundamental frame of reference which conditions all experience. This is our sense of identity.

The way in which we appreciate ourselves affects not only our experience but also our thinking and the way we act. It is the dominant psychological model which underlies and conditions all mental activity. In this respect it is a mental paradigm. But it is unlike an ordinary paradigm in that it underlies all thinking and not just thinking in one particular field. Moreover it even underlies the generation of paradigms themselves. Since it is something beyond an ordinary paradigm I shall call our sense of identity a *metaparadigm*.

The current metaparadigm is one of an individual self distinct from the rest of the environment. This egocentric model has been very useful both for biological survival, and on a wider scale, for evolutionary progress. Until recently there has been little reason to question it – indeed most Western cultures have strongly supported it. But now that rapidly approaching global crises have forced us to examine the consequences of this model in much greater depth, its fundamental flaws and paradoxical conclusions are becoming increasingly apparent. In this situation a paradigm shift (or rather a metaparadigm shift) is needed. We need to restructure our thinking so as to include our essential unity with the whole of nature as a fundamental element. We need to know not just as an understanding but as an immediate awareness that all aspects of the environment are as much a part of oneself as the body is. It will then become as difficult indiscriminately to cut down a forest or otherwise upset the overall balance of the biosystem as it would be to chop off one's own finger.

Gregory Bateson, the anthropologist, psychiatrist and ecologist, has come to very similar conclusions:[3]

> If this ['I versus It' model] is your estimate of your relationship to nature *and you have an advanced technology*, your likelihood of survival with be that of a snowball in hell. You will die either of the toxic by-products of your own hate, or, simply, of over-population and over-grazing. . . .
>
> If I am right, the whole of our thinking about what we are and what other people are has got to be restructured . . . The most important task today is to learn to think in a new way. Let me say that *I* don't know how to think that way. Intellectually I can stand here and I can give you a reasoned exposition of this matter; but if I am cutting down a tree, I still think 'Gregory Bateson' is cutting down the tree. I am cutting down the tree.

But although he comes to the same conclusion as to the type of change necessary, Bateson seems to make the error of expecting an identity between the individual and the outside world. But this experience, although possible, is not the same as the experience of union to which I have been referring. In the state of unity consciousness all sense of separation with the outside world is retained. Added to this, is an awareness of the underlying harmony of all creation. The union is not on the level of thought as a unity between an individual self and the rest of creation, but on the level of the Self which underlies both. There is no loss of diversity in enlightenment. So even when Bateson does reach this level of consciousness he will still find that '*I* am cutting down the tree', and added to this there will be the awareness that in essence I and the tree are one. His difficulty is brought out clearly when he says '*I* don't know how to think that way'. He is looking for a unity on the level of thought rather than on the level of Being.

Let me repeat, the structuring of a holistic and ecological consciousness within ourselves does not begin on the level of understanding, nor on the level of the individual ego. It must come from the very centre of our being.

A Shift in Metaparadigm

If the change cannot be brought about by merely thinking about it and if the old model is firmly entrenched from childhood onwards, there may seem to be little chance of ever developing an alternative. Some insight into how such a change might occur comes from looking at how ordinary paradigm shifts occur.

Paradigms are built up as the result of experience and retain their status through their continued ability to explain new facts and solve problems within their given field. When the model fails badly a paradigm shift begins and the new paradigm gains status through its ability to account for the observations which could not be accommodated by the old.

The same is true with the metaparadigm. The egocentric, 'I versus It' model is built up during the first two years of life as the child begins to break away from the mother and starts functioning as an autonomous unit. The child begins to experience a duality between itself and the rest of the environment, and builds up a model of the world on this basis. Now the one experience which most shakes this model is the personal experience of a unity with the rest of creation. This cannot be incorporated within the 'I versus It' model and starts a shift towards a new metaparadigm.

It is precisely this experience of unity that TM brings about. Comparing the situation with that of a paradigm shift in science we could say that the experiment which brings about the new observation is the process of meditation; the observation which does not fit in with the old model is the experience of oneness found in transcendental consciousness; and the new model which begins to develop, in this case the new metaparadigm, is a higher state of consciousness.

Now the change is by no means immediate. One of the central points of Kuhn's thesis is that paradigm shifts do not happen overnight. Scientists seldom give up their old views of the world without considerable resistance. Throughout scientific history the older generation of scientists have clung rigidly to their models of the world in spite of all the evidence accumulating for the new one. Rather than reject the old paradigm they have frequently preferred to reject the new evidence. A similar phenomenon will undoubtedly occur with a shift in metaparadigm. It is one thing to have experienced one's essential unity with the rest of nature: it is quite another to restructure one's thinking accordingly. People do not easily let go of their presuppositions: their minds adhere to the familiar modes of experience which have served them so well for so long. The change will be gradual and will require the constant repetition of the experience of oneness if this is to coexist along with the equally real experience of diversity. Hence the need for regular daily meditation.

Revolution or Evolution

I am not trying to suggest that a general raising of the level of consciousness will by itself cure all our problems. Nor for that matter is Maharishi. All that is being suggested is the general principle that if a large proportion of the population are living in a higher state of consciousness we should be in a better position to find more realistic, co-operative, long-sighted and less selfish answers to the problems now facing mankind. As Maharishi comments:[4]

Although there are certainly many things in the world to be put right, we shall not be able to accomplish this humane ideal by merely reshuffling the environment. It will never humanly succeed until we can see and appreciate that environment at its full value, until we can envision all its possibilities with expanded mind and heart so that they may be actualized to the advantage of everyone and everything in nature.

Some Marxists may doubt whether it is possible for such an

approach to bring about a true change in society. 'Social being determines consciousness' is the cry and only by first producing a profound social and political change will the situation be resolved (whether Marx himself took this line is another question). On the other hand, Freud argues that it is the individual's need to repress his lower instincts which is the principal cause of a repressive social structure, i.e. that individual being determines society.[5] The two might seem to be in opposition, but probably they are both right to some extent: the way we are being partly determined by the structure of society and the structure of society being partly determined by the way we are. It's a chicken and egg situation, and you don't break the cycle by getting rid of the chicken because the egg will still hatch, nor by cracking the egg because the chicken will only lay another. Both aspects of the problem have to be treated simultaneously.

The sense in which I have been talking of changing consciousness is different from both the Marxist and the Freudian models. By 'consciousness' or 'self' they are referring to aspects of individual consciousness – and as far as the interaction of the individual self with society is concerned their conclusions may well be correct – but this individual self is not the same as the pure Self, or pure consciousness. The pure Self, by definition, is unconditioned and attributeless. It can neither be changed by the external environment nor does it have any attributes which might condition the external world. In a sense it lies beyond both. But, one effect of gaining an awareness of this pure Self is that perception and thinking both become clearer, and the person with an expanded awareness is in a better position to deal with both the chicken and the egg. John White puts it very succinctly in the Introduction to his book *The Highest State of Consciousness:*[6]

It is only through a change in consciousness that the world will be 'saved'. Everyone must begin with himself. Political action, social work, this *ism*, that *ology*, are all incomplete, futile actions unless accompanied by a new and elevated mode of awareness. The ultimate action, then, is no action at all except to change consciousness. In other words, *the true revolution is revelation*. When that has occurred on a global scale, the old problems and prejudices and inhumanities will vanish, and revolution will become evolution – but not until then.

Towards a High Synergy Society

The term synergy was coined by Ruth Benedict, the American anthropologist, in 1941.[7] She was studying aggression in various tribal communities and found that societies in which aggression was low or absent had a social structure such that actions which advantaged the individual also advantaged the group as a whole. She called such social orders high synergy societies. Conversely, a low synergy society is one in which an individual while acting for his own good is likely to be acting to the detriment of the group. Such societies tended to be very aggressive.

Since Benedict the term 'synergy' has been extended to many other systems beside societies. The healthy body is a fine example of a high synergy system, the functioning of each cell serving both the needs of the cell and the needs of the body as a whole.

Now the essential point about a high synergy system is that there is no difference between acting for oneself and acting for the good of the whole. Each component of the system may seem to act totally for itself. A muscle cell in your leg, for example, is not concerned at all with the welfare of a cell in the retina of the eye, nor with the welfare of the body as a whole: it has a job to do and gets on with it. But because the healthy organism is a high synergy system the cell is also acting for the good of the whole, which is itself for the good of the cell. Similarly in high synergy societies, the individual is acting for the good of the group not because he is unselfish and puts social obligations before personal desires, but because the good of the individual *is* the good of the group.

Biologically speaking the characteristics of a high synergy system are essentially the characteristics of a healthy organism. This has led several people to consider human societies in terms of organisms. If the parallel holds then it readily becomes apparent that our present social organism is not in a very healthy state. As far as the planet as a whole is concerned many human societies are like giant cancerous growths. Indeed, as Konrad Lorenz points out, there is an astonishing similarity between a picture of a malignant tumour and an aerial photograph of a modern suburb eating its way into the surrounding countryside.[8]

Cancer is a low synergy phenomena in that individual cells are no longer acting for the good of the body. A malignant cell is one in which the genetic processes are disturbed. The genes control the functioning of each cell and since the same genes are found in every cell of the body they tie the individual cell back to the system as a whole. Without this order the malignant cell no longer performs its proper role in the community but goes off on its own ruthlessly multiplying at the expense of the rest of the organism.

We, as cells of the biosystem, have similarly lost the knowledge of our relationship to the system as a whole. In this case the knowledge resides not in the genes but in the mind. That which is common to all people and which transcends individuality is the experience of oneness, the pure Self. Without this awareness we see ourselves only as isolated 'cells' and go off on our own with almost total disregard for the system as a whole.

In such a low synergy system the individual actions appear to be entirely selfish. But it is not the selfishness which is at fault, the fault lies in our only appreciating ourselves as 'skin-encapsulated egos'. The solution therefore is not to try and subdue our very natural self interest but to expand our awareness of the self. The enlightened man still acts for the good of himself but since he now appreciates himself and everything else in terms of the Universal Self he has gained the awareness which ties him back to the whole and his actions are spontaneously for the good of himself *and* for the good of the whole. This is the beginning of true altruism and an altruism that is not opposed to selfishness. Selfishness and selflessness have become the same. This is the natural and only genuine basis for a high synergy society: a collection of individuals working together not because they are 'do-gooders' but because they are spontaneously in tune with the whole.

Pierre Teilhard de Chardin put forward very similar ideas. He saw two complementary trends in evolution: a tendency towards 'extreme individuation' and a simultaneous tendency towards 'extensive interrelation and co-operation'.[9] In his scheme, evolution is a 'convergence' towards the development of a 'super-consciousness ... a harmonized collectivity of consciousness', in which both trends will reach their full expression: 'the plurality of individual reflections grouping themselves together and reinforcing one another in the act of a single unanimous reflection'.[10] This he sees being brought about by a *megasynthesis* – 'a super-arrangement in which all the thinking elements of the earth find themselves today individually and collectively subject'.[11] But this synthesis will not, he emphasizes, be achieved by any superficial link-ups but by a synthesis of centres: 'it is centre to centre that they must make contact and not otherwise'.[12]

If by centre he means the centre of consciousness, the pure Self, then this is exactly what Maharishi is saying. We must not try to gain a superficial understanding of our mutual interdependence but a direct personal awareness of our common cores 'so that our individual purposes flow in harmony with all other purposes'.[13]

It is sometimes feared that a society of enlightened men would be a society of sheep. But this is not so. Living for the good of the whole involves no forsaking of individual autonomy and integrity, for, as we have already seen, the experience of unity in no way compromises the experience of diversity: each strengthens the other and both are lived to the full. An 'enlightened' society would be a society of diverse but integrated individuals; a true 'body of people'.

The Force of Evolution

Evolution is a rapidly accelerating process. Each new step occurs in only a fraction of the time that it took for the previous step.

Cosmologists currently put the age of the Universe at around 40,000,000,000 years. This is an incomprehensible stretch of time so in order to get some grasp of it let us imagine it to be contracted into the more familiar period of one year. During the first ten and a half months of that year the earth itself did not exist (it only came into existence some 4,500,000,000 years ago). The first signs of life were single-celled algae and bacteria and these probably appeared about one month ago. About two weeks ago these simple cells began organizing themselves into more complex multi-cellular organisms, but creatures did not start crawling out of the sea until three or four days ago. This was already very late in the history of the planet. Dinosaurs roamed the planet for most of yesterday and during this time the first mammals began to appear. Human beings have been on the scene for about fifteen minutes. Most of this time they have spent as hunters, only beginning to farm the land a few minutes ago. The first civilization did not appear until the last five seconds of the year and our present industrialized-technological society is less than a quarter of a second old. We have only to look at the tremendous advances that have been made in our own lifetimes – a mere few hundredths of a second in that entire year – to see that this rapid acceleration in development shows no signs of abating. What then do the next few thousandths of a second hold in store for us? To see let us go back and look at the pattern behind this evolutionary explosion.

Each major step in evolution has been one of progressive organization and increased complexity. Hydrogen atoms condensed from interstellar space to form the more complex atoms of which our planet is composed. Later, in the 'primordial soup', different atoms became organized into more complex organic molecules, these molecules grouped together to form living cells, and more complex organisms evolved as the individual cells grouped themselves together in more organized systems. Indeed, to be an organism means to have become organized, and the tendency towards increased organization appears to be not only the force behind evolution but the principle of life itself.

If this tendency is to continue it would be tempting to suggest that the next major step in evolution would be a grouping together of individual organisms into well-integrated social units. The trend over the last few thousand years has certainly been in this direction. Over the last two centuries it has been accentuated by the mutual interdependence forced upon us by large-scale industrialization, and more recently technological developments have led to a massive increase in communication between both individuals and groups. Whether this trend results in a state of 'friendly fascism' where the whole world is controlled by a few multi-national industrial corporations, or whether it culminates in a true high synergy society, is up to us. For the first alternative we need do nothing. For the second each individual needs personally to raise his level of awareness and become an active (and conscious) participant in the evolutionary process.

It is impossible to separate the personal development of consciousness from the progressive organization which underlies physical evolution. The two are complementary perspectives of the same process. Consciousness in the mental world is the complement of organization in the physical world. Thus the development of a higher state of consciousness is a manifestation of the 'force of evolution' on the mental level.

This complementary relationship of organization and consciousness might lead one to suggest that some higher degree of organization within social groups would lead to the emergence of a corresponding higher order of consciousness – a social consciousness or group mind. Since this would be the natural counterpart of a high synergy system it would be a social consciousness which was in perfect accord with the consciousness of the individual.

Sociologists tend to reject such theories on the grounds that most of the knowledge collected within the social sciences shows no evidence of any such 'group mind'. But this is only to be expected. Although the number of people in the world is the same order of magnitude as the number of neurons in the brain (3.6 thousand million people compared to about ten thousand million neurons) the degree of organization and interaction between human beings is nothing compared to the incredibly complex and sophisticated network of communications between neurons in the brain. Thus if some group or social mind is in the process of developing it is probably comparable to the consciousness of an earthworm at present and we would hardly expect to be able to detect it. Nevertheless, it may well be that Jung's collective unconscious is the individual manifestation of some rudimentary form of group mind.

Judging from the rate at which evolution has been consistently speeding up, this next step, if it occurs, will come in the next decade or two. This would be what Teilhard de Chardin referred to as the *Omega Point:* the point where 'the Universal and the Personal ... culminate in each other'.[14]

But it would be wrong to think of this omega point as any end point to evolution or human progress. It would represent the addition of another dimension to evolution. And new dimensions, by the very virtue of being dimensions, cannot be expressed in terms of the previous frame of reference. So from our present position it is probably impossible for us to conceive what this new level of evolution would be like. Perhaps this is why Maharishi always talks of it in terms of infinites.

A Sociological Phase Transition

This may all sound highly optimistic; looking at the rapidly approaching global crises there would seem to be very little chance of humanity surviving long enough to reach this transition point. Certainly the threat is very great and the vast majority of people still support the egocentric-exploitative models which are leading straight to their own destruction. Yet with many other transitions in nature there is often no inkling of the coming change until the transition begins. Take the case of boiling water, for example. As the water begins to heat up a few but increasing number of molecules escape to form water vapour. As the water is heated up further the number of molecules escaping gradually increases until, at the boiling point, there is a sudden change in which the molecules boil off very rapidly and restructure themselves as a gas. There is said to have been a phase transition from water to steam. It is possible that as more and more individuals move into higher states of consciousness society will reach a point at which it undergoes a similar phase transition – a 'sociological phase transition'. But if so there would be little overall sign of the coming change until it actually occurred. The old trends would dominate right up to the transition point just as water remains water from 1°C right up to 99°C.

Maharishi sees this phase transition in terms of a spread of orderliness and coherence throughout society, and it will come, he says, as the result of a spread of growth and orderliness within the individual. Drawing a parallel with coherent phenomena in physics, Dr Lawrence Domash, a professor of physics at MIU, has pointed out that only a small proportion of the elements of a system need to display coherence for the effect to be felt throughout the whole.[15] Whereas random fluctuations largely tend to cancel each other out, coherent activities tend to add up and soon become noticeable. Calculations from physical phenomena such as coherent light generation (i.e. lasers) show that if the number of elements in a system is 'n' then the number of elements that need to be functioning coherently for the effect to begin to become noticeable is of the order of the square root of 'n'. (I have already looked at how this accounts for the emergence of individual consciousness from a brain in Chapter 3.) Domash applies this to a society containing meditating, though not necessarily enlightened, individuals on the assumption that during meditation the increased coherence of brain wave activity is having a similar ordering effect on other individuals (and there is now growing evidence that this is occurring). He allows for the fact that people are only meditating for a small fraction of the day by multiplying by a factor of 50 – presumably if the individuals in question were enlightened this would be unnecessary – and comes up with a figure of $50/\sqrt{n}$ for the fraction of the population that need to be practising TM for the social effect to be noticeable. For a country the size of the United States this fraction is about $\frac{1}{4}$ per cent, and for England it is about 1 per cent. These figures, it is argued, represent the threshold for a 'sociological phase transition'.

Recent studies suggest that this idea is not quite so far-fetched as it might at first appear. There are now quite a few cities in the United States in which the number of people practising TM has exceeded this theoretical threshold. Looking at the official crime rate statistics for these cities it has been found that there was a decrease of 8.8 per cent, and this at a time when for the nation as a whole the crime rate in cities was increasing at six per cent per year. There was also found to be a significant correlation between the proportion of people meditating in each city and the specific decrease in crime rate in that city.[16] Any study of this kind must of course be viewed with caution. There are inevitably many uncontrolled variables which make it difficult to prove any cause-effect relationship. Nevertheless the results were remarkably consistent over many cities, and, if further research bears them out, they offer some support for Maharishi's claim that if only a small percentage of the world practised TM the course of history would be changed.

Alpha or Omega?

Kenneth Boulding, the economist and futurist, writes that 'the twentieth century marks the middle period of a great transition in the state of the human race. It may properly be called the second great transition in the history of mankind.'[17] And John R. Platt comments that 'the act of saving ourselves, if it succeeds, will make us participants in the most incredible event in evolution.'[18] But whether we rise to the challenge and move on, through the omega point, to a new era of evolution, or whether civilization as we now know it extinguishes itself as some evolutionary blind alley is up to us.

If the challenge is met we will pass through a major cultural revolution – a Revolution of Consciousness. And a revolution to which the Industrial Revolution, the Russian Revolution and the Einsteinian Revolution were only prologues.

In the true sense of the word revolution the Self will return to take its rightful place at the centre of consciousness just as in the Copernican Revolution the sun resumed its rightful place at the centre of the solar system. But the Copernican Revolution did not come about by destroying the falsely placed earth or holding the sun still, and the Revolution of Consciousness will not come about by destroying the falsely placed ego or holding on to an idea of the Self: it will only come as a result of personal experience. Thinking about it, writing about it, talking about it will not by themselves produce the necessary changes in consciousness. In this respect the present book, or any other book for that matter, can be of little help. It is only more words about that which is essentially beyond words.

The evolution of consciousness must move out of the speculative, philosophical realm and into the empirical. And when I say 'must' I do not mean it as a logical necessity – it could well not happen – but as a cosmic imperative. If we delay a hundred or even fifty years it will almost certainly be too late.

Every major step in evolution has been built upon the foundations laid down by the previous changes. The last major change was the emergence of individual self-awareness in which man became conscious of himself as a thinking being. He thereby gained the ability to make conscious decisions about his own future. This must now become the basis for the next step. Thus the fundamental difference between the coming step and all previous ones is that we, and this means each and every one of us, are now responsible for seeing the process through.

But just the ability to choose is not enough. We cannot make decisions without a knowledge of what is possible. We need an image of the future, a vision of possibilities, to draw us on in the right direction, and some means to make this image an actuality. Here I can do no more than point a direction and suggest a path. In this respect the present book may serve as a first step. The next step, however, is up to you.

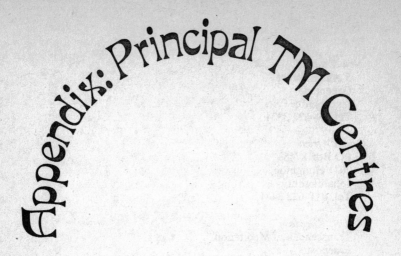

Appendix: Principal TM Centres

TM is now taught in most countries throughout the world. The following list contains addresses of the major national and international administrative centres.

Australia
  TM Centre Australia
  68 Wood Street
  Manly
  Sydney
  NSW 2095
  Tel. 02–977 5066

India
  World Capital of the Age of Enlightenment
  Maharishi Nagar
  Noida
  Ghaziabad
  201 307 UP

New Zealand
  5 Adam Street
  Greenlane
  Auckland 5
  Tel. 09–523 3324

South Africa
  PO Box 87483
  2041 Houghton
  Johannesburg
  Tel. 011–622 3444

United Kingdom
  Transcendental Meditation
  Freepost
  London SW1P 4YY
  Tel. (Freephone) 0800 269303

United States
  National Capital of the Age of Enlightenment
  14th Street NW
  Washington
  DC 20011
  Tel. 202–723 9111

  Transcendental Meditation Center
  Maharishi International University
  Fairfield
  Iowa 52556
  Tel. 515–472 5031

For addresses of other national centres contact:
  Maharishi Continental Capital for the Age of Enlightenment
  Postbus 700
  6400 AS Roermond
  The Netherlands
  Tel. 4752–3014

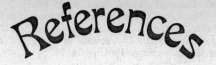

Chapter 3: The Nature of the Mind

1. Maharishi Mahesh Yogi, *The Science of Being and Art of Living*, SRM Publications, London, 1966, p.54.
2. Peter Russell, 'Transcendental meditation and conscious experience', paper presented at Brain Research Association Conference on Transcendental Meditation, Exeter, 1973.
3. Maharishi Mahesh Yogi, *Bhagavad-Gita, A New Translation and Commentary, Chapters 1-6*, Penguin Books, London, 1966, p. 470.
4. Idries Shah, *The Exploits of the Incomparable Mulla Nasrudin*, Dutton, New York, 1972, pp.26-7.

Chapter 4: The Technique of TM

1. Quoted in William James, *The Varieties of Religious Experience*, Fontana, London, 1960, p.385.
2. Anonymous, *The Cloud of Unknowing*, transl. C. Wolter, Penguin Books, London, 1961, ch.52.
3. Maharishi Mahesh Yogi, *Bhagavad-Gita, A New Translation and Commentary, Chapters 1-6*, Penguin Books, London, 1966, p.432.
4. Lyle Watson, *Supernature*, Hodder & Stoughton, London, 1973, pp.105-7.
5. E. Bryhni, A. Fjeld and A. Løvlie, 'Mechanical shocks induce phenocopies of developmental mutants'. *Nature*, vol. 248, pp. 794-5.
6. Roberto Assagioli, *Psychosynthesis*, Viking, New York, 1965, pp.237-66.

7. Hans Jenny, *Kymatics*, Basilius Press, Basle, 1967.
8. Shankara, *The Crest Jewel Of Discrimination*, Advaita Ashram, Almora, India, 1970, p.22.
9. Maharishi Mahesh Yogi, *The Science of Being and Art of Living*, SRM Publications, London, 1966, pp.58, 59.

Chapter 5: The Psychophysiology of Meditation

1. John Allison, 'Respiratory changes during Transcendental Meditation', *Lancet*, 1970, vol. i, p.833.
2. R. Keith Wallace and Herbert Benson, 'The physiology of meditation', *Scientific American*, vol. 226, no. 2, pp.84-90.
3. R. Keith Wallace, 'Physiological effects of Transcendental Meditation', *Science*, vol. 167, pp.1751-4.
4. R. Keith Wallace, 'The physiological effects of Transcendental Meditation: a proposed fourth major state of consciousness', Ph.D. thesis, Department of Physiology, University of Calif., 1970.
5. Herbert Benson and R. Keith Wallace, 'Decreased blood pressure in hypertensive subjects who practised meditation', *Circulation*, vols 45 and 46, supplement II.
6. Tom J. Routt, 'Low normal heart and respiratory rates in practitioners of Transcendental Meditation', to be published in Orme-Johnson and Farrow, below; and Benson and Wallace, op. cit.
7. Wallace and Benson, op. cit. and R. Keith Wallace, Herbert Benson and Archie F. Wilson, 'A wakeful hypometabolic physiologic state', *American Journal of Physiology*, vol. 221, no. 3, pp.795-9.
8. Wallace, Benson and Wilson, op. cit.; and David W. Orme-Johnson, 'Autonomic stability and Transcendental Meditation', *Psychosomatic Medicine*, vol. 35, no. 4, pp.341-9.
9. David W. Orme-Johnson and John T. Farrow, *Scientific Research on Transcendental Meditation: Collected Papers*, vol. 1, MIU Press, New York, 1975.
10. Elmer E. Green and Alyce M. Green, 'Volition as a metaforce in psychophysiological self-regulation', paper delivered at Sixth Annual Medical Meeting of the Association for Research and Enlightenment, Phoenix, Arizona, 1973.
11. Wallace, Benson and Wilson, op. cit.
12. Robert E. Ornstein, *The Psychology of Consciousness*, W. H. Freeman, San Framcisco, 1972.
13. Gillian Cohen, 'Hemispheric differences in serial versus parallel processing', *Journal of Experimental Psychology*, vol. 97, no. 3, pp.349-56.
14. Bernard Glueck, 'Biofeedback and meditation in the treatment of psychiatric illness', *Comprehensive Psychiatry*, vol. 16, no. 4, p.310.
15. J. P. Banquet, 'Spectral analysis of the EEG during meditation', *Electroencephalography and Clinical Neurophysiology*, vol. 35, pp.143-51.

16. Mark Westcott, 'Hemispheric symmetry of the EEG during Trans-cendental Meditation', in Orme-Johnson and Farrow, op. cit.
17. Paul Levine, *et al.*, 'Immediate EEG changes with the Transcendental Meditation technique: case study of a new meditator', MERU Report 7501, in Orme-Johnson and Farrow, op. cit.

Chapter 6: The Relief of Stress

1. Peter Blythe, *Stress Disease*, Arthur Barker, London, 1973, pp.17-19.
2. Lennart Levi, *Stress and Distress in Response to Psychosocial Stimuli*, Pergamon, London, 1973.
3. Una Kroll, *TM: A Signpost for the World*, Darton, Longman & Todd, London, 1974.
4. David W. Orme-Johnson, 'Autonomic stability and Transcendental Meditation', *Psychosomatic Medicine*, vol. 35, no. 4, pp.341-9.
5. Denver Daniels, personal communication.

Chapter 7: Health, Creativity and Intelligence

1. Elmer E. Green, *The May Lectures*, Brunel College, London, 1974.
2. See Peter Blythe, *Stress Disease*, Arthur Baker, London, 1973, pp. 34 and 62; and O. Carl Simonton, and Stephanie S. Simonton, 'Belief systems and management of the emotional aspects of malignancy', *Journal of Transpersonal Psychology*, vol. 7, pp.29-47.
3. Frank Papentin, 'Self-purification of the organism and Transcendental Meditation', in Orme-Johnson and Farrow, *Scientific Research on Transcendental Meditation; Collected Papers*, vol. 1, MIU Press, New York, 1975.
4. Quoted in *The Psychology of Transcendental Meditation: A Literature Review*, eds Demetri P. Kanellakos and Jerome S. Lukas, W. A. Benjamin, Menlo Park, Calif., 1975, p.132.
5. Harold Bloomfield, Michael Cain and Dennis Jaffe, *TM: Discovering Inner Energy and Overcoming Stress*, Delacorte, New York, 1975.
6. Daniel Goleman, 'Meditation as meta-therapy: hypotheses toward a proposed fifth state of consciousness', *Journal of Transpersonal Psychology*, vol. 3, pp.14, 15.
7. John Graham, 'Auditory discrimination in meditators', in Orme-Johnson and Farrow, op. cit.
8. Michael Pirot, 'Transcendental Meditation and perceptual auditory discrimination', in Orme-Johnson and Farrow, op. cit.
9. Frederick M. Brown, *et al.*, 'EEG kappa rhythms during Transcendental Meditation and possible perceptual threshold changes following', paper presented at the Kentucky Academy of Science, USA, November, 1971.
10. Robert Shaw and David Kolb, 'One-point reaction time involving meditators and non-meditators', in Orme-Johnson and Farrow, op. cit.

11. Karen Blasdell, 'The effects of Transcendental Meditation upon a complex perceptual motor task', in Orme-Johnson and Farrow, op. cit.
12. Peter Russell, 'Transcendental meditation and conscious experience', paper presented at Brain Research Association Conference on Transcendental Meditation, Exeter, 1973.
13. André S. Tjoa, 'Some evidence that the practice of Transcendental Meditation increases intelligence as measured by a psychological test', in Orme-Johnson and Farrow, op. cit.
14. Maharishi Mahesh Yogi, *Maharishi International University Catalogue*, MIU Press, Los Angeles and Seelisberg, Switzerland, 1974, p.37.
15. Erwin Schrödinger, *What is Life?*, Cambridge University Press, London, 1969, p.78.
16. Michael J. MacCullum, 'Transcendental Meditation and creativity', in Orme-Johnson and Farrow, op. cit.; and Howard Shecter, 'The Transcendental Meditation program in the classroom: a psychological evaluation of the science of creative intelligence, ibid.

Chapter 8: The Fourth State of Consciousness

1. Swami Prabhavanda and Frederick Manchester, *The Upanishads*, Mentor, New York, 1957, p.51.
2. Quoted in Walter T. Stace, *Mysticisim and Philosophy*, Macmillan, London, 1961, p.104.
3. Quoted in J. E. Coleman, *The Quiet Mind*, Rider, London, 1971, pp.83, 87.
4. Quoted in Una Kroll, *TM: A Signpost for the World*, Darton, Longman & Todd, London, 1974, pp.103-4.
5. Quoted in Stace, op. cit., p.87.
6. Quoted in Abraham Maslow, *The Farther Reaches of Human Nature*, Penguin Books, London, 1973, p.194.
7. Swami Prabhavanda and Manchester, op. cit., p.21.
8. *The Gospel According to Thomas*, transl. A. Guillaumont, *et al.*, Harper & Row, New York, 1959, p.3.
9. Aldous Huxley, *The Perennial Philosophy*, Fontana, London, 1958, pp.17-18.

Chapter 10: Self-Realization

1. Maharishi Mahesh Yogi, *Bhagavad-Gita, A New Translation and Commentary, Chapters 1-6*, Penguin Books, London, 1966, p.142.
2. Quoted in Jack Forem, *Transcendental Meditation*, Dutton, New York, 1973, p.183.
3. Sidney Spencer, *Mysticism in World Religion*, Penguin Books, London, 1963, pp.72-5.

4. See Maharishi, op. cit., p.282.
5. Lao-Tsu, *Tao-Te-Ching*, transl. Jane English and Gia-Fu Feng, Wildwood House, London, 1973, ch. 15.

Chapter 11: Higher States of Consciousness

1. John Sinclair (transl.), *The Divine Comedy of Dante Alighieri*, vol. 3, John Lane The Bodley Head, London, 1946.
2. Jacob Böhme, 'The Key', unpublished, transl. by P. Malekin, 1974, ch. 9, para. 68.
3. Quoted in Evelyn Underhill, *Mysticism*, Dutton, New York, 1961, p.251.
4. Walt Whitman, *Leaves of Grass*, McKay, 1891, p.323.
5. Quoted in Rudolph Otto, *Mysticism, East and West*, Macmillan, New York, 1932, p.61.
6. *The Gospel According to Thomas*, transl. A. Guillaumont, *et al.*, Harper & Row, New York, 1959, p.43.
7. Maharishi Mahesh Yogi, *The Science of Being and Art of Living*, SRM Publications, London, 1966, p.250.
8. Sidney Spencer, *Mysticism in World Religion*, Penguin Books, London, 1963, p.9.
9. F. C. Happold, *Mysticism: A Study and an Anthology*, Penguin Books, London, 1963, p.351.
10. Lao-Tsu, *Tao-Te-Ching*, transl. Jane English and Gia-Fu Feng, Wildwood House, London, 1973, ch. 38.
11. Maharishi Mahesh Yogi, *Bhagavad-Gita, A New Translation and Commentary, Chapters 1-6*, Penguin Books, London, 1966, pp.12-17.

Chapter 12: Some Psychological Perspectives

1. Abraham Maslow, *Toward a Psychology of Being*, Van Nostrand, Reinhold, New York, 1968, p.25.
2. W. Seeman, S. Nidich and T. Banta, 'The influence of Transcendental Meditation on a measure of self-actualisation', *Journal of Counseling Psychology*, vol. 19, no. 3, pp.184-7.
3. W. Seeman, S. Nidich and T. Dreskin, 'Influence of Transcendental Meditation: a replication', *Journal of Counseling Psychology*, vol. 20, no. 6, pp.555-6; and Philip C. Ferguson and John C. Gowan, 'The influence of Transcendental Meditation on anxiety, depression, aggression, neuroticism and self-actualisation', paper presented at California State Psychological Association, Fresno, Calif., January, 1974.
4. Ibid.
5. William P. Van den Berg and Bert Mulder, 'Psychological research on the effects of Transcendental Meditation on a number of personality variables using the NPI', in Orme-Johnson and Farrow,

Scientific Research on Transcendental Meditation: Collected Papers,
vol. 1, MIU Press, New York, 1975; and Theo Fehr *et al.,* 'Study of
49 practitioners of Transcendental Meditation with the Freiburger
Personality Inventory', in Orme-Johnson and Farrow, op. cit.
6. Lawrence Farwell, 'Effect of Transcendental Meditation on level of
anxiety', in Orme-Johnson and Farrow, op. cit.; Ferguson and
Gowan, op. cit.; and Larry A. Rjelle, 'Transcendental Meditation
and psychological health', in Orme-Johnson and Farrow, op. cit.
7. Colin Wilson, *New Pathways in Psychology,* Gollancz, London, 1972,
p.16.
8. Abraham Maslow, *Religions, Values and Peak-Experiences,* Viking,
New York, 1970 (new introduction).
9. Daniel Goleman, 'Meditation as meta-therapy: hypotheses toward a
proposed fifth state of consciousness', *Journal of Transpersonal
Psychology,* vol. 3, p.4.
10. *Journal of Transpersonal Psychology,* Statement of Purpose.
11. Roberto Assagioli, *Psychosynthesis,* Viking, New York, 1965, p.18.
12. Herbert Benson, R. Keith Wallace, *et al.,* 'Decreased drug abuse with
Transcendental Meditation – A study of 1,862 subjects', International
Conference on Drug-Abuse Problems, Ann Arbor, Michigan,
November, 1970.
13. Eva Brautigam, *Effect of Transcendental Meditation on Drug Abusers,*
Malmo, Sweden; W. Thomas Winquist and G. T. Slatin, 'The effect
of Transcendental Meditation on students involved in the regular use
of hallucinogenic and "hard drugs" ' and Otis, 'Reduced use of
non-prescribed drugs', Stanford Research Institute, 1972 (copies of
these papers available from SIMS, Los Angeles); and M. Shafii, R.
Lavely and R. Jaffe, 'Meditation and Marihuana', *American Journal
of Psychiatry,* vol. 131.1, pp.60-3.
14. Winquist and Slatin, op. cit.

Chapter 13: The Means and the Ends

1. Ram Dass, Lecture at the Maryland Psychiatric Research Center,
reprinted in *Journal of Transpersonal Psychology,* vol. 2, p.194.
2. Roberto Assagioli, *The Balancing and Synthesis of Opposites,*
Psychosynthesis Research Foundation, New York, 1972.
3. Christmas Humphreys, *Basic Buddhism,* Buddhist Society, London,
1963, p.10.
4. *The Gospel According to Thomas,* transl. A. Guillaumont, *et al.,*
Harper & Row, New York, 1959, p.17.

Chapter 14: The Knower and the Known

1. Alvin Toffler, *Future Shock,* Pan, London, 1971, p.371.
2. A. N. Whitehead, *The Aims of Education,* Ernest Benn, London,
1950, p.1.

3. Quoted in Paul Goodman, *Compulsory Miseducation*, Penguin Books, London, 1971, p.9.
4. Aldous Huxley, *The Perennial Philosophy*, Fontana, London, 1958, p.9.
5. Aldous Huxley, *The Doors of Perception*, Penguin Books, London, 1959, pp.60-5.
6. *Maharishi International University Catalogue* (1st edition), MIU Press, Seelisberg, Switzerland, 1974, p.9.
7. Roy W. Collier, 'The effect of Transcendental Meditation upon university academic attainment', *Proceedings of the Pacific Northwest Conference on Foreign Languages*, Seattle, Washington (in press); and Dennis P. Heaton and David W. Orme-Johnson, 'Influence of Transcendental Meditation on grade point average: initial findings', in Orme-Johnson and Farrow, *Scientific Research on Transcendental Meditation: Collected Papers*, vol. 1, MIU Press, New York, 1975.
8. *Maharishi International University Catalogue* (2nd edition), p.4.
9. Ibid., p.14.

Chapter 15: The Art of the Impossible

1. Alice Lovat, *The Life of Saint Theresa*, Herbert & Daniel, London, 1911, p.377.
2. Scothill and Hodous, *Dictionary of Chinese Buddhist Terms*.
3. Tony Schmid, *The Eighty-Five Siddhas*, Shambala.
4. Geoffrey Clements and Steven L. Milstein, *Auditory Thresholds in Advanced Participants in the Transcendental Meditation Programme*, MERU Report 7702, Seelisberg, Switzerland, 1977.
5. *A Course in Miracles*, Foundation for Inner Peace, New York, 1977.
6. David W. Orme-Johnson, Geoffrey Clements, Christopher T. Haynes and Kheireddine Badaoui, *Higher States of Consciousness: EEG Coherence, Creativity, and Experience of the Siddhis*. MERU Report 7701, Seelisberg, Switzerland, 1977.

Chapter 16: The Consciousness Revolution

1. Thomas Kuhn, *The Structure of Scientific Revolutions*, University of Chicago Press, 1970.
2. Willis Harman *et al.*, 'Changing Images of Man', Stanford Research Institute Center for the Study of Social Policy, Policy Research Report no. 4, 1974.
3. Gregory Bateson, *Steps to an Ecology of Mind*, Paladin, London, 1973, p.437.
4. Maharishi Mahesh Yogi, *Creative Intelligence*, journal published by SRM, London, no. 3, p.2.
5. Sigmund Freud, *Civilisation and Its Discontents*, Hogarth, London, 1930.
6. John White, *The Highest State of Consciousness*, Anchor, 1972, p.ix.

7. Quoted in Abraham Maslow, *The Farther Reaches of Human Nature,* Penguin Books, London, 1973, p.210.

8. Konrad Lorenz, *Civilised Man's Eight Deadly Sins,* Methuen, London, 1974.

9. Pierre Teilhard de Chardin, *The Phenomenon of Man,* Fontana, London, 1965, p.21.

10. Ibid., pp.27, 277.

11. Ibid., p.268.

12. Ibid., p.290.

13. Maharishi, loc. cit.

14. Teilhard de Chardin, op. cit., p.285.

15. Lawrence Domash, MIU video tape: 'Solution'.

16. Garland Landrith and Candace Borland, 'Improved Quality of City Life: Decreased Crime Rate', in Orme-Johnson and Farrow, *Transcendental Meditation: Collected Papers,* vol. 1, MIU Press, New York, 1975.

17. Kenneth E. Boulding, *The Meaning of the Twentieth Century: The Great Transition,* Harper & Row, New York, 1964, p.1.

18. John R. Platt, 'The step to man', *Science,* vol. 149, p.607.

Index

ARKANA – NEW-AGE BOOKS FOR MIND, BODY AND SPIRIT

A selection of titles

With over 200 titles currently in print, Arkana is the leading name in quality new-age books for mind, body and spirit. Arkana encompasses the spirituality of both East and West, ancient and new, in fiction and non-fiction. A vast range of interests is covered, including Psychology and Transformation, Health, Science and Mysticism, Women's Spirituality and Astrology.

If you would like a catalogue of Arkana books, please write to:

Arkana Marketing Department
Penguin Books Ltd
27 Wright's Lane
London W8 5TZ